THE ANUNNAKI CONNECTION

T0383893

THE ANUNNAKI CONNECTION

Sumerian Gods, Alien DNA & the Fate of Humanity

FROM EDEN TO ARMAGEDDON

HEATHER LYNN, PhD

This edition first published in 2020 by New Page Books, an imprint of
Red Wheel/Weiser, LLC
With offices at:
65 Parker Street, Suite 7
Newburyport, MA 01950
www.redwheelweiser.com

Copyright © 2020 by Dr. Heather Lynn

All rights reserved. No part of this publication may be reproduced or
transmitted in any form or by any means, electronic or mechanical, including photocopying, recording, or by any information storage and retrieval
system, without permission in writing from Red Wheel/Weiser, LLC.
Reviewers may quote brief passages.

ISBN: 978-1-63265-173-0
Library of Congress Cataloging-in-Publication Data available upon request.

Cover design by Kathryn Sky-Peck
Cover photograph montage uses images from Marc Ward/Stocktrek
Images/Getty and *Adam and Eve* by Lucas Cranach the Elder
Interior photos/images by TK
Interior by Maureen Forys, Happenstance Type-O-Rama
Typeset in Baskerville 120, Copperplate Gothic, and Chalet Comprime

Printed in Canada
MAR

10 9 8 7 6 5 4 3 2 1

Dedicated to those
who stay up late to dream
when the rest of the world remains
asleep in the darkness.

TABLE OF CONTENTS

PREFACE

A s finite humans in an infinite cosmos, we continually seek to understand our place therein. To the ancients, the human experience was dual in nature, whether as good vs. evil, light vs. dark, or heaven vs. earth. According to the great mythologist and scholar Joseph Campbell, "everything in the field of time are pairs of opposites" (Campbell, 2012, 125). Our history is rooted in duality, but as Campbell also points out, mythic thought transcends duality. It is through mythic thought that we can fully appreciate our deep connection to the Anunnaki. This book will treat the subject of the Anunnaki, the origins of humankind, and extraterrestrials with the respect and seriousness it deserves. But before attempting to understand this study's proposed connections, we must first address what is meant by the term *myth*.

It is commonly accepted that myth was how ancient people explained the unexplainable. However, this interpretation is not entirely satisfactory and gives insufficient credit to our distant ancestors. I argue that myth is not the search for meaning, as meaning is a product of the rational mind—more specifically, the left hemisphere. It is this part of the brain that is logical, connecting details from the present to categorize and organize information. The left hemisphere thinks in terms of language and is our inner voice that makes meaning between our internal world and external world. Myth, by its very nature, has the power to transcend even this inner duality. The language of myth is by no means rational, but neither is it irrational. It is *pre*-rational. Myth is the language of dreams, symbols, and archetypes. It is how the ancients shared their universal truths and worldviews with each other—and eventually us. Thus, the gods and myths of the ancient past should not be judged on rationality alone. Rather, myth should be cherished for its ability to transcend both time and space. It is this transcendent nature of myth that can open the door to humanity's own ascension.

ACKNOWLEDGMENTS

I would first like to thank everyone at Red Wheel/Weiser, especially my editor for New Page Books, Michael Pye, whose faith and patience will never be forgotten. Thank you to the many alternative researchers who have inspired me to ask more far-reaching questions, especially Michael Cremo for encouraging me to push the envelope. Thank you to Gary A. David, for his devotion to his research and sharing it with me and the world. Thank you to Dr. John DeSalvo, who has been a sage and, more importantly, a friend. Thank you also to the incomparable Edmund Marriage. Finally, but most importantly, thank you to my readers for being brave enough to venture outside of the established historical narrative to explore radical ideas and earth-shattering possibilities.

THE ANUNNAKI CONNECTION

INTRODUCTION:

Connecting the Dots

The omission is the most powerful form of lie,
and it is the duty of the historian to ensure that those lies
do not creep into the history books.

—GEORGE ORWELL, British novelist

For the past two hundred years, ancient Egypt has captured our imaginations. Napoleon's Egyptian Campaign in the Ottoman territories of Egypt and Syria—an expedition that led to the discovery of the Rosetta Stone—set in motion a phenomenon known as *Egyptomania*. This widespread fascination with ancient Egypt swelled with Howard Carter's discovery of King Tutankhamun's tomb in 1922. And Egyptomania is still recognizable in postmodern culture in everything from entertainment to architecture.

In this new millennium, a different and more ancient civilization known as the Sumerians has also captured the imaginations of people all over the world, launching us into another mania: *Sumer-mania*. Information about the Sumerians, particularly their pantheon of gods known as the Anunnaki, is everywhere, thanks to the internet. At the time of the writing of this book, one search of "Sumerian" on YouTube resulted in over 762,000 hits, with the term "Anunnaki" offering over 509,000 results. It is a burgeoning fascination in almost all media. What was once a subculture is becoming increasingly mainstream—and for good reason. The Sumerians were truly exceptional in ways that you will discover throughout this book. They were so exceptional that even academia has been haunted by unresolved questions about who the Sumerians really were and where in the world they came from. Scholars believe that all groups of known people in Mesopotamia spoke Semitic languages, but the Sumerians did not. This leads us to "The Sumerian Problem."

First proposed by Professor Jonathan Ziskind in 1972, the Sumerian Problem addresses how the Sumerian language could be unique among the peoples of the ancient Near East: they must have migrated from somewhere far away (Ziskind, 1972, 41). But the Sumerian language is not the only thing that sets this ancient civilization apart from all others. Their knowledge of the cosmos was mind-blowing in its accuracy, so much so that it would later influence advancing civilizations like the Egyptians, Greeks, and even our own modern culture. It is easy to understand why the Sumerians are so fascinating!

However, the growing obsession with the Sumerians and Anunnaki provides more questions than answers. While self-proclaimed experts have proposed intriguing alternative theories about the Anunnaki, many of these theorists do one of a handful of things that undermine their arguments. First, they support, without question, the work of Zecharia Sitchin, an economist and amateur Assyriologist who gave a unique interpretation of the Sumerian myths that promoted paleo-contact theory, or as some in the mainstream entertainment industry now call it "ancient astronaut theory." There are also conventional academics studying the Sumerians and Anunnaki, most of whom are employed in tenured positions at universities and do not entertain alternative ideas. The absolute debunking put forward by those few researchers does little to connect the dots for the growing number of people demanding to know the true history of the Anunnaki. This sort of close-minded view only serves to further divide the issue. It also makes it appear that they are hiding something deep within the Ivory Tower. The only thing gained by this type of secrecy is increasingly extraordinary speculation.

In her infinite wisdom, my little old Appalachian grandmother always used to say that those who have nothing to hide, hide nothing. So what could they be hiding then? This growing division and secrecy have created a chasm that opportunistic people now seek to fill with absolute fantasy in order to sell countless books, DVDs, guided tours, and more. Popular beliefs range from the mundane to the fantastic: evidence of giants, extraterrestrials, ancient technology, and so on. What is the truth? Humanity has a right to know.

We are now living in an era when few people are genuinely trying to solve ancient mysteries. Those intellectual pioneers who risked it all to bring us new ways of questioning ancient texts, lost civilizations, and the truth about human origins have all but vanished. There are a few who still fight for what they believe, but there is no denying the very short window of time they have left. For those still following their work, it has become an all-too-common occurrence to wake up on a given morning to learn of the passing of another great researcher.

Where does that leave those of us who still wonder about these great mysteries? Turn on cable television on any given day and you will find marathons of programming that embellish the work of these researchers, some going so far as presenting it in an almost comical way. Has the study of this great civilization really come down to cable TV asking us to believe that the Sumerians rode dinosaurs and made contact with Wild West cowboys? (Yes. That was a real program.)

What has happened? With the mainstream media mocking this great mystery and the old-guard academics ignoring it, where does one turn? To the internet, of course. While the internet has indeed helped researchers connect with each other and make their findings available to the public, it has also had the unfortunate consequence of creating a climate of disinformation and false news, as well as a platform for snake oil salesmen. So for the seekers looking for the truth about the Anunnaki, how do we connect the dots to create the most accurate picture?

Access to evidence regarding the Anunnaki and their connection to human origins is still restricted by an elite control mechanism that author Michael Cremo has called "The Knowledge Filter" (Cremo and Thompson, 1993). The Knowledge Filter is very real and something I have personally witnessed in action during my time as both an undergraduate student and doctoral candidate. However, based on this personal experience, I build on Cremo's concept and even take it a little further. I think that this Knowledge Filter is a compartmentalized arm of a larger control mechanism I refer to as the academic industrial complex. As a result of this behemoth of secrecy, there is evidence that cannot yet be examined until it is disclosed or somehow released to the public. Thus, I cannot claim that this book will definitively satisfy all the questions you have about the Anunnaki. I can only hope to provide more dots—or historical data points, as we historians call them—because the more dots we have, the clearer the picture becomes. As a historian, I have been educated and trained in a conventional way.

However, I take an unconventional approach when studying the mysteries of the ancients.

While working as an archaeologist, I discovered that much of what we know about our history is based on the consensus of elite and often politically motivated individuals and institutions. After this revelation, I embarked on a spiritual journey, leading me to break away from the mainstream to go in search of the truth behind human origins. I have discovered a world of deceit. In the cavernous lower levels of museums around the world, thousands of artifacts are hidden from public view because they are considered "too threatening" to the established historical narrative. Meanwhile, secret archaeological excavations are routinely funded by shadowy organizations and multinational corporations who launder money through universities. On my quest, I have infiltrated secret organizations, deciphered ancient texts, and investigated myriad declassified government documents. In this book, we will investigate the Anunnaki connection to uncover the truth behind the Anunnaki, including:

- Who are the Anunnaki, really?
- How accurate are the current Sumerian text translations, and how do we know for sure whom to believe?
- What role might they have played in human origins?
- Is there a connection between the Anunnaki and other gods? What about demons?
- Where are the Anunnaki now? Could their return spell the end of our world?

Given the vast amount of information out there on the Anunnaki, this quest may seem like an ambitious endeavor. Perhaps it is, but I believe it is the duty of both the historian and archaeologist to find the truth and clarify the past through the expulsion of permissible systemic lies. As E. B. Tylor, the father of cultural anthropology, once said, "every possible avenue of knowledge must be explored, every door tried to see if it will open." This is exactly why I will present to you the absolute facts as we know them today, as well as the theories of both the fringe and the mainstream so that you will be able to make up your own mind.

CHAPTER 1

Civilization Suddenly Appears

Civilization began the first time an angry person
cast a word instead of a rock.
—SIGMUND FREUD, Austrian neurologist
and the father of psychoanalysis

wo hundred million years ago, Earth's two ancient supercontinents, Laurasia in the north and Gondwana in the
south, began moving closer to one another. As they continued moving, their eventual collision caused them to split
into many coastal masses, resulting in the creation of what we
now know as the Near East. The shifting of the Arabian Plate
forced the Iranian Plate downward, creating the Persian Gulf
and the Mesopotamian lowlands. This same process forced
land upward, forming the Zagros mountain range.

Sea-level changes continued over hundreds of thousands of
years. Then, something significant happened at the end of the
last Ice Age. Massive ice fields that covered the polar regions
melted, causing the sea level to rise at what we now know was
an astonishing rate. In a study published in the journal *Global
and Planetary Change*, researchers found that the sea level rose by
an average of about three feet per century at the end of the last
Ice Age, with intermittent periods of increase to eight feet per

century (Stanford et al., 2011). This process lasted until about 6,000 years ago, until the Ubaid period (ca. 6500 to 3800 BCE), about the time that the ancient Sumerian city-state of Ur was originally settled. At that time, the Persian Gulf's water level was much higher than it is today. In addition to the change in landscape, the climate became warm and wet, contributing to the growth of dense forests east of this region in the Zagros Mountains in present-day Iran. These deciduous and coniferous trees included pine, juniper, oak, and cedar, which is also referenced in the world's oldest known literary work, The Epic of Gilgamesh. The Near East became a land rich in fertile plains and eventually home to various land-based animals like gazelle, sheep, goats, and cattle. This inevitably attracted stone-age humans to the region, as it was a land of opportunity and growth. The area referred to by scholars as the "Fertile Crescent" was home to many prehistoric people. This general area known as Mesopotamia is the region between and around two rivers, the Tigris and the Euphrates, which have their source at the borders of present-day Syria and Turkey, cross the current Iraq in the northwest and southeast, and throw themselves into the Persian Gulf. It is near these two rivers, in the fertile valleys, where the very early main city-states of the region developed: Kish, Lagash, Ur, Uruk, then Akkad, and later Babylon.

Before the rise of Sumerian civilization, no known permanent and organized settlements are found in the archaeological record. Both stunningly complex and primitive societies were formed by hunter-gatherers. Hunter-gatherer sites like Göbekli Tepe show possible evidence of feasting, dancing, celebrating, and spirituality. Stonehenge, as well, appears to have been a massive ritualistic meeting place of significant spiritual importance. However, it is important to remember that these sites, though absolutely fantastic, are not considered permanent settlements or urban centers, there being no traces of domesticated plants or animals yet found at Göbekli Tepe (Peters, Schmidt, Dietrich, and Pöllath, 2014). This is one of the primary pieces of evidence, though circumstantial, to support symbolism and religion as leading to the development of agriculture and domestication and not the other way around (Peters, Schmidt, Dietrich, and Pöllath, 2014). So while there were arguably advanced cultures of hunter-gatherers in the region much farther back than the Sumerians, they were all missing the key attributes of what scholars define as *civilization*.

Archaeologists and historians have a technical set of features that together constitute a definition of civilization. Most of these features were catalogued by archaeologist V. Gordon Childe (1892–1957), who taught at Edinburgh. According to Childe, for a group of humans to be considered a civilization, rather than, say, a tribe or band, they must have (Trigger, 2010):

- Large urban centers
- Full-time specialist occupations
- Primary producers of food paying surpluses to a deity or ruler
- Monumental architecture
- A ruling class, exempt from manual labor
- A system for recording information (writing)
- Development of exact, practical sciences
- Monumental art
- Regular importation of raw materials
- A class structure (peasants, craftspeople, rulers)
- A state religion/ideology
- Persistent state structures

Some organized bands of humans shared *some* of these features. The Ubaid culture, for instance, had painted pottery, terra-cotta tools, and the beginnings of a distinctive temple architecture. Nevertheless, they did not possess all the necessary features such as having a large urban center or monumental art. The Ubaidians are believed to be the first culture to act as a civilizing force in the region because they developed agricultural techniques, trade, and certain industries. But as advanced as the Ubaidians were, they pale in comparison to the Sumerians.

The discovery of the Sumerians rattled preexisting beliefs about the rise of human civilization. Who were these people, and why had they been left out of the archaeological and historical record for over 2,000 years (Kramer, 1963)? There is no doubt that ancient people were intelligent, creative, and highly complex, just like modern people, but the Sumerians stand out above all others as the most unusual. Scholars describe the Sumerians as exhibiting an "unusually creative intellect" (Armstrong, 2015). This becomes clear when considering that in a mere 300 years after the Ubaid period—a historical blink of an eye—huge complex structures, theology, advanced technologies, science, math, and government emerged. These were inventions unlike anything the world had previously known, and they would forever change the course of human culture.

The following is a list of some inventions and technologies with which the Sumerians are credited (Kramer, 1988):

- The invention of time based on increments of sixty
- Astronomy
- Weights and measures
- Mathematics
- Geometry
- The 360° circle
- The wheel
- Wheeled vehicles

10

- Sailboats
- Maps
- Wind power
- A bicameral congress having a senate and a house of representatives
- Libraries
- Schools and universities
- The concept of professional careers
- Clergy
- Economists
- Philosophers
- The concept of an end to the work or school day
- Labor unions
- Surgery
- Dentistry
- Optometry
- Pills
- Credit and financing
- Lawyers
- Bankers

As you can see, these inventions are not stone tools or grass huts. These are all highly intellectual and teachable skills, rooted in a deeper, more conceptual way of thinking. By at least the fourth millennium BCE, the first urban center had formed. These early civilizations began with the Sumerians and would later include the Akkadians, Babylonians, and Assyrians. This incredible leap from hunter-gatherer group to a more modern civilization confounds scholars, but that's not the only thing they have difficulty explaining. The most controversial aspect, thus far, pertains to the distinctiveness of the Sumerian language. In fact, the Sumerian language is so troubling, it has been dubbed "the Sumerian Problem." What exactly is it that makes the Sumerian language a problem?

Sumerian does not fit into any of the major linguistic groups, prompting scholars to conclude that since all other groups in Mesopotamia spoke Semitic languages, meaning the branch of the Afroasiatic language group originating in the Middle East, then the Sumerians must have migrated from somewhere far away (Ziskind, 1972). Researchers discovered the Sumerian Problem when French and American archaeologists at the end of the nineteenth and early twentieth century found vast hoards of cuneiform tablets in the ancient cities of Lagash and Nippur, similar to what was already known from Akkadian tablets. When the scholars finally deciphered these tablets, they found that numerous words and syllabic values did not completely fit with previously understood Semitic grammar and vocabulary. They soon realized that what they had deciphered was not Akkadian at all, but rather a completely unknown language type. The Sumerian language was and still is an enigma, even more than 100 years after its discovery.

To be clear, the Akkadians came after the Sumerians, when Sargon of Akkad (the Great) took over Sumer and reigned over Mesopotamia, creating the world's first empire, the Akkadian Empire in 2334 BCE. Yet the Akkadians continued to use Sumerian on their tablets, much as Latin was used in the Middle Ages and early modern era. The Sumerian language was preserved as a "language of learning and high cultural interchange" (Ziskind, 1972, 3), a testament to the Akkadians' respect for this advanced culture.

But to get back to our main issue, what prompted this shift in culture from hunter-gatherer to a society with features recognizable to any modern person?

The generally accepted theory posits that increased competition for resources created a need for more workers. This new working class required managers, leading to a development of a state superstructure or government. Subsequently, the bureaucracy introduced by this new government system would need a supporting physical structure like temples and administrative centers. Further, the increased centralization of economic activity demanded the development of more detailed methods of record keeping, thus giving rise to the invention of writing, math, and so forth. These skills needed to be transferred, so schools were developed to train a specialized workforce. People were taught to be scribes, managers, skilled craftspeople, builders, physicians, scientists, priests, and others at high levels of government. By now, a complete transition from clan or tribal law to a more recognizable modern state of governance occurred. This shift is referred to by archaeologists as the *Urban Revolution*.

Copy of a bilingual (Sumerian-Akkadian) votive inscription from Rimush, King of Akkad. Circa 2270 BCE.

The Holy Sumerian Trinity: Laying the Foundation

Symbolism and religion first led to the development of agriculture and domestication and not the other way around (Peters, Schmidt, Dietrich, and Pöllath, 2014). Religion was the catalyst for everything prior to the Urban Revolution. To understand this concept is to grasp how vitally important religion was to the Sumerians. We can deduce that hunter-gatherers and pre-civilized cultures also highly valued ritual and spirituality. At some point though, most likely with the Sumerians, ritual became organized into a religion. Sumerians had a clear structure to their spirituality and rites. We know this thanks to the writings they left behind. Those Mesopotamian myths that have come down to us today are the written stories originally perpetuated by an oral tradition. Therefore, we must try to understand their meaning in a broader context because of the greater subtext understood within the society that was never put down. It also doesn't help that many of the tablets on which these myths were recorded have been broken, so missing pieces are a common occurrence when studying the Sumerian texts—indeed, with all ancient texts. As you read on, remember that the following overview of the Sumerian religion is the generally accepted scholarly understanding and interpretation. This is not the full story or the only possible interpretation. Nevertheless, it is necessary to establish a baseline narrative for the Mesopotamian gods so that you will have a better point of reference when we discuss alternative interpretations of these myths as this chapter progresses.

While there are volumes of Sumerian texts just waiting to be studied, of those currently translated, more than fifty tell the story of the Sumerian gods known as the Anunnaki. These stories are always fragmentary and, of course, do not form a coherent whole since there are different versions or variants in the stories, the divine genealogies, etc., and they sometimes refer to other tales that have yet to be found. Hence, the difficulty we face in clearly understanding their beliefs. Still, numerous great figures emerge with some consistency from the historical record.

The Mesopotamian religion is not only polytheistic, it has many gods. Contrary to common belief, it is quite difficult to know their exact number because it is not always easy to determine if a name represents a god still unknown or only qualifies a god already known. As more texts are discovered and deciphered, a clearer picture emerges, but this takes time. The city-states of Mesopotamia, from the third millennium, seem to have agreed on a common pantheon, completed for each by a local pantheon. The gods were hierarchical according to the model of royal power, particularly when differentiating between the Anunnaki, the "great" gods, and Igigi, the "little" gods. The god exercising supreme power was Enlil, whose sanctuary was at Nippur as the religious, but not political, capital of the country. It appears that, over time, the Mesopotamian religion concentrated around a smaller number of great divine figures, as the "great" gods absorbed into themselves the prerogatives of many less important deities and developed a personality of their own. Eventually, in Babylon there would be a more pointed focus on a single new god, Marduk, whom the Babylonians viewed as the spiritual successor of Enki, especially in his role in the creation of men. While this is not yet monotheism, all the supreme powers are gathered in the hands of only one supreme god.

When studying the Anunnaki, one common lament is that it is difficult to keep track of who's who. Much of the time, the names of gods are given both in Sumerian and Akkadian, in just the same way as with the Greek and Roman gods. For instance, the Greek goddess of love, Aphrodite, was also known by the Romans as Venus. Accordingly, the names of the primary gods are often presented as Sumerian name/Akkadian name. This may seem confusing at first, but rest assured after reading this book, you will have a far greater understanding of their nature. Chapter 3 will take you through the profile and description of each Anunnaki god and serves as a handy reference guide that will help you in your further study. For now, let's just look at some general points so we can build a better understanding of the Sumerian worldview.

A bit similar to the Christian faith, the Sumerians had a holy trinity. This trinity is An/Anu, Enlil/Ellil, and Enki/Ea. The three main gods of the Mesopotamian pantheon were recognized as supreme by the city-states and always quoted in their descending order of importance. An/Anu was the father god to Enki and Enlil, with whom he would later be syncretized. Religious syncretism is when one religion's symbols, deities, myths, or rituals are combined with another religion's or a combination of components of different religions to make a new system. The term *syncretism* goes back to the Greek συγκρητισμός and denotes a union. This is why, when reading about the Sumerians, you may see references to An and Anu meaning the same god.

Enki is often described in very real, biological terms, whereas Enlil is described as a spirit, or "Lord Ghost." The Sumerian word *líl*, whose Akkadian equivalent is *zaqíqu*, means "ghost, phantom, haunted" (Michalowski, 1989, 98; Tinney, 1996, 129–30; Michalowski, 1996). Some scholars argue that this cannot be a correct translation, because it does not seem to make sense in the context of his mythological capabilities. We will look at this more closely in chapter 4. However, what does stand out in this context is the likely Sumerian origins of a paternal trinity comprised of a heavenly father, son, and holy ghost, all of whom had equal but shared power over humanity.

These were the main three deities. Still, An would go on to create more progeny, and the subsequent children of An would become known as the Anunnaki. It is unclear to scholars whether or not the Anunnaki were true gods. Details surrounding this mysterious group are scattered. In fact, no one even knows for sure just how many Anunnaki there were in total. One text suggests there are about fifty, while another refers to only seven. An entirely separate account describes how Marduk assigned 300 Anunnaki for duty in the heavens and 300 the netherworld, totaling 600 Anunnaki beings. Thus, there is no consensus on a final number.

The main purpose of these beings, as described in the Sumerian myth *Enki and the World Order*, was to decide the fate of humans. They are also described as residing in the netherworld. Many modern popular accounts depict the Anunnaki as having been worshipped. While this could make some sort of logical sense, there is no hard evidence for their adoration in the archaeological record, with the exception of only three attestations in administrative texts from the Ur III period, which hint that offerings were made to Anunna (Anunnaki). In the myths of Mesopotamia, their importance does shift. For example, Enki was initially portrayed as less supreme than An and Enlil, and in some cases like the flood myth, Enki intervened. An was the god of the "on-high." He was the first god to rule the universe, the founder of the cosmic order, but in most accounts, he is presented as more withdrawn, leaving the power to his son Enlil.

Enlil's main sanctuary was in Uruk, where he ruled over the people. He was bound to heaven and to air and was similar to the Greek god Zeus in that he was the supreme leader of the gods. But the comparison stops there: Enlil was not the strongest of the gods, and he was far from being the wisest. Several myths give Enlil a surprisingly small role in the creation of the universe. Some myths even portray him as clumsy or brutal. The chief sanctuary of Enlil was the Ešumeša temple in Nippur. Enlil had a wife, a goddess deity called Ninlil. Together, Enlil and Ninlil formed a royal couple, comparable to Zeus/Hera.

Enki/Ea is often portrayed as the more intelligent and cunning god, exercising the technical function of power. He is often called *Nudimmud*, "the one whose business is to manufacture and produce." Divine power symbols representing, apparently, various aspects of civilized life "concretized" in the aspect of jewelry or talismans would increase the power of a god when granted by another god. Enki had an important sanctuary in Eridu. In the mythical world geography, An and Enlil resided in the palace of heavenly gods, An situated higher than Enlil, while Enki, even though he frequently moved to the gods above, had a separate residence, called the Abzu, which is characterized as underneath the freshwater table on which floats the flat disk of the Earth where humans live. Enki also created the Apkallu, the Seven Sages, "very experts" from Abzu, taking the form of fish with a second head having a human face. Enki used the Sages as intermediaries to establish culture and bring civilization to men. According to the myth, the Apkallu were saved from the Great Flood, the same deluge scholars believe was the original source myth for the Great Flood of the Bible. There are many other great Sumerian gods and myths that have a direct relationship with the stories of the Old Testament. This biblical connection is one reason of many that the gods of Mesopotamia warrant further study—not merely to bolster the claims of any one religion, but rather to make clear the incontrovertible fact that these

Anunnaki retain their connection to humanity even after thousands of years.

The preceding is the generally accepted narrative of the
Mesopotamian gods, but this is by no means the only interpretation. Despite the importance of the Sumerian texts, historians have not come close to deciphering all that have been
excavated. This leaves a considerable gap in our collective
knowledge base, which has widened over many years. It seems
just as one mystery gets solved, another emerges. Scholars
have not been able to agree on many aspects of the Sumerian
Problem—an issue far greater than a single question of origin.
As such, others have stepped in to offer their theories and interpretations of Sumerian myths, sometimes still leaving more
questions than answers. One of the most popular figures in
this quest for understanding is Zecharia Sitchin.

A Novel Perspective

A growing number of people have now heard of the Anunnaki either from mainstream academic accounts or the popular
media. The Anunnaki and their related myths entered public
awareness after author Zecharia Sitchin reinterpreted the myths
in his book *The 12th Planet* in 1976. It was in this book, as well
as his subsequent novels, that Sitchin presented an alternative
cosmology for the Anunnaki. Sitchin is, to some extent, a controversial figure. Most scholars discount his interpretations of
Sumerian tablets and deem his theories pseudoscience. Others
respect him for his passion and dedication, as well as bringing
the Sumerians myths to the fore. Who was this man?

Zecharia Sitchin was born in Baku, the capital and largest
city of Azerbaijan, in 1920. He lived for over thirty years in

Palestine before finally moving to the United States. During his stay in the Middle East, Sitchin learned ancient Hebrew. He studied economics from the University of London and was an editor and journalist in Mandatory Palestine before moving to New York in 1952, where he worked as an executive for a shipping company. Although he had a rather mundane job, he remained passionate about history and archaeology and was deeply religious. Sitchin devoted much of his youth to gathering material on the prehistoric cultures and eventually engaged in self-study of Sumerian.

The Sitchinian theory is quite nuanced and explained over seven books in part of a series called *The Earth Chronicles*. His reinterpretation of the Sumerian myths is clearly influenced by the preceding work of authors believing in paleocontact theory, also popularly known today as either ancient astronaut theory or ancient alien theory. The influential works of ancient astronaut theorists like Erich von Däniken and Immanuel Velikovsky suggest that extraterrestrial beings played a significant role in ancient human history. All of these theorists reinterpret the myths of Mesopotamia from a modern, space age perspective, which may be why they share common attributes. We will examine the theories of Immanuel Velikovsky in the next chapter, but first, let's take a look at a very condensed version of Sitchin's views.

According to Sitchin, the universe has not always been as we know it today. Originally there was a cosmic egg, the concentrated atomic mass that exploded after reaching the theoretical "density limit," some fifteen billion years ago. This massive event hurled cosmic debris throughout space. Some of these fragments remained incandescent and formed the stars, while others cooled and formed planets and meteorites. These bursts, traveling in space, ended up forming the galaxies that make up the universe. The gravitational forces of our solar system drew in a reddish planet called Nibiru. This planet traveled in our solar system, below the elliptical, passing through the orbits of Neptune and Uranus.

The intensity of its magnetic field shifted Uranus to its side, allowing Nibiru to pass. At that time there was no planet Earth, but rather a much larger Tiamat. Tiamat was covered primarily by water. In the course of its trajectory, one of Nibiru's moons struck Tiamat, dividing it into two parts. It pulverized the half where it struck, creating the asteroid belt between Mars and Jupiter, and pushed the other half into a lower orbit, the current path of Earth. During this process, Earth's gravity captured one of Nibiru's moons, taking it as its own satellite. The first passage of Nibiru was responsible for the current configuration of our solar system. Pluto was a moon of Saturn that was torn from its gravity and pushed into the present orbit. Nibiru has an orbital period of 3,600 years and moves around two suns. Sitchin postulates that the Sumerians described Nibiru as four times larger than the Earth and responsible for great catastrophes on our planet during its passage through our solar system. He explains that the approach of this planet was the cause of the deluge in both the Mesopotamian myth and the Bible, due to a polar displacement on Earth.

In Sitchin's account, Nibiru was the home planet of a people described by the ancients as a "race of gods," or Anunnaki. These gods have visited Earth in the past, influencing human culture. Per Sitchin's own translations, *Anunnaki* means "those who descended from the heavens," also known to the Hebrews as Nephilim or Elohim and the ancient Egyptians as Neter. These alien gods landed in ancient Mesopotamia about 450,000 years ago and colonized the Earth for the purpose of extracting large quantities of gold. Anu, Enki, and Enlil descended to southern Mesopotamia where they established Eridu, which according to Sitchin's translation means "home away from home."

Sitchin goes on to recount that the Anunnaki began the construction of the establishments necessary for mining and colonization. Needing resources, like food and water, they created Eden, a field of agriculture and farming. They soon discovered abundant gold deposits in southern Africa. Satisfied, Anu left the command of the mission to Enlil, while Enki directed the gold mines in present-day Zimbabwe. But the accompanying Anunnaki, who were used for hard labor, soon refused to work, which is similar to the biblical account of a rebellion against the Elohim.

During this time, groups of *Homo erectus* lived in southern Africa. Observing them, Enki realized that these primates were suitable for their mining operation. He captured a female and brought her to Enlil. From this point, Sitchin reinterprets the creation story as one with more science than story. He continues by claiming that the Anunnaki genetically manipulated an egg of this female, grafting it to Enki's wife Ninhursag's DNA. Thus, about 200,000 years ago, a sterile, male, physically strong and intelligent hybrid was born. The Anunnaki called it Lulu and went on to clone many more. These Lulu were created with the sole purpose of obeying and working. Excited and amused by this experiment, Enlil ordered his Anunnaki scientists to create new beings by mixing Lulu's DNA with that of other animals on Earth, creating a herd of chimera.

The creation of these chimera purportedly explains the abundance of anthropomorphic primitive gods, as well as the half-human, half-animal versions. Since these creations were genetically modified clones, they could not breed, so Enki decided the Lulu needed the ability to procreate. Enlil disagreed on this point, fearing uncontrollable growth of beings capable of rebellion and potentially harming the Anunnaki mission. Enki retorted that with the limited number of Lulu available, the mission would surely fail. Then, against his will, Enlil ended up approving the fertilization of Lulu and the generation of early man or Adamah (origin of the name Adam).

The idea that the Adamah could be dangerous due to retained hunter-gatherer attributes and behaviors divided the Anunnaki. Enlil was supported by the royal family and the military, all of whom wanted to eliminate the Adamah in favor of the more controllable and docile Lulu clones. Enki, supported by the scientists, believed that a more educated Adamah were a valuable resource for the Anunnaki and in the future it would be up to these humans to rule the land when the Anunnaki returned home. Unfortunately for the Adamah, when Enlil learned that the humans and Anunnaki had been engaging in sexual intercourse and even procreating, he was enraged. He accused the human females of original sin, and in an effort to prevent the problem from reaching Eridu, he gave orders to drive human beings out of Eden. In the Bible, this is the expulsion from the earthly paradise.

Meanwhile, in Africa, Enki began passing on knowledge to certain humans to establish the first kings. Enki bestowed the title of priest on these first rulers and established the original mystery school. His rule was complete and total obedience or face the punishment of death. This concept of absolute power was adopted by the kings, who went on to exploit their subjugated workers and use violence to control them. Slaves were harvested among primitive humans and genetically manipulated.

Then the alien colonization system began to decline because of low productivity and the rebellions of human slaves, especially in the mines. Lineages of kings were established and recorded on what we know as the Sumerian King List, possibly considered the direct progeny of the Anunnaki themselves. These kings were the first mystery school initiates, versed in sciences such as mathematics and astronomy and knowledgeable in medicine, architecture, and engineering.

By Sitchin's timeline, 100,000 years ago Anu died. Enlil inherited the position of king of the gods and decided to go back to Nibiru. Enki, as Enlil's half brother and son of a concubine, knew that he would not be able to ascend to the throne, so he refused to leave, feeling that he already had his own dominion on Earth. Enlil got angry and departed. Enki did not know what to do with all the abandoned gold, so he began to give it as gifts to the most faithful of men. Then, about 50,000 years ago, Enki left Africa and headed to Eridu, accompanied by loyal kings, priests, initiates, and their people, constituting the first major human migration from Africa to the Middle East. Eventually, a revolt broke out on Nibiru, and Enlil was exiled by his own royal family. Enki was then urgently recalled to Nibiru as heir to the throne. With that, the Anunnaki abandoned Earth about 5,000 years ago.

Panspermia

Sitchin, who died in 2010, was not alone in believing that humankind was somehow genetically manipulated by extraterrestrial intervention. Extraterrestrial genomic theories reach as far back as the classical era. The Greek philosopher Anaxagoras laid the foundation for the ancient astronaut hypothesis with his concept of Panspermia. He proposed that there were tiny seeds, or *spermata*, which were all over the cosmos, hence the prefix *pan-*. In the eighteenth century, Benoît de Maillet expanded on this idea by claiming that these "seeds" fell from space and into the ocean. The basic premise of Panspermia, in general, is that primitive life, originating from another planetary body, was deposited on Earth by way of a comet, asteroid, or other type of space debris.

Panspermia provides an alternative to what scientists call abiogenesis, or the generation of life from nonliving matter. Under this hypothesis, primitive life may have originally formed somewhere else in the universe. The foundations of life could have been seeded on Earth as well as on other habitable planets. In 1903, Svante Arrhenius (1859–1927), the Nobel Prize–winning Swedish physicist and chemist, formalized the concept of Panspermia, theorizing that microbe spores were propelled through space by radiation emitted by stars and were possibly the seeds of life on the primitive Earth (Arrhenius, 1908).

The Panspermia theory gained further interest during the nineteenth and twentieth centuries from several researchers—most notably, Leslie Orgel and his colleague, the late Nobel Prize–winning British scientist Francis Crick. Although Crick is primarily remembered for codiscovering the double helical structure of the DNA molecule, Orgel and Crick took the theory of Panspermia and expanded upon it. They proposed the theory of Directed Panspermia. Thus, one of the scientists responsible for discovering the structure of DNA was one of the very first ancient astronaut theorists. Let that sink in for a moment.

How did two very serious, acclaimed scientists conclude that there was alien intervention in the genetics of humankind?

After researching the structure of DNA, Crick started to have serious reservations about the possibility of DNA evolving naturally, due to its complexity. He and Orgel claimed that small granules of DNA could be rocketed out into space and would then have a chance at colonizing a different planet. This would allow future civilizations to pass on their genetic material in the face of a potential Earth catastrophe.

In 2018, thirty-three scientists from well-respected universities had a paper published in the peer-reviewed journal *Progress in Biophysics and Molecular Biology* that sent shock waves throughout the scientific community. The paper, entitled "Cause of the Cambrian Explosion—Terrestrial or Cosmic?" presents some of the incredible evidence of Panspermia since the 1970s. While it has come under scrutiny, the paper had undergone a year of intense peer review before getting published. The controversial theory challenges the more accepted hypothesis of abiogenesis, which suggests that at a point in the most ancient history, the conditions on Earth made possible a series of complex organic chemical reactions that led to the first primitive life-forms. From this "primordial soup" emerged self-replicating RNA within an 800-million-year period following the stabilizing of the Earth's crust (Steele et al., 2018). While this process is plausible and the potential well-understood by scientists, what is still unclear is how exactly the information became encoded into nucleic acids like DNA and RNA, subsequently forming a system of genetic inheritance and expression. Still, many scientists agree that abiogenesis is the best hypothesis for the origin of life on Earth that we have.

However, this new research into Panspermia relied on key experimental and observational data gathered over the past sixty years consistent with or predicted by the Hoyle-Wickramasinghe

(H-W) thesis of Cometary (Cosmic) Biology (Steele et al., 2018). The H-W model suggests:

> *that life was seeded here on Earth by life-bearing comets as soon*
> *as conditions on Earth allowed it to flourish (at or just before 4.1*
> *billion years ago); and living organisms such as space-resistant*
> *and space-hardy bacteria, viruses, more complex eukaryotic cells*
> *and organisms, . . . perhaps even fertilised ova and plant seeds,*
> *may have been continuously delivered ever since to Earth helping*
> *to drive further the progress of terrestrial biological evolution*
> *(Steele et al., 2018, 4).*

What the researchers argue is that abiogenesis did not happen on Earth and, instead, the source of genetic diversity and seemingly out-of-place species is a rain of living extraterrestrial organisms that integrated here on Earth and used a process known as horizontal gene transfer to transfer their RNA and DNA into the genomes of terrestrial life. This would mean that abiogenesis is wrong and life on Earth is not caused by the selection of naturally occurring advantageous mutations (Steele et al., 2018). This new way of understanding the origins of life explains how various epidemics are caused by the arrival of retroviruses from space, suggesting that it was an extraterrestrial retrovirus that drove the Cambrian explosion.

A retrovirus is a special category of RNA viruses that requires reverse transcription of the single-stranded RNA genome to a double-stranded DNA intermediate (Actor, 2012). *Reverse transcription* is the term used to describe the synthesis of a DNA copy of an RNA molecule. Retroviruses can transform cells because they must insert or integrate their genomes into the host cell chromosome, causing a mutation before viral replication can take place (Payne, 2017).

As evidence, the researchers point to known retroviruses utilizing horizontal gene transfer to integrate their own genetic material into the infected host in order to reproduce. Horizontal gene transfer is the nonsexual transmission of genetic material between unrelated genomes, allowing genetic material to be passed across species boundaries (Choudhuri and Kotewicz, 2014). An "infected" organism will transmit the retrovirus to its descendants if the virus has infected germ line cells, sperm, or ova, resulting in the acquired genetic material becoming part of the offspring's inheritance, replicating over and over again through generations.

The researchers believe that since retroviruses are dependent on their host to be successful, they could not have independently appeared at the same time. Further, scientists are able to determine that these retroviruses do not predate the Cambrian explosion, but rather they appear after a mass extinction event at the end of the Ediacaran period about 542 million years ago (Steele et al., 2018). This supports the researchers' implication that these complex early viruses are indeed extraterrestrial and came to Earth on comets that caused the Ediacaran extinction. That would make these retroviruses the main driver of the Cambrian explosion. They integrated themselves into the genomes of countless terrestrial species, introducing novel genetic material that resulted in an explosion of diversification of living forms.

The implications of the H-W Panspermia hypothesis are extraordinary. It would mean that the entire galaxy constitutes a single connected biosphere, making all life—whether terrestrial or extraterrestrial—related!

So where is the evidence? The researchers point to the octopus as a prime example of how this viral Panspermia took place. Cephalopods, the group comprised of the squid, octopus, and nautilus, have baffled scientists due to their confusing evolutionary tree. These creatures first appeared in the Late Cambrian

Period and were thought to have descended from the primitive nautiloid. However, the octopus is very differently evolved and indeed quite bizarre. Its complex nervous system, high intelligence, and ability to camouflage seem to have appeared suddenly, as opposed to evolving over a long period of time due to adaptations. Further, there is evidence of extensive changes in the RNA found in the neural structures of octopuses that could not have come from simple adaptation because these genes are nowhere present in the primitive ancestors but just sort of popped up out of nowhere, adding to the researchers' belief that these genes came from "a far distant 'future' in terms of terrestrial evolution, or more realistically from the cosmos at large" (Steele et al., 2018, 11). Could the octopus really be proof of extraterrestrial life? Considering that over 80 percent of our oceans is unmapped, unobserved, and unexplored (NOAA, 2009), there is no telling how many more secrets they may hold. Our search for extraterrestrial life may actually yield more results by focusing on terrestrial exploration first.

Ideas like Panspermia can be quite compelling because they do not rely on a religious dogma nor on myths and legends to help explain the science. Still, there are clear differences between a theory like Panspermia and Sitchin's. Although Directed Panspermia is arguably a more accepted theory in the mainstream than Sitchin's, it is still highly controversial and even ridiculed. Thus, if a theory like Directed Panspermia, which is supported by numerous scientists, spanning as far back as classical antiquity and including contemporary Nobel Prize–winning scientists, is still ridiculed in the halls of academia, then how well-received do you think Sitchin's theory is? As you would imagine, Sitchin is thought of as, at best, a pseudoscientist and, at worst, a liar. But where does that leave the general public?

It most certainly leads to a huge gap in both understanding and communication. As a result, people are measured against one of only a few sides of a potential story. With time, this leads to people being placed into one "camp" or the other. They are either believers in a specific version of an interpretation, like Sitchin's, or they are part of the mainstream. We are left with the "believers" and the "nonbelievers," as the gap between us widens. It is only through daring to cross this gap that we can get closer to the truth behind who the Anunnaki were and what their relevance may be now.

Why Consider Alternative Theories?

Alternative theories and diverse interpretations are vital to discourse and debate. More and more, empirical research leans on Cartesian-style Reductionism, which proposes that complex systems can be explained by simply cutting them down to their most basic parts. While this method can work for hard sciences, it is not the most effective approach when dealing with social sciences because of the numerous data points that must be in place for Reductionism to work well. When studying the past, historians do not have the luxury of a wealth of data points. Much of our past has been lost, buried under the sands of time. Furthermore, variables in history are mostly dependent and causal. To isolate one as independent is to alter the nature of historical development.

There is a valid need to generalize based on variables and their connections to gain a more holistic view of past events. Why does this matter? Because researchers are constantly fine-tuning techniques for drawing inferences about the likely effects of theories. In the hard sciences like computer development or chemistry, statisticians try to develop mathematical formulas to identify causality from data. The problem that statistics faces is that the numerical results can confuse actual causation with simple difference-making. Jonathan M. Livengood, associate professor of philosophy at the University of Illinois, argued that "ordinary causal judgments are closely connected to broadly moral judgments" (Livengood, 2011, 4). What this means is that when scholars are still undecided over the correct theory of actual causation, it results in misguided scientists' "intuition-fitting" (Livengood, 2011, 4). How scientific is that really?

I believe that natural systems and their properties should be viewed as wholes, rather than simply a collection of parts. Thus, I prefer looking at data more holistically because humanity is an extremely complex system whose function cannot be fully understood by its pieces alone. We need creative dot connectors, including Zecharia Sitchin, Erich von Däniken, Immanuel Velikovsky, Ignatius L. Donnelly, and others, to open our minds to possibilities outside of our own intellectual comfort zones. Even some of the most respected minds in history, like Isaac Newton, entertained fantastic theories that people of their day deemed superstitious or even heretical and were not afraid to challenge preexisting beliefs. It is the renegades who break barriers and forge new paths.

Paleocontact, in any form, is a truly fantastic idea with huge implications for humankind; but how much of it is true? Does *anyone* actually believe these theories? Sure, a theory like Directed Panspermia has its merits, but what about Sitchin's version, which may read like an interstellar fairy tale? What about the work of Erich von Däniken, who has spent over sixty-five years trying to prove that extraterrestrials visited Earth long ago and helped to shape humanity? He argues that "the evidence that human beings have been influenced by extraterrestrials throughout history to present day is becoming more compelling by the day" (von Däniken, 2018, 199), explaining that specific artificial mutations can be seen not only in the human genome, but also in our traditions (von Däniken, 2018). It may be easy to think that for anyone to believe in such alternative theories, they must be uneducated, gullible, or naive, but there are scientists, university scholars, theologians, philosophers, historians, and multinational corporations that take this account very seriously—so seriously that they sometimes pledge both their money and lives to searching for the truth. What if the answer has been right before our eyes, towering over us in megalithic fashion? The depth of humanity's roots is almost unimaginable to modern scientists, yet it was written in numerous ancient texts found all over the world.

As you will see, there is much more to our history than we are led to believe, starting with the fact that Earth's great civilizations share a common spark, one that science has only began to scratch the surface of. What they are about to discover will surely change everything.

CHAPTER 2

Primordial Beginnings

In all chaos there is a cosmos, in all disorder a secret order.
—CARL JUNG, Swiss psychiatrist and psychoanalyst

J ust as our last chapter started with a recounting of the two-hundred-million-year-old formation of Earth's continents from the collision of the two ancient supercontinents Laurasia and Gondwana, we will begin here by discussing a collision, not on Earth, but rather in the heavens. While the theories we will examine have flaws, they are important to address. A quote sometimes attributed to the Augustan period Roman poet Quintus Horatius Flaccus, better known as Horace, says, "Begin, be bold, and venture to be wise." By beginning with a critical examination of the bold cosmologies of Zecharia Sitchin, and now Immanuel Velikovsky, we also venture to become wise.

Clash of the Titans

Immanuel Velikovsky (1895–1979) was a Russian-American scientist and true polymath. He studied law and ancient history, as well as medicine. After receiving his medical degree in

1921, he emigrated to Germany, eventually traveling to Vienna to study psychoanalysis under the guidance of the first student of Sigmund Freud, Wilhelm Stekel. In 1939, after learning psychoanalysis from the masters, he moved to the United States and began delving into the three archetypes of interest to Freud: Moses, Akhenaten, and Oedipus. Velikovsky went on to study ancient texts, which led him to his radical theory that Earth has experienced a number of catastrophes caused by the collision of Venus and Mars. According to Velikovsky's understanding of ancient manuscripts, this violent planetary collision was witnessed by the people of Earth and subsequently recorded by numerous and disparate ancient civilizations.

Over the course of his research, Velikovsky stumbled upon a translation of one of the key texts of ancient Egypt, which his translator Alan Gardiner dated to the end of the Middle Kingdom. The papyrus described a number of catastrophic events almost identical to those mentioned in the Book of Exodus. Similarities included the accounts of water turning into blood, livestock disease and boils, fiery hail, darkness, and more. These and other striking coincidences between the biblical and Egyptian texts led this scientist to put forward the hypothesis that the story in Exodus was not fiction or allegory, but rather a real event of a celestial nature.

According to Velikovsky, a little more than 4,000 years ago there was an explosion on Jupiter, resulting in a planet-size fragment separating from it—what we would now call Venus. This new comet rushed toward the sun and entered an elliptical orbit crossing the Earth's. Around 1500 BCE, Earth entered the comet's tail. At first, the atmosphere was filled with fine red dust that fell to the surface of the planet, painting the ground and polluting the water. When the Earth came closer to the head of the comet, large particles fell, hurling at the Earth a fierce meteor shower, even hail, which undoubtedly caused great destruction. A huge amount of hydrocarbon was released into the atmosphere in the form of rains, some of which reached the ground and leached into the depths, forming modern oil reserves; however, the worst thing was that part of the oil falling from the sky was ignited by lightning, so it appeared as though fire fell from the sky.

Velikovsky believed that this celestial catastrophe explains the prominent role that Venus has played in a huge number of myths, legends, and ancient astronomical and historical texts. The Persian accounts tell of a day that lasted for three days, and then changed over to a night, which lasted three times longer than usual. The Chinese also wrote about a time when the whole Earth was burning and the sun did not set for several days. During this time, most of the world's population was destroyed or starved due to famine. The first part of the Mexican Codex Chimalpopoca called the Anales de Cuauhtitlan (Annals of Cuautitlán) reports that there was a cosmic catastrophe in the distant past resulting in an extended period of night. In the recorded legends of pre-Columbian Central America, it is said that fifty-two years before there had been a catastrophe, which coincided with a darkened sun.

There are so many other interesting connections made by Velikovsky, but another thrust of his arguments was that electromagnetic forces, rather than gravity, determined events within the solar system. Velikovsky wrote a letter to his friend Albert Einstein arguing that space is not a vacuum and that electromagnetism plays a fundamental role in the solar system and the entire universe. Einstein did not agree with Velikovsky, which was common between the two friends who had discussed theories together for a number of years. Velikovsky knew that he needed evidence. He predicted that if astronomers could detect radio emissions from Jupiter, this would support his theory, and in 1955, astronomers at the Carnegie Institution were, in fact, stunned to detect strong radio signals emanating from Jupiter.

The greatest objections from the scientific community were based around rejecting that electromagnetic forces were so influential. Velikovsky was ridiculed by the scholars of his day. Yet, you can see how Einstein, father of the general theory of relativity, was at odds with Velikovsky, but they still corresponded and discussed their theories without resorting to personal attacks. This sort of open-minded civil discourse is growing hard to find these days. If only all scientists were as willing to discuss so-called fringe ideas, but many modern scholars are not as secure as Einstein was. Einstein knew his own intellect and was not threatened by those who thought differently.

Clearly, Velikovsky's theory has flaws, like his overall chronology or timeline of events. Much of what he theorized depended on biblical texts, particularly those of the Old Testament. As such, there are contradictions. For example, there is a written testimony about the scientific breakthrough of the Babylonians in about 1600 BCE discovering that Venus is not two celestial bodies—the morning and evening star—but one. However, Moses was supposedly dodging the fiery comet trail from the Venus protoplanet in about 1200 BCE. Of course, this may be splitting hairs. Consider also that the mass of Venus is much larger than that of any comet, so if Velikovsky's theory is correct, then there is one big problem with the statement that Venus, no matter how much it weighed, passed close to Earth: the moon is still in its orbit. If Venus had indeed moved between the Earth and the moon, this would have inevitably led to the moon being hurled into space.

I do not point this out to debunk Velikovsky. I am only a historian and archaeologist, not a physicist or astronomer, and I have never had personal correspondences with great scientists like Einstein, as Velikovsky did. As a social scientist, what I hope to make clear is this: there are and have been learned individuals who propose bold theories that challenge the accepted historical or even prehistorical narratives. A theory that is bold will also be flawed. It takes courage to make mistakes. A quote often attributed to Einstein points out, "Anyone who has never made a mistake has never tried anything new." Velikovsky was not afraid to make errors, and neither was Sitchin. In science, many of the greatest discoveries were accidental.

A Sumerian Cosmology

Velikovsky's account is similar to Sitchin's in a lot of ways. In Sitchin's view, ancient humans and their civilizations were almost completely wiped out by the collision of the Earth with the planet he called Tiamat, after the Sumerian god. According to this theory, Earth is littered with traces of this apocalyptic event. Today, excavations around the globe are increasingly showing off the destruction that Tiamat caused. Many ancient writings are full of reports of this disaster, just as Velikovsky discovered.

Initially, the idea of the presence of unknown planets in the solar system did not come from scientific hypothesis, but a myth. From the middle of the twentieth century, alternative theories mention Nibiru, a planet supposedly positioned between Mars and Jupiter. Sitchin argued that the Sumerians knew about a "wandering planet," which they called Nibiru. He argued that it was an absolutely real celestial body, but went even further, declaring that Nibiru was inhabited by the civilization of the Anunnaki, the mysterious ancestors of humankind who created *Homo sapiens* for exhausting work in gold mines in Mesopotamia and Africa, based on his translations. Multiple mainstream scholars of Near Eastern history and linguistics vehemently oppose Sitchin's translations. However, while there are numerous errors in Sitchin's direct translations of the Sumerian language, it is a mistake to throw out his entire theory. It goes back to the point made about Velikovsky's theories: to be a pioneer, you have to be bold enough to make a few mistakes.

Correct Translations?

In his book *The 12th Planet*, Zecharia Sitchin contended that the Sumerian texts had been mistranslated and were accounts of ancient extraterrestrial contact. He argued that the texts referred to technologically advanced aliens coming to Earth in spaceships more than 400,000 years ago to mine for gold to take back to their home of Nibiru to replenish that planet's depleted atmosphere. Hence, they genetically modified humankind to be their slave species to mine the planet's natural resources. As a result, these aliens or Anunnaki became our overlords.

Allow me to address some of the main criticisms of Sitchin's work. Sitchin claimed he was one of the few people in the world able to read Sumerian; however, this is an exaggeration. It is widely known that the ancient Mesopotamians had their own dictionaries. Many ancient textbooks have been found, as well as tablets used by students to practice their writing. These have been translated and are continuing to be translated since the mid-twentieth century. Not only have they been translated, but also published. I personally own a number of these publications, including one by William Nesbit, put out in 1914 by Columbia University Press, called *Sumerian Records from Drehem*. It contains a treatise by Nesbit, as well as the Sumerian records from the Drehem site, located in present-day Iraq. These tablets unearthed more than a century ago mainly concern the management of livestock near Nippur. They do not tell of ancient spacecraft; however, they do tell us that the settlement, then called Puzrish-Dagan, was a place of importance during the twenty-first century BCE. This sort of administrative record keeping is what many discovered texts are about. In addition to a number of old books available, there are online resources now accessible to anyone. The Electronic Text Corpus of Sumerian Literature (ETCSL) maintained by Oxford University is the very best up-to-date online resource for Sumerian translations. It is searchable and freely available to all researchers.

Modern experts have shown that Sitchin's translations do indeed contain errors. The most vocal of them is Dr. Michael Heiser. In fact, Heiser, a credentialed scholar specializing in the Hebrew Bible and ancient Semitic languages, runs an entire website devoted to refuting Sitchin's theory. He points out that Sitchin made many translation errors and offered to debate him on the late-night radio show *Coast to Coast AM* with the late Art Bell. Heiser, while offering solid research-based criticism of Sitchin's work, could also be considered biased. In addition to his enthusiasm to debunk Sitchin, it should be noted that his own books have been published by Lexham Press, part of the Faithlife Corporation. According to its website, Lexham Press "seeks to increase biblical literacy, thoughtful Christian reflection, and faithful action around the world by publishing a range of evangelical Bible study materials, scholarly works, and pastoral resources" (*lexhampress.com,* 2018). Heiser views his work through an evangelical Christian lens, which, like any lens, can limit your sight and result in biased conclusions.

Herein lies the problem: Sitchin's work is so divisive that there is seemingly no middle ground. Those who follow Sitchin tend to do so unquestionably. Those who refute Sitchin also do so unquestionably. This division creates a huge gap in our understanding of human history. In splitting hairs over every translation in this way, we lose the opportunity to make meaningful connections. Getting tripped up over small matters keeps us from looking at the bigger picture, and this is how we miss the truth. The truth is a bigger, more complex image visible to all if we could just look past our own limited views and come together to see what is hidden in plain sight. Of course, there are many who make a living now pushing a one-sided view of reality, so it is in their interest to keep up the walls. Divide and conquer has always been an effective strategy. It is for this reason that in my research, I prefer not to get caught in arguing one variation of a translation over another, unless it is essential to the context and meaning of an entire passage.

Instead of referring to Sitchin's work as a translation of the Sumerian texts, I believe it is more accurate and helpful to refer to it as *an interpretation.* This is not meant to disparage his efforts; quite the opposite. It is my position that most of the trouble in discussing Sitchin's work comes when people try to either prove or discount everything he theorized based only on the practice of linguistics. (And many who oppose Sitchin's views come from this field.) Linguistics is a complex field of study, but its complexity and use of scientific methods do not mean that it is a quantifiable science in the same way as mathematics or physics.

The Art of Translating

Even specialists in the field of linguistics do not agree with viewing it as a hard science. In an article published by the Linguistic Society of America, scholars questioned whether linguistics belongs to the natural sciences, biology, or social sciences. They argued that because the linguistic processes use scientific techniques, it is easy for people to believe that it is a science. The study of language seems very different from cultural anthropology or archaeology because its rigid parameters within the structures of grammar stand in contrast to the "free and undetermined behavior of human beings studied from the standpoint of culture" (Sapir, 1929, 213). These scholars determined that language is primarily a cultural product and must be understood as such, and that the development of languages depends on *interpretation*, much like art, another product of culture (Sapir, 1929).

What does this all mean? The study of language, like archaeology, is not a science, even though scientific techniques are used by its practitioners. The study of language is more akin to an art. Therefore, interpretation is a valid way to engage with language since language is a cultural artifact. In order to accept Sitchin's account, one would need to look at the interpretation, rather than reduce it to simply a translation, because his actual scholarly translations have proven to be wrong. Therefore, anyone who wishes to believe in Sitchin's account does so on the basis of belief, which is the realm of faith and not science. Is there anything wrong with interpreting ancient texts in such a way that it requires faith to accept? You would have to ask the over six billion people in the world who depend on the interpretations of some form of ancient religious text as a foundation of their belief.

With that in mind, let's look at the Babylonian creation epic, The Enûma Eliš, and learn how Sitchin's interpretation of this important text could give us insight into the birth of the cosmos.

The Enûma Eliš, Tiamat, and Nibiru

The history of our solar system is told in the Enûma Eliš. The creation story shares remarkable similarities with that in Genesis, only the Enûma Eliš is much older. It consists of seven tablets corresponding to the seven days of Creation from Genesis, and just as with the seventh day of rest in Genesis, the seventh tablet is dedicated to the glorification of the Babylonian creator deity. The order of creation also corresponds in both Enûma Eliš and Genesis, as the gods discuss the creation of man. Also in the Enûma Eliš, the planets are referred to as gods who were involved in an epic battle. According to Sitchin, at the time the Earth did not exist, and there was a planet called Tiamat between Mars and Jupiter about the size of Uranus. A strange planet called Nibiru came from outside of our solar system—making it a wandering planet—and escaped from another solar system. Nibiru was caught in the gravity of our solar system and caused, among other things, the tilting of Uranus and Pluto becoming a separate planet in orbit around the sun, as it used to be a moon of Saturn. Nibiru also exerted its gravity on the various planets in our solar system. One of the moons of Nibiru collided with Tiamat, and later Nibiru collided with Tiamat. The fragments of Tiamat formed the Asteroid Belt and possibly various comets and loose asteroids, and the remainder was hurled into orbit around the sun and became the planet Earth, while another moon of Tiamat became our current moon. Nibiru settled in a contrarian elliptical orbit around the sun rising from below through the Asteroid Belt between Mars and Jupiter in an orbit of 3,600 years. This means that a Nibiru year is equivalent to 3,600 Earth years.

Due to the clashes of Tiamat with Nibiru, Nibiru is referred to as the bringer of "the elixir of life" or "the seeds of life" as evolution on Earth was set in motion. According to the fossil record, there was no life on Earth for the first 600 million years. About four billion years ago, the first life began to emerge, after which it began to develop rapidly.

Nibiru came to be known as the Twelfth Planet, as the sun and moon were also taken into account. When one does not include the sun and moon, Nibiru is also called the Tenth Planet or Planet X. This is, of course, before a group of astronomers decided that Pluto could no longer be counted as a full-fledged planet. The X also stands for "the unknown planet." Supposedly, the Twelfth Planet is responsible not only for the fluctuations caused in the orbit of the planets, but also for many Earth catastrophes whenever it makes its journey through the inner part of the solar system, such as so-called pole shifts (north becomes south and south becomes north), changes in the precession of the Earth, tectonic plate shifts, earthquakes, tidal waves, volcanic eruptions, and a scale of climatic changes. On a more human level there are mass mortality events, crop failures, famines, disease, and wars. The biblical flood may have been caused by the Twelfth Planet—and possibly the exodus of the Hebrew people from Egypt and the associated ten plagues, as Velikovsky argued.

It is important to keep in mind that when reading these texts, god/gods had multiple meanings in the Sumerian mythology, similar to other religions.

MEANING 1:

Designation for a planet, star, moon, comet, or celestial body to which divine qualities were granted. We not only see this in the Enûma Eliš when talking about Tiamat and Marduk, but also at other places in clay tablets that talk about Nibiru as "the Lord of Heavens" and "the Heavenly Judge."

MEANING 2:

Name for settlers from another planet. As humankind are the kind of the Earth, the gods are the kind of the Twelfth Planet.

MEANING 3:

A spiritual being or quality. This can be divided into a, b, and c.

a. For Christians and other believers in monotheism there is an omnipotent Supreme Being, the almighty Creator, usually in the masculine role. In polytheistic religions like Hinduism there are also female goddess roles with multiple gods who are subordinated to a head god or goddess. In some views, the different gods are part-identifiers of the same god.

b. In some views, spiritual angels are appointed over a certain time period and territory and become the god for that epoch or age. These may then carry the title of god, usually lord, but remain subordinate to the Almighty God.

c. The Cosmos, the Architect, the Source, the All, the Universe, etc. (This being can take rather vague forms.)

Sitchin's history of Sumerian mythology continues with the description of how the inhabitants of this Twelfth Planet Nibiru colonized Earth to extract raw materials. These extraterrestrial settlers were called the Anunnaki. The first group was charged with setting up the necessary systems so that other beings of extraterrestrial origins could follow. Of course, by this account, the Anunnaki would have to be technologically advanced. According to Sitchin's calculations outlined in his book *The 12th Planet*, the Anunnaki may have been capable of space travel 500,000 years ago and may have come to Earth around 432,000 years ago (Sitchin, 2016). This estimation of between 400,000 and 500,000 would put their arrival shortly before the start of what scientists call the Phanerozoic eon.

The Phanerozoic eon gets its names from the Greek for "visible life," which refers to it being a time when there was a sharp increase in the number of organisms on Earth. With the advent of the Phanerozoic eon, there was a sudden appearance in the fossil record of a number of biological species and organisms with skeletons. This was the time on the Earth when animals and humans "appeared." The history of the development of the Earth is divided into four eons, with the first three combined into one era. The very first eons are the Hadean, when Earth formed, the Archean, when the Earth crust formed, and the Proterozoic, when oxygen appeared in Earth's atmosphere. All three of these eons are grouped into one era called the Precambrian. The Precambrian era lasted from 4.6 billion years ago up to about 542 million years ago. After the Precambrian came the Cambrian period, the first period of the Paleozoic era and the beginning of a new eon that we are currently in, the Phanerozoic. This period is known for the incredible, abrupt, and rapid development of living organisms, a phenomenon called the "Cambrian explosion."

From their interpretations of the Sumerian texts, alternative theorists like Sitchin have calculated the time intervals and approximate dates of the Anunnaki's activity on Earth. These dates roughly correspond with known geological timelines:

- **450,000 years ago**: Entities who fled from Nibiru discovered gold on Earth.

- **445,000 years ago:** The first group of Anunnaki, headed by the entity Enki, landed on Earth. They laid the foundation for the first city on Earth, Eridu, in the southern part of Mesopotamia off the coast of the Persian Gulf.

- **416,000 years ago:** More Anunnaki, headed by Enki's brother Enlil, came to develop a mining operation in Africa. The supreme ruler Anu, father of Enki and Enlil, handed over the rule of the Earth to his youngest son Enlil.

- **400,000 years ago:** The Anunnaki built the city of Sippar, which is located southwest of present-day Baghdad in central Iraq.

- **300,000 years ago:** Enki decided to create primitive workers for the mining operation, referred to as *ùĝ saĝ gíg ga*, meaning "the black-headed people." These were the first *Homo sapiens*, who were genetically modified primates.

- **200,000 years ago:** Earth entered a new glacial period.

- **100,000 years ago**: Earth's climate changed again, this time warming.

- **75,000 years ago:** More climate catastrophe as the last Ice Age moved in. Life on Earth concentrated only in central latitudes, closer to the equator. Cro-Magnon survived in middle latitudes.

- **55,000 years ago:** The climate stabilized, and the Anunnaki married Earth women. Their descendants began governing over early humans.

- **30,000–20,000 years ago:** The world's population was multiplying uncontrollably. Enlil decided to destroy humanity. Droughts, floods (including the Great Flood), and epidemics began. Nevertheless, people survived.

This timeline coincides with a lot of what scientists now know about the chronology of the Ice Age, putting *Homo sapiens sapiens* in the middle of a treacherous period of global instability. Imagine how many times during this harsh period humans came perilously close to total extinction. Such extensive and chronic trauma may have given rise to the many myths of cataclysm and creation that most scholars believe to be just stories. However, stories *are* histories. The word *history* is from the Old French *estorie*, meaning "story, chronicle, history," and from Late Latin *storia*, shortened from Latin *historia*, "history, account, tale, story" (*etymoline.com*, 2018). Historians generally regard stories from oral traditions as true even though they are passed on through many generations. Why couldn't these stories of ancient cataclysmic events and strange visitors be accurate accounts of real events?

The conventional narrative would have you believe that these ancestors were violent, primitive, half-naked cave dwellers who simply worshipped a nature they could not comprehend. However, the truth is that very little is known about early humans, and most of what is believed is based on scant evidence and biased interpretations of data. This bias can be seen every time an archaeologist finds something of cultural significance and concludes, without enough measurable data, that it is of ritual significance. This thinking has permeated the field from the start.

Take Henri Breuil (1877–1961), a French archaeologist, anthropologist, and devout Jesuit priest, who studied cave art throughout Europe and Asia. He graduated from the Seminary of St. Sulpice and was such a religious zealot, his colleagues referred to him as an "irascible and egotistical man" (Bahn, 62). In addition to being a Jesuit, Breuil worked with the Ahnenerbe or "Inheritance of the Forefathers," a Nazi research institute founded by Heinrich Himmler. The purpose of the Ahnenerbe was to find the supposed archaeological and cultural history of the so-called Aryan race.

Breuil's judgments were taken as almost infallible. Scholars even called him the "Pope of Prehistory" (Bahn.). However, his work was littered with bias and speculation, the most notable example being his theories of hunting magic and the Paleolithic cave art found in the Sanctuary at Trois-Frères in Ariège, France. It was in these caves that Breuil came upon an incomplete drawing of a horned humanoid figure, known today as "The Sorcerer." Breuil sketched what he thought the rest of the figure should look like and later published that drawing in the 1920s. Breuil claimed that the humanoid depicted a shaman that was seen in the trances of early humans. These early humans would go to the deepest parts of the cave, enter into a trance, and emerge to paint images of their visions on the cave walls in the hopes that they could draw power out of the cave.

This theory, sketch, and the credibility of Breuil have been the subject of much debate. Breuil's drawing takes too many liberties when compared with the actual painted image, which was barely an outline. Is it any surprise that someone with such religious zeal would literally fill in the blanks using his own beliefs? The theory that the humanoid figure may be a shamanic one may not be incorrect; however, considering that the sup-posed evidence for Breuil's theory is his own speculation, it becomes clear that academia has not always been fair or even trustworthy. Nevertheless, Breuil's theory has now become the accepted narrative for Upper Paleolithic cave art. Where is the rest of Breuil's evidence to support his claims about these spe-cific early humans and their trances? How could he surmise all of these details from simply one half-drawn image?

Archaeological discoveries such as these can be like a Ror-schach test. When looking at something vague like this, you will project your own ego onto the image. The truth is that the further back you go in history, the less you can know for sure. Physical evidence degrades, languages disappear along with texts, and nature reclaims her dominion from humankind. This is how civi-lizations become lost. It is sheer hubris on the part of academics to believe that they can know the answers with such little data.

Breuil's depiction of the Shaman. (from The Shamans of Prehistory *by Jean Clottes and J. David Lewis-Williams)*

49

Archaeologists still tend to project religious implications and meanings onto what may be secular depictions. This is how settlements become temples, and local traditions, religious rites. While it is enticing to assign an otherworldly significance to a buried statue, not every find is a religious relic.

The Sumerian civilization developed around 4000 BCE during a time of considerable intellectual advancements. Only around 300 years had passed since the humans became a modern industrialized civilization, which is trivial on a geologic scale. It may not seem so, but even the Phanerozoic eon—the entire span that complex life has existed on the Earth's land surface—is still a small fraction of the time frame in which the Earth has existed. Given that industrialized human civilization has only occupied such a small range of geologic time, it raises the question as to whether a civilization such as this could have happened on this planet before. Could there have been a lost highly advanced civilization on Earth so ancient that the archaeological or even the fossil record could not show a trace of it? Researchers at NASA are wondering the very same thing.

Lost Civilization

Do we really know everything there is to know about the progression and stages of life on this planet? Researchers at NASA recently questioned the very possibility of an undetectable ancient industrial civilization. In a paper published by the International Journal of Astrobiology called "The Silurian Hypothesis: Would It Be Possible to Detect an Industrial Civilization in the Geological Record?" (named after the ancient race of intelligent subterranean reptilians from the show *Doctor Who*), scientists at NASA's Goddard Institute for

Space Studies and the University of Rochester ask whether humans were not the only advanced civilization to have existed on our planet (Schmidt and Frank, 2018).

The study claims that since the fossil record doesn't go back further than 2.6 million years, we would not be able to actually detect such an ancient civilization. Anything earlier than 2.6 million years would have already turned to dust by now. Everything before this time period has already been lost to time. Using the Drake equation to estimate the number of active, communicative extraterrestrial civilizations in the Milky Way galaxy, the researchers used the letter N to represent the number of possible civilizations, "which was equal to the product of the average rate of star formation, R*, in our galaxy; the fraction of formed stars, f_p, that have planets; the average number of planets per star, n_c, that can potentially support life; the fraction of those planets, f_l, that actually develop life; the fraction of planets bearing life on which intelligent, civilized life, f_i, has developed; the fraction of these civilizations that have developed communications, f_c, i.e., technologies that release detectable signs into space; and the length of time, L, over which such civilizations release detectable signals" (Schmidt and Frank, 2018). Thus, the equation looked like this:

$$N = R^* \cdot f_p \cdot n_e \cdot f_l \cdot f_i \cdot f_c \cdot L$$

Using this mathematical model, the researchers determined that if ancient civilizations went to space and left artifacts on other planets, it would be easier to find the evidence of these civilizations than it would be on Earth (Schmidt and Frank, 2018). This is because erosion and tectonic activity would erase the evidence of an extremely ancient civilization. They go on to cite the example of the dinosaurs, stating that "for all the dinosaurs that ever lived, there are only a few thousand near-complete specimens, or equivalently only a handful of individual animals across thousands of taxa per 100,000 years" (Schmidt and Frank, 2018, 5). As such, it is highly unlikely that physical artifacts of a lost civilization this old could have survived. Even early human technological devices like the Antikythera mechanism (ca. 205 BCE) have barely made it. However, the researchers propose that more research should be conducted on elemental and compositional anomalies in current sediments because they may show signs of a previously unknown ancient civilization, like iridium layers, shocked quartz, microtektites, and magnetites (Schmidt and Frank, 2018, 17). On one hand the researchers seem optimistic at the possibility for an extremely ancient technologically advanced civilization to have existed on Earth—or even other celestial bodies, for that matter. The study also mentions interest in abiogenesis, the belief that life evolved from inorganic or inanimate substances, and the possibility of a "shadow biosphere," which would be "composed of descendants of a different origin event from the one which led to our Last Universal Common Ancestor (LUCA)" (Schmidt and Frank, 2018, 4).

While the researchers at NASA point to a belief in the possibility of advanced extraterrestrial life, they stop short of saying it could have come here, stating that they "strongly doubt that any previous industrial civilization existed before our own" (Schmidt and Frank, 2018, 18). Yet, their research uses a flawed theoretical framework to discount the possibility of such an ancient lost civilization: the Drake equation. To understand how the Drake equation may not be the proper framework on which to examine the possibility of ancient planetary life, we must first look at the work of the SETI Institute and Frank Drake, after whom the equation is named.

The Search for Extraterrestrial Life

Throughout history, those who pondered whether there is life beyond Earth have also questioned whether or not extraterrestrial life could be intelligent and perhaps even capable of communication. The nonprofit Search for ExtraTerrestrial Intelligence Institute (SETI Institute) is attempting to resolve these questions by setting out to "explore, understand and explain the origin, nature and prevalence of life in the universe" (SETI, 2018). While the mission statement is clear, the search for extraterrestrial life has proved challenging for a few notable reasons. Firstly, SETI Institute's mission is fundamentally flawed due to its anthropocentric nature. Secondly, SETI's resistance to utilizing new technology decreases its likelihood of success.

The founders of SETI lack the diversity in their backgrounds to fully assess the plausibility of communicating with extraterrestrial life. Currently, SETI "employs over 150 scientists, educators and support staff" (SETI, 2018). While employing scientists is of course essential, there is still not a significant focus on attracting a more creative and diverse staff. The majority of people involved are in such disciplines as mathematics, physics, and astronomy. These professionals are well respected in their fields and have much to contribute to humanity's search for life beyond Earth. However, there are many more aspects to consider when resolving a question of this magnitude. For instance, extraterrestrial civilizations may have unique cultures, languages, ethics, and philosophies, all of which need to be taken into account by professionals in their respective fields. By engaging more professionals in diverse fields such as anthropology, history, and philosophy, SETI would greatly enhance its efforts. There are more factors to consider when trying to identify and understand extraterrestrial life, as cosmic evolution has not one, but three components: astronomical, biological, and cultural (Dick, 2008). Scientists from SETI concern themselves primarily with the first two based on their specific training. They tend to ignore the third, critical, component of culture.

The SETI Institute, initially founded by astronomers, started taking form as far back as 1961, thanks to Frank Drake, a U.S.-born radio astronomer. Drake offered a mathematical equation to support the possibility for extraterrestrial life. He began by introducing his theories at a conference at the National Radio Astronomy Observatory in Green Bank. This event would later be known as simply "The Green Bank Conference" (Clark, 2000, 32). Drake, as the organizer of this event, sat down to set an agenda for the meeting. As Drake compiled the important points to be discussed, he decided to assign each point a symbol, turning the agenda into an equation. This equation, known as the Drake equation, became the cornerstone of the SETI Institute.

During the Green Bank Conference, Drake communicated his ideas to many experts in the field of astronomy, including Carl Sagan. Sagan had been interested in the search for extraterrestrial life for quite some time, so he was quick to lend his support. Likewise, support for the new SETI Institute initiative echoed almost worldwide due to the public perception of Sagan and the respect that he had earned in the scientific community (McDonough, 1987). Sagan was viewed as an intellectual—witty and charismatic. He was able to explain science in a way the average person could easily understand it. This helped him to become a popular figure on television. Thanks to his fame, scientists from all parts of the world started to accept the idea that extraterrestrial civilizations might exist and be worth looking for (McDonough, 1987). Sagan was a driving force

in the establishment of the SETI Institute's credibility, leading to the involvement of more mathematicians, astronomers,
and scientists. To this day, SETI commemorates the legacy of
Sagan in the name of its anchor center: the Carl Sagan Center
for the Study of Life in the Universe, in which Drake is the
director (SETI, 2018).

Since its founding, the SETI Institute has not positively
detected any extraterrestrial life. The use of the Drake equation
to support its research assumes that life is rare in the universe
and that the same evolutionary conditions that took place on
Earth would have to transpire for life to occur outside of Earth
(Ćirković, 2004). But SETI should not presuppose that all
creatures would have undergone the same evolutionary processes humans have. There are other factors to consider. Due to
the need for special planetary conditions, along with a random
set of events that have contributed to our biological evolution,
it comes as no surprise that SETI has "failed to make a positive
detection" (Clark, 2000, 182). Is there a potential flaw in the
foundation of SETI's mission? Clark argues, "we [scientists]
simply lack the theory to attach warranted values to most of the
terms in the Drake equation" (Clark, 2000, 34). Drake, sitting
alone and working out a mathematical formula to support the
existence of extraterrestrial life without the input of a diverse
group of professionals, is not a strong enough foundation for
an ambitious organization such as the SETI Institute.

Furthermore, the founders of SETI have suggested that
creatures existing in this galaxy would have made the same
technological advancements as humans. There is no substan-
tive basis for this claim. Many scientists believe the galaxy is
uniformitarian. In this sense "advanced technological communities could arise at any point in the Galactic history"
(Ćirković, 2). We do not have concrete evidence to support

that evolution is consistent, much less predictable—quite the contrary. Clark questions what triggered the Cambrian explosion that propelled "increasingly complex life-forms" away from five million years of evolution, as proposed by Darwin (Clark, 2000, 181). There are simply too many variables involved in life's origins and what technologies could be possessed by extraterrestrials. Clearly, we cannot begin to understand the development of advanced technology without some knowledge of its scientific components—represented in the Drake equation as symbols that can only be hypothesized but not truly known.

It may sound silly to point this out, but the SETI Institute is inherently disadvantaged because it is comprised of humans rather than extraterrestrials. In other words, by thinking only from a human perspective, members of SETI are limited in their understanding of extraterrestrial communications. The SETI Institute operates on the basis that extraterrestrial life must indeed have parallel cultures to humans because humans are in the universe and so are extraterrestrials, and since both life-forms would exist in the universe, the universal laws of both science and math must apply (Basalla, 2006). The position that SETI takes on this matter is unbalanced and unfounded. Its mission is greatly compromised from the very beginning due to these types of misinterpretations. There is more of a focus on the specialized fields of interest and individual assumptions of its members than on recognizing the holistic nature of life. Humans cannot fully understand the potential thought processes, cultural differences, or philosophies of extraterrestrial life. The idea that humans can, and do, have the objectivity and knowledge to grasp what it would take to communicate with extraterrestrials is anthropocentric. There are too many variables that need to be assessed by professionals in a number of nonmathematical or astronomical fields, such as anthropology and philosophy.

Such diverse approaches are vital to the success of the SETI Institute's mission. The basic belief that humans will be able to communicate with extraterrestrials is not just a matter of reconciling equations, it is also riddled with philosophical difficulties (Basalla, 2006). These philosophical questions may, in and of themselves, determine whether SETI will succeed. For example, even if extraterrestrial life does have the technological ability to communicate with life on Earth, they may not have the desire to do so. Another possibility is that their belief system could have philosophical ideals culturally prohibiting communication with Earth. Many humans face these same philosophical dilemmas. Often the prospect of communication with extraterrestrials is believed to be "anti-biblical" (Peters, 2017). With a philosophical consensus not having been met by the civilizations on Earth yet, SETI must realize the even if extraterrestrials have evolved parallel with humans, there are too many philosophical components to be resolved using human perspective and science alone.

Since the SETI Institute proceeds under the assumption that technological advancement among extraterrestrial civilizations would occur parallel to the advancements of humans on Earth, the primary approach its members are using to communicate with extraterrestrial life is outdated. SETI relies on radio signal-processing technology pioneered in 1959, because radio waves can "travel through interstellar space with relative ease" (Clark, 2000, 58). In spite of this benefit of the use of radio signals in the search for extraterrestrial life, there are also factors inhibiting progress. Radio signals only target specific stars and are beamed to other stars without significant motion so this method "does not provide any scanning" and leaves the detection of advanced extraterrestrial civilizations up to chance (Zaitsev, 2008). Alternative technologies exist that could improve the SETI's efforts for possible extraterrestrial communication. For the SETI Institute's mission to succeed, a more modern approach must be considered.

The SETI Institute uses an algorithm known as the "Fast Fourier Transform (FFT)" to try to decode signals from the cosmic background noise it receives through radio wave technology (Griggs, 2008). Alternatively, the use of an algorithm known as the Karhunen-Loève Transform (KLT) to detect spread spectrum signals has been suggested by scientists since the early 1980s. The computing power required to interpret these algorithms would be burdensome, even by modern standards; however, a possible solution offered at a meeting in Paris called Searching for Life Signatures suggests that "the KLT should be programmed into computers at the new Low Frequency Array telescope in the Netherlands and the Square Kilometre Array telescope, due for completion in 2012" (Griggs, 2008). As computing power increases, so does the pressure for SETI to use this method. Senior SETI astronomer Seth Shostak agrees that the KLT could offer better insight into extraterrestrial communication, but does not think that abandoning existing efforts would lead to a discovery any sooner. He holds firm to the belief that even if extraterrestrials communicated in such an advanced way that it could be detected with KLT, it is safer to assume that extraterrestrials "might use a 'ping' signal that has a lot of energy in a narrow band—the kind of thing the FFT could find" (Griggs, 2008). Whether or not this is the right approach has yet to be proven.

Still, SETI continues to use technology proposed almost fifty years ago by Frank Drake and other radio astronomers.

An even more modern approach should be considered by SETI to bring the goal of extraterrestrial communication within reach. Using pulsed laser signals that are beamed by a large telescope across the galaxy could streamline the search for extraterrestrial life. Lasers can cover a greater distance than radio waves. According to Jeff Hecht, "the advantages of using a laser, rather than radio waves, is that with the naked human eye, the distances of about 0.1 light year could be detected" (Hecht, 1996). Furthermore, with a relatively good telescope acting as a receiver, a laser beam "could be detected up to distances of about 100 light years" (Hecht, 1996). At a rate such as this, SETI could cover more cosmic distance than it does by targeting radio waves at distant stars.

Another benefit to using laser beams instead of or in addition to radio waves is that laser beams can carry far more information than a radio wave alone. This is exemplified in the preference for cable communications on Earth (Clark, 2000, 111). Clearly, SETI would benefit from the new technologies available today. The chances of making contact with extraterrestrial life would increase significantly, based on probability alone, with more and different methods employed. Understandably, funding is a major concern at SETI, since it is a non-profit organization. However, this is another reason the SETI Institute should expand its current search methods. Using a laser would be more cost-effective since it can reach a greater distance. Also, according to Hecht, the telescopes required for detection of this laser do not need to be of a high optical quality, nor must they be large. Money could be saved since the telescopes would only serve as a "light bucket" for SETI observations (Hecht, 1996). With so many options, SETI has a lot to consider if progress is to be made.

The efficacy of a search for extraterrestrial life remains an ongoing debate. In light of the anthropocentric foundation of the SETI Institute, the organization has earned the support of a large group of important figures. Some of its sponsors include NASA Headquarters, the Department of Energy, the International Astronomical Union, and Hewlett-Packard, along with many others (SETI, 2018). It is logical to surmise that even at its current pace, progress in the form of extraterrestrial communication is still possible. However, out of respect for its sponsors, the memory of its founders that have passed, and all of the individuals that have invested so much into the mission, the SETI Institute has a moral obligation to examine any and all methods that would increase its likelihood of success.

By engaging the help of a more diverse group of professionals, particularly one that represents the fields of social sciences, humanities, and philosophies, a more inclusive, holistic approach could make the difference as well in whether or not extraterrestrial communication occurs in the next fifty years. Likewise, realistically exploring new technologies would lead to a more fiscally responsible, results-oriented SETI Institute, thereby laying a new foundation that could reasonably support the hopes and dreams of future generations who believe there is life beyond Earth and that communication is not only possible, but necessary for understanding humanity's place in the universe. While the researchers at NASA "strongly doubt that any previous industrial civilization existed before our own," broadening the field beyond a flawed theoretical framework could change the probability of making contact with ancient lost civilizations.

What Is the Anunnaki Connection?

To set the stage for my own theory on the Anunnaki, we have reviewed the ideas of alternative researchers like Zecharia Sitchin and Immanuel Velikovsky, but these two are by no means the only ones to pose cosmologies. There are many independent scholars who have worked to answer some of the questions that traditional academics refuse to even entertain. These scholars seem to agree on one central premise: the ancient world still holds more secrets than we are led to believe.

What I believe is that these secrets can be answered by examining what these ancient enigmas have in common. There seems to be a universal connection underpinning everything from the monuments of the Giza necropolis to the blue stones of Stonehenge. Ancient cultures from all parts of the world share similar origin stories, deities, and beliefs even though they supposedly never had contact with one another. What is this connection? It appears that civilization as we know it stemmed from an extraordinarily ancient source that has yet to be identified. This ancient source bestowed technical and practical knowledge, as well as elements of high culture, on otherwise primitive humans.

Nature and the cosmos are comprised of energies of different types, but the essence of these energies is, no doubt, the same. The energies that come from the farthest planets and stars do not differ from those energies that comprise humankind. In this sense, man himself is a small celestial body, like a planet or star. We shine with our own light or sometimes reflect the light of others, almost like an avatar. The most important thing to understand is that the world turns into a single network through which an infinite amount of energy circulates. The universal wisdom of the ancients is based on this idea: that the small connects to the large, and the large connects to the small. Due to this interplay of energy, there is a connection.

Historically, those who understood this ancient principle have grasped the essence of cosmic laws and have been able to establish contact with celestial forces through the base materials on Earth, such as stones, metals, and plants, which are inherently connected with the energy of certain celestial bodies. These were the shamans, humans with the extraordinary capability to connect with both an inner and outer conscious experience. Could these ancient shamans have been in communication with the beings Sumerians called the Anunnaki? The answer depends on not just who, but *what* the Anunnaki really are.

CHAPTER 3

Anunnaki Gods

Archaeology does not supply us with certitudes,
but rather with vague hypotheses. And in the
shade of these hypotheses some artists are content
to dream, considering them less as scientific
facts than as sources of inspiration.
—IGOR STRAVINSKY, Russian composer

Sumerian texts are filled with the stories of the gods and their lives. In these stories, the gods create and destroy and exhibit drunkenness, promiscuity, anger, envy, selfishness, and arrogance both among themselves and between people and demigods. Despite their supposed power, their actions are far from ideal and bear out the baseness and earthly character of biological animals. Of course, this would not necessarily mean they were immoral or evil. There are many stories of the gods helping people in every way, treating illnesses, and saving lives. Moreover, the gods were teachers. Besides identification with celestial bodies, the gods had other functional characteristics partly connected with the elements of nature. They were engineers, erecting civilization not only through a philosophical or ideological influence, but also physically with their massive building projects.

The face of an Anunnaki god? (© Can Stock Photo Inc.)

Physicality

With wide eyes, sharp features, and intricately styled hair and beards, the Anunnaki are striking in appearance and larger than life. At times, they appear nonhuman. Their depictions, created around six thousand years ago, were crafted by a people of unknown nationality who came to Mesopotamia from an unknown land. To the Sumerians, these gods were the masters of earth and sky, having power over both life and death. Immortalized in stone, they look very different from the prehistoric deities that early humans appeared to regard as sacred before civilization. Rather than the simplicity of primitive cave art, these stone masterpieces convey a complex message of high culture and technological advancement. Is this how the gods of humankind's first civilization really looked? What other physical attributes might they have had?

Given the details of the reliefs left behind, the answer may seem obvious. Clearly these gods were anthropomorphic. Yet, art is often a stylized depiction of the world rather than a photorealistic one, so their humanlike appearance could be more of a projection of the artists. Consequently, modern alternative researchers have taken a lot of creative liberty with the Anunnaki. This has been confusing for many who simply want to know what the Anunnaki looked like. Ufologists tell us about gray aliens, while conspiracy theorists portray them as shapeshifting reptilian creatures. Some researchers believe that in ancient times there were several different types of humanoid creatures walking the Earth.

Fish Men

One example might be the Mesopotamian fish men called Oannes, who were part of a group of demigods called Abgal in Sumerian, or Apkallu, in Akkadian. According to the legend, these fish-human hybrids were wise gods or sages that came to teach humans the fundamentals of civilization—an idea we will revisit in chapter 6. These beings were said to have emerged from the water and taken human form during the day among the people and then disappeared into the night.

Some researchers have suggested that these creatures were not truly amphibious humanoids, but rather ordinary humans wearing fish suits. The Chaldean scribe Berossus said of the Oannes that he had a fish head but also a second head. He also had both the feet of a man and the tail of a fish. He shared the language of man but ate no food (Cory, 1828). If taken

65

literally, this creature sounds like an abomination. However, when looking at the surviving depictions of this monster, could it be that the Oannes is a man simply wearing a fishlike costume?

Oannes figure appears to be wearing
a fishlike costume. (John Ashton [public domain])

Giants

One of the more popular claims is that the Anunnaki were giants. Some of these theories are due in part to images like the Tablet of Shamash, on which a large seated figure of the god Shamash is offering the rod and ring (a symbol of power and justice) to a standing Hammurabi, the sixth king of the First Babylonian Dynasty, who reigned from 1792 BCE to 1750 BCE.

The Tablet of Shamash. Natritmeyer (CC BY-SA 4.0, creativecommons.org)

According to the accounts on the Code of Hammurabi stele, a seven-foot piece of basalt now at the Louvre in Paris, Shamash, the god of justice and equity, gave the code of laws to Hammurabi. The stele states, "Hammurabi, the king of righteousness, on whom Shamash has conferred right (or law) am I" (King, 2018) to establish who is in the picture. Sometimes, people get Shamash and Marduk confused. Perhaps that comes from elements in Hammurabi's Code that refer to Marduk, as when Hammurabi says, "By the command of Shamash, the great judge of heaven and earth, let righteousness go forth in the land: by the order of Marduk, my lord, let no destruction befall my monument" (King, 2018). It goes on to say, "Hammurabi is a ruler, who is as a father to his subjects, who holds the words of Marduk in reverence, who has achieved conquest for Marduk over the north and south, who rejoices the heart of Marduk, his lord, who has bestowed benefits for ever and ever on his subjects, and has established order in the land" (King, 2018). The stele establishes that Marduk, in addition to other gods, bestowed many gifts upon Hammurabi, and the ruler is a grateful and loyal servant to Marduk. But it is clear in the text and the depiction of the rod and ring that the actual conferring of the rule of law was by Shamash. Thus, the seated figure is a very powerful and prominent Shamash.

The additional celestial symbol of the eight-pointed star represents Shamash's twin sister Inanna (later syncretized to Ishtar), goddess of Heaven. They were both Enki's offspring. The text reads, "May Ishtar, the goddess of fighting and war, who unfetters my weapons, my gracious protecting spirit, who loveth my dominion, curse his kingdom in her angry heart; in her great wrath, change his grace into evil, and shatter his weapons on the place of fighting and war.

May she create disorder and sedition for him, strike down his warriors, that the earth may drink their blood, and throw down the piles of corpses of his warriors on the field; may she not grant him a life of mercy, deliver him into the hands of his enemies, and imprison him in the land of his enemies" (King, 2018). Inanna/Ishtar was a protector, and her celestial symbol appears to denote her guarding presence overseeing the exchange of power between her brother Shamash and King Hammurabi. A detail that is also important to note is that Shamash is usually depicted with four horns wrapped around his head.

What we see here is a common portrayal of a seemingly giant deity in the presence of smaller mortals. However, conventional belief is that whenever there is a discrepancy of scale in ancient art, it is meant to communicate the importance of the figure rather than relative size. So here it would mean that the artist or artisan of this image meant to convey that Shamash was the most important figure on the tablet. While this is a logical and consistent theme carried out through many cultures and art forms, it has not been enough to convince some researchers who feel the size differences depicted in ancient art should be taken as a literal account of scale, implying that the gods of old were, in fact, giants.

Giants are one of the most common motifs of ancient legends. A great many creation myths speak of giant gods. The Bible references the Nephilim as the giant offspring of the sons of God who mated with human females, also known as the "Watchers" in the Book of Enoch. Genesis 6:4 says:

> *There were giants in the earth in those days; and also after that, when the sons of God came in unto the daughters of men, and they bare children to them, the same became mighty men which were of old, men of renown (KJV).*

Notice that the text says the giants were *in* the earth, rather than *on* the earth. Could this suggest these beings were interterrestrial, rather than extraterrestrial? We will come back to that idea. For now, consider the plausibility of giants. Thanks to gravity, living beings cannot grow to arbitrary sizes. Creatures like dinosaurs and megafauna are believed to have been able to grow to enormous heights due the Earth's gravity being weaker millions of years earlier. Given today's gravity, modern giants like elephants and giraffes pale in comparison to creatures of the past. For truly giant humanoids to have existed on this planet, it would have had to have been many millions of years ago.

Abrahamic religions are not the only ones that speak of giants, though. The ancient Greeks had Titans, a race of giants born to Ouranos and Gaia. In Central America, there was the giant white god Quetzalcoatl who, like the Greek Titan Atlantis, was depicted holding the Earth upon his shoulders. There is also the figure Cú Chulainn, known as the Irish Hercules, whose story is amazingly similar to the Greek hero Heracles, the Persian hero Rostam, and the Germanic Lay of Hildebrand. While such parallels point to a common origin, archaeologists do not believe there is enough evidence to prove such a connection (Beck, 2000).

Perhaps the giants of legend were not as extreme in size as we now imagine. In a time where people may have stood under five feet, a human of more than seven feet would have been the stuff of legends and would definitely warrant storytelling. So it is possible legendary giants were not massively tall by today's standards, as these myths are oral traditions reaching back millions of years. If ancient gods *were* taller than average, their maximum growth probably did not exceed ten feet.

Strange Skulls

Misshapen skulls have led researchers to speculate on extraterrestrial ties. The Starchild Skull is a small, deformed 900-year-old bone skull found in Mexico in 1930. A teenage girl exploring in a mine tunnel about 100 miles southwest of the city of Chihuahua discovered it in a shallow grave, lying next to a normal human skeleton. Further DNA testing has determined a high percentage of unusual DNA in the Starchild Skull. However, just because the skull is not normal does not make it extraterrestrial. Such an extraordinary claim requires extraordinary evidence.

About 200 miles from where the Starchild Skull was found is the small Mexican village of Onavas. In 1999, a 1,000-year-old cemetery was uncovered there during the building of an irrigation canal. The site, referred to as El Cementerio, contained the remains of twenty-five human burials. Thirteen of them had skulls that were elongated and pointy at the back. Of the twenty-five burials, seventeen were children between five months and sixteen years of age. In these cases, the cranial deformation was intentional. Could these two discoveries be connected? If the ancient people of Mexico were practicing cranial deformation, what might be the motivation?

Artificial cranial deformation or modification is a practice seen in many cultures throughout history, but especially in ancient Mesoamerican populations. Historically, the Nahuatl people of Mesoamerica saw the human skull as the seat of the soul, a vessel for the spirit. They called this spirit *tonalli*, the root of which, *tona*, indicates a connection to the sun. In their belief system, the soul drew its energy and power from the heat of the sun and was contained in a person's skull. So when children were born, the Nahuatl believed the gods breathed the *tonalli* into them. The breathing in of the *tonalli* awakened the infant's consciousness and made him one with his soul's destiny.

However, all infants have a membranous gap between the cranial bones, which allows the skull to fit through the birth canal and then stretch in response to the natural expansion of the brain during development. Having this fontanel made infants especially vulnerable to losing the *tonalli* from that opening, or perhaps worse, evil spirits could possess the infant by entering the skull. To safeguard the infant's *tonalli*, the head would be tightly bound, and the pressure would gradually push the skull into a conical shape. Thus, elongated skulls or other deformations have yet to show extraterrestrial origins.

Nevertheless, it makes one wonder if there could be more to the motivation behind the body modifications. Some have suggested that these ancient people were emulating their gods. While science has discredited extraterrestrial claims for many elongated skulls, it has yet to explain away the ubiquitous practices of artificial cranial deformation.

True Blue

Another strangely common theme for deities—and one of the most distinctive features of the gods of India—is blue skin. Blue-skinned gods have been found in Egypt and even in South America. Some researchers have claimed that the Anunnaki were also blue. Is the blue color of the skin simply an artistic element or could it mean something more? Let's say for a moment that the gods could actually have blue skin. This could mean that the skin itself is not blue, but rather the blood. A fair-skinned human has a pinkish hue to the skin because human blood is red. If the skin of the gods seemed blue, could the blood of the gods have been blue? You have probably heard the old description "blue-blooded." To be blue-blooded meant to be of noble origin. Representatives of aristocracy and royalty were said to have blue blood. Is the term *blue blood* just an out-of-date colloquialism denoting noble birth, or could the term refer to genetic ancestry?

One of the main functions of blood is transport, i.e., the transfer of oxygen, carbon dioxide, nutrients, and products throughout the body. Oxygen is the basic element necessary for a living organism to function and provides its energy, obtained as a result of complex chemical reactions. A living, breathing organism should typically consume oxygen and emit carbon dioxide. There are elements of blood that contain pigments. In humans, the respiratory pigment of blood is hemoglobin, which consists of ions of divalent iron. It is thanks to hemoglobin that our blood is red. But even with iron as the base, respiratory pigments can still be a different color, and the transfer of oxygen and carbon dioxide may well be carried out with respiratory pigments based on other metals apart from iron. For example, in ascidians (a type of marine invertebrate) the blood is almost colorless. It does however contain a green protein called hemovanadins, which has vanadium ions. This color gives the blood a hemocyanin pigment based on copper. This pigmenting is very widely distributed making some snails, crustaceans, and octopuses blue in color. Thus, it is possible for a living organism to be blue. Could ancient gods have had a similar molecular composition? Could they have really been blue or is this just another artistic convention?

The Engineers

As soon as these beings set foot in Mesopotamia, construction began. Cities grew like weeds. The temples of the Sumerians were huge and majestic. Sited after magicians and intermediaries to the gods had consulted the stars and planets for the ideal location, they were erected in the form of stepped pyramids called ziggurats. Each new tier was stacked upon the other until they joined at the top in an open area where it was equally possible to appeal to a jubilant crowd, watch the stars and moon phases, or communicate with the gods.

The Sumerians believed that the god to whom the temple was dedicated actually lived in it. The god defended the city from all threats and troubles, and the city pledged to worship that god. A specific ritual was intended for each deity with mysteries, chants, collective worship, and obligatory sacrifices. According to the Sumerian understanding of the natural order, humans existed only to serve deities. Part of serving these gods included offering gifts, such as feeding the gods. Considering the otherworldly nature of the Anunnaki, it might be difficult to imagine what they would have eaten. Thankfully, we do not have to simply guess. The historical record tells us exactly what the Sumerian gods did and did not like to eat.

The Anunnaki Diet

Components of the divine diet and eating habits of Mesopotamian gods and goddesses were preserved in Sumerian texts. From this it is clear that their nourishment was important to not only survival of the gods, but also their appeasement. Initially, the gods were vegetarian, possibly vegan. They only began to eat meat after the creation of humankind. They used their human slaves to produce their food, hence the development of agriculture (Nowicki, 2014). A fragment from the *Debate between Grain and Sheep* indicates that after eating sheep and grain, the Anunnaki were not sated (Nowicki, 2014). Even after they consumed the "sweet milk of their holy sheepfold" they were not sated. As a result, they gave these to human-kind as sustenance (Nowicki, 2014).

The lands of Sumer provided a bounty of food. Sumerians grew millet, wheat, rye, and rice and made many different types of bread. They also grew many fruits and vegetables, including apples, apricots, beets, cabbage, cherries, chickpeas, figs, grapes, lentils, lettuce, melons, mulberries, onions, pears, plums, pomegranates, radishes, and turnips (Krasner, 2016). Meat was also eaten, but primarily offered to gods and royalty. Sources included beef, chicken, ducks, fish, geese, goats, sheep, and turtles. The gods preferred their meats roasted and were especially fond of roasted goat. They did not like their meat boiled or fried.

It seems as though once they settled into their lives with humans, vegetarianism became passé, with some going so far as to consume human flesh. While there are texts that suggest this was rare, there is at least one case of the gods eating human flesh in an incantation from the maqlfi ritual. In this text, a person who had been the victim of witchcraft and manipulation by black magic called out to Gibil, son of An and Ki and the god of fire and metallurgy, commanding him to: "Devour my enemies! Eat who is evil to me!" (Nowicki, 2014). However, some scholars have argued that this fragment does not mean literally to eat, but to burn in the sense that fire "eats" everything in its path. While this straightforward interpretation makes sense at first, Stefan Nowicki of the University of Wroclaw argues that fire is viewed as the *carrier* of offerings, so if fire was supposed to be the one normally *eating* everything, then there would be no burnt offerings since the fire would devour everything before it ever reached the intended recipient (Nowicki, 2014). Thus, there is a possibility that the Anunnaki ate humans, likely roasted.

The gods also had a sweet tooth. They would sweeten their foods with grape and date syrup, as well as honey. Desserts were among their favorite offerings, especially cakes made from butter, flour, honey, and various fruits (Nowicki, 2014). Enki knew his daughter Inanna loved butter cake, so when she would visit, he would order the preparation of cakes, cold water, and beer to properly welcome her. The moon god, Suen, also loved cakes and beer.

This of course brings us to brewing. What divine cuisine would be complete without alcohol? Goddesses and gods loved to drink different alcoholic beverages. Enki knew a special process of brewing a strong beer from emmer sweetened with date syrup. In fact, the Sumerian word *kas-dé-a*, usually translated as "banquet," actually means "the pouring of beer," referencing the libations of alcohol in a celebration or feast (Nowicki, 2014).

Interestingly, leeks, onions, garlic, and fish were banned from meals before the undertaking of any worship or ritual activities because the Anunnaki did not like how these smelled on the breath of humans as they praised them. Likewise, the Anunnaki would have abstained from eating these on a regular basis so as not to offend each other with bad breath. This royal protocol has continued to modernity. It is widely known that Queen Elizabeth has ruled that she and the royal family cannot have onions, fish, and pungent flavors, especially garlic, which she calls "anti-social" (Willgress, 2016). The queen's daughter-in-law, Camilla Parker Bowles, Duchess of Cornwall, confirmed that the royal family is indeed not supposed to eat garlic, as does her son Tom Parker Bowles, food writer and critic. It looks like royal breath has been a concern for at least six thousand years!

However, not all supernatural creatures in Sumerian mythology required food. According to the fragment of *Inanna's Descent to the Nether World*, demons did not eat:

> *Those who accompanied her, those who accompanied Inanna,*
> *knew no food, knew no drink, ate no flour offering and drank*
> *no libation. They crushed no bitter garlic. They ate no fish,*
> *they ate no leeks. They, it was, who accompanied Inanna*
> *(Nowicki, 2014).*

This leads us to believe that there was something very real about the Anunnaki. They were seen as actual beings dwelling on a physical plane, somehow similar to humans and different from creatures like demons. In antiquity, it was said that the gods walked among us. Who were these gods?

The Pantheon

To list all the deities of Sumer is impossible not simply because of their great numbers but also because there are many we still have not fully identified. What we do know is that the Sumerian gods had a huge heavenly family, a forerunner to the Greek pantheon. And like that better-known pantheon, these gods had both good and evil qualities. The Sumerian gods loved and laughed, lied and betrayed, and committed heinous acts like murder and rape. They often disregarded family loyalties but were also clearly harsher with humans than with each other.

The ancestors of the entire pantheon were the divine couple made up of Abzu/Apsû and Tiamat, considered the most popular deities of high rank in Sumer. Abzu was the god of the freshwater underworld, the primordial chaos. The word *Abzu* actually meant these freshwater bodies; however, the

Babylonian creation story did not just refer to the Abzu as a natural phenomenon or feature, but rather deified it. Abzu's main temple was in the city of Eridu. Tiamat was the goddess of salt waters, the oceans of the world. Each compound of Abzu and Tiamat caused chaos. According to mythology, the solar god Marduk, who later became the supreme deity of the Babylonians, cut the progenitor Tiamat into two parts: the sky came from the top; the ground came from the bottom. Chaos was over.

Chief among the Sumerian gods was the sky god Anu, consort of the goddess Ki, father of Enlil (god of air), Enki (god of the seas and fertility), and Inanna (goddess of war and love). Anu was involved in a love affair with Inanna; therefore, she is called either his daughter or his wife. The children of Anu also gave birth to a new generation of gods: Enlil had a daughter named Nanna (goddess of the moon), who then had a son, Adad (god of storm). These descendants of Anu were called the Anunnaki. Their offspring also belonged to the Anunnaki and occupied a special position in the Sumerian pantheon.

The Anunnaki were served by the gods of a lower order, Igigi, created only for the care of the supreme gods. According to Sumerian mythology, the Igigi at first tolerated the Anunnaki's poor and unjust treatment, but eventually rebelled. Until their uprising, the Igigi formed the land, laid the riverbeds, erected and demolished mountains, planted flora, grazed animals, and served the gods in every way. But instead of gratitude, they only got ridicule, reproaches, and beatings. The Igigi finally declared that they would no longer work for the gods and were also gods themselves. The Anunnaki were shocked at what they saw as ingratitude on the part of the Igigi, so they decided to create a new slave species: humans.

Ancient Mesopotamia is revealed to scholars by its recorded history, including numerous works of art and literature. From within these artifacts, we have uncovered and interpreted a surprisingly large and complex mythology spanning millennia. The polytheistic religion consisted of hundreds, and possibly thousands, of gods, goddesses, and demons of varying degrees of significance. Cities, towns, and villages throughout the region worshipped different patron deities, each one featuring unique powers or capabilities. The most important deities had their central places of worship—for instance, Enlil in Nippur, Enki in Eridu, Marduk in Babylon, Inanna in Uruk, and so on.

It is worth noting that kinship is not always clear even to experts in the field, so if you find yourself getting lost as you study the gods of Sumer, don't feel bad. In the texts, individual deities had several names. For instance, in inscriptions of the kings Sennacherib, Esarhaddon, Ashurbanipal, and others, the names Asur, Sin, Samas, Bel, Nabu, Nergal, and Istar all represent Marduk (Clay, 1907). Additionally, the names Enlil, Ellil, or Illil can all refer to the god of Nippur (Clay, 1907). While this is and has been a confusing aspect of translating ancient Near East texts, new research resulting in new discoveries is happening every day, which continues to connect the dots between these somewhat enigmatic deities. Inanna, for example, is called the daughter of Nanna, then Anu, and then sometimes Enlil. Even with *Inanna's Call to Enki*, he is named "The Father," yet this is taken to mean "father" as a title or status and not his direct kinship and biological position. For the older gods, all the younger gods were children. It is also worth considering that there were hundreds of Sumerian gods. With time, study, and familiarity, Mesopotamian myths do become easier to understand. Often Sumerian literary texts only refer to a few dozen gods.

The Shining Ones

The Anunnaki have been connected to the Elohim of the Bible. The word *Elohim* has been translated by some alternative researchers to mean "bright" or "shining ones." These shining ones were purportedly beings from an advanced civilization who came to give humanity laws, agriculture, and various technologies. They were culture bearers who took sage knowledge around the world over a period of two thousand years—an idea we will explore further in the next chapter. While this is an intriguing thesis, some scholars say it is based on a faulty premise in the translation of *Elohim*: the conventional translation of the word does not equate to "shining ones." While the Hebrew *el* does correspond to the Akkadian *il* (which is also sometimes spelled with two lls, as in *illu*, depending on form and context), when it is used in the word *Elohim*, it is made up of different cuneiform signs. The cuneiform spelling for *ill* is not the same as for "god." The cuneiform for god or deity is often *illu* and not *ill*. This is apparent when you are actually looking at the original, which can be done by going to the Pennsylvania Sumerian Dictionary Project (*psd.museum.upenn.edu/*), a free site provided by the University of Pennsylvania Museum of Anthropology and Archaeology. The main god An (in Sumerian) was later known as Anu or Ilu in Akkadian. However, some point to Ilu or Illu as proof of a connection to the word *illuminate*, indicating light. Others argue that these pronunciations are indeed similar, but they do not indicate a link, since they are not related in the appearance of the original cuneiform.

Nevertheless, there are many accounts in ancient texts from all around the world referring to gods as somehow illuminated and often directly associated with light. This is frequently the case with religions worshipping the sun. A common feature of sun-worshipping groups is to revere earthly materials reminiscent of the sun or having light-reflecting capabilities. This is why you will see gold and other bright metals so highly valued. This begs the question, what if a primitive tribe of people encountered a highly advanced group of beings who perhaps wore items of metal? Ancients not only wore metal adornments, they even dusted themselves in gold, like in the legend of El Dorado wherein an initiate chief would be covered in gold dust and sent out on a raft into the middle of Lake Guatavita. This would be quite a shock to a group of people still using stone tools. It would appear as though these beings were robed in the light of the sun and stars. As Arthur C. Clarke noted: "Any sufficiently advanced technology is indistinguishable from magic" (Clarke, 1982).

Gods with a Thousand Faces

No one says it better than author Graham Hancock when he declares that we are a "species with amnesia" (Hancock, 1996). Perhaps the gods depicted in ancient myths come from our collective memory. We could spend a lot of time considering the possible physicality of the Anunnaki, looking at the many interpretations spanning many years. I know this is a topic that interests a lot of people, but I think there is not much use to debating how the Anunnaki appeared because I believe there is an element of truth to each—not literal truth, but a mythological truth. As I mentioned in the beginning of this book, myth is how the ancients shared their universal truths and worldviews with not only each other, but also us.

In his popular book, *Hero with a Thousand Faces*, Joseph Campbell (1904–1987) presents his theory of the monomyth through comparative mythology. He describes the journey of an archetypical hero present in many world mythological and religious systems. Campbell's seminal work was inspired by the theories of Freud, Jung, and Arnold van Gennep, as well as the research of the ethnographers James George Frazer and Franz Boas and the psychologist Otto Rank. Exploring the myths of the peoples of the world, Campbell concluded that most of the legends have a common plot structure, which he called the monomyth. Moving from the psychological to the metaphysical plane of analysis, Campbell presented the heroic journey as a cosmogonic cycle. Having passed through the tests of initiation, having crossed the threshold between being and nothingness, the hero, as the embodiment of the microcosm and the macrocosm, dissolves into the higher self, thereby completing his path.

This mythic archetype is seen in all cultures. It is a truly universal story. In addition to religious heroes like Jesus or Moses, modern entertainment includes such deeply archetypal characters as Harry Potter, Frodo Baggins, and Luke Skywalker. While these figures differ in detail like appearance, culture, time, environment, etc., at their heart they are the same archetype, hence the thousand faces in the name of Campbell's book.

The Anunnaki also differ in appearance. They change and develop from Sumerian myths to Akkadian and Babylonian. Eventually, they influence the gods of Egypt and those of Olympus. Through syncretism, as we previously discussed, these gods survived for many years. Though they too may have had a thousand faces, *who they are* is the real truth we are seeking. Furthermore, as we have learned from studying the Sumerian Problem, the Sumerians came from a foreign land. So it would be logical to surmise that the stories of the Anunnaki did not originate in Sumer—or even Mesopotamia, for that matter. The myths reported in the Sumerian texts were likely much older oral traditions that traveled with these migrants to Sumer, where they eventually were assimilated. Could the Anunnaki and the gods of Sumer have been literary iterations of antediluvian deities? Or were they the actual survivors of an extinction-level cataclysm that occurred somewhere between 12,800 and 11,600 years ago?

A Brave New Worldview

Thus far, we have explored a range of existing theories, each with its own flaws and points of intrigue. I thought it was important to include all the prevailing alternative narratives. As an alternative researcher and renegade archaeologist myself, I am asked about the veracity of these claims everywhere I go. One evening, I sat in on a radio show that took live questions from callers. One of the callers told me to "quit sitting on the fence and pick a side already!" Caught a bit off guard, I stopped for a moment to consider what the caller was asking of me. He was not interested in only hearing me present exciting narratives, alternative or otherwise. Rather, he was looking to me to share my personal and professional conclusions given the available data. At that point, unfortunately, I did not have a solid theory of my own to present. So I stated that clearly but shared my opinions to the best of my ability, discussing some of the strengths and weaknesses I saw in theories like Sitchin's. It was admittedly not the most satisfying answer to his question, but it was honest. I vowed to never disparage another researcher and to always consider all sides of the story. Besides, how effective is it to tear apart the theories of others without having an alternative of your own to offer?

Since then, I have continued my research and pondering. It was and is important to me to avoid "picking a side" for the sake of argument. This line of thinking is not only ripping apart the fabric of the research community, it is dividing us all. Just as I will not simply go along with mainstream narrative, I will not go along with any one alternative narrative, especially when I have come to my own conclusions regarding what *really* happened in Sumer all those years ago. In the pages that follow, I will share these conclusions, the evidence, and the implications. What you are about to read will require an open mind and willingness to set aside what you think you already know about the origins of humankind.

A Possible Interpretation

Based on the evidence in the archaeological, geological, climatological, historical, and literary records, what I believe to be facts about the Anunnaki are as follows: There was indeed a group of advanced living beings who settled in a mountain valley in the Near East around 8200 BCE, bringing never-before-seen technologies to the sedentary Late Epipaleolithic hunter-gatherer groups like the Natufians. These individuals had advanced knowledge of the arts and sciences characteristic of high culture. They were displaced from some northern homeland more than ten thousand years ago due to a climatological disaster, perhaps triggered by a meteor. As a result, they sent their best and brightest minds to various parts of the world, including Mesopotamia, to resettle. During their diaspora, they encountered tribes who saw them as shining gods because of their metallic adornments and ability to seemingly control nature through agricultural methods like irrigation and artificial pollination.

This power over the primitive peoples had an effect on certain members of the advanced civilization, leading them to dehumanize those they referred to as the "black-headed people" and "Adamah" (the red people). They would eventually enslave some of these locals using controlling techniques including religion and superstition. They forced these individuals to "worship" or work for them in physically laborious roles in agriculture and construction, making sure to keep the majority ignorant, as knowledge is indeed power. They allowed a select few of the local tribal leaders to learn writing and other skills so that they could act as an interpreters and middlemen. These became the priest class. The labor of the newly organized and unified masses under the direction of a technocratic elite created an economic boom as had not been seen previously. This could explain the rapid advancements in the region. Good ideas are only ideas if there are not enough people to put them into action. This handful of sages would go on to ignite the locals, creating an engine of civilization fueled by cheap labor. It was progress at the expense of justice.

However, dissenting members of this sage group objected to this unfair treatment of the locals and were benevolent, eventually defying their own to teach local tribal leaders the great arts and sciences of high culture such as agriculture, mathematics, astronomy, medicine, and writing. This is often expressed as the work of one individual, known almost ubiquitously in global mythology as the bringer of fire or knowledge: Enki to the Sumerians, Prometheus to the Greeks, Lucifer to the Gnostics, Mātariśvan to the Vedics, Loki to the Nordics, Nanabozho to the Ojibwe, Māui to the Polynesians, and the list could go on.

After bestowing this forbidden knowledge, the rebel "gods" started to assimilate and be absorbed into the local culture through intermarrying. This interbreeding was frowned upon by some of the less benevolent "gods," who felt the need to preserve their royal blood through breeding only with each other. This led to the practice of sibling marriage, as seen in ancient Egypt. After dying, these beings took on a godlike status and were revered. However, they were physical beings, a point that gets lost as they were later deified in the memory of their people. Their technological contributions were so great, they took on a legendary status.

While this is certainly an oversimplified narrative, it can begin to shape ongoing discourse about who and what the Anunnaki were. It is clear that these advanced beings indeed came from a faraway place. The texts do not dispute this Sumerian Problem. The real question remains: Where did they come from? A secondary question can also be asked: Where had these advanced emissaries received their knowledge? This second question may not be so easily put to rest with the existing evidence, but clues can be found in the spiritual traditions of both the ancient and modern world. This spiritual aspect will be addressed in detail in chapter 6. For now, let's continue to focus on the evidentiary connections found in the archaeological and historical records.

What we can truly know about the Anunnaki comes from three primary sources: Sumerian tablets from the Library at Nippur; the biblical Book of Genesis, where they were known as the Elohim; and the Hebraic Books of Enoch, where they were known as the angels. We also know that there is still no archaeological evidence for the immigration of any known culture that would explain the sudden spark of innovation and culture in the indigenous peoples of Mesopotamia. Scholars agree that the Sumerians themselves did not take credit for their own success but rather attributed all of their progress to the influence of the Anunnaki. Likewise, ancient people like the early Hebrews, and even those as far west as the Celts, credited their gods with helping them develop their civilizations. Could this one small group of ancient cultural engineers have been responsible for the spark of genius seen in the archaeological record? Yes. According to my research, the Anunnaki were very much physical living beings.

CHAPTER 4

Origin of Man

*A myth is far truer than a history, for a history only
gives a story of the shadows, whereas a myth gives a
story of the substances that cast the shadows.*
—ANNIE BESANT, British theosophist

I magine, for a moment, an alternative setting for the Anunnaki, one that does not include old-fashioned 1950s rocket technology and modern Western military titles and notions like "captain" or "commander." Set aside the iconography of a cold war era space race and big-budget visual creations from Stanley Kubrick and George Lucas. Instead, come with me to a very real time in human history when living gods walked beside man.

Homo sapiens, meaning "man who knows" in Latin, is the scientific name for the general modern species of humans. *Homo* is the genus, or the taxonomic category that is positioned above species and below family. This includes Neanderthals and Denisovans, as well as many others of our extinct cousins. In fact, *Homo sapiens* is the only surviving species of the genus *Homo*. Modern humans are classified even further as the subspecies *Homo sapiens sapiens* as the system branches out further and further whenever a new specimen is found. Sometimes a specimen that does not neatly fit into this ongoing jigsaw puzzle gets conveniently forgotten in museum basements.

Some refuse to accept that these ancestors are related to modern humans; thus their existence does not factor into the equation. However, I ask you to consider the Omo remains, discovered in Africa between 1967 and 1974 at the Omo Kibish sites near the Omo River, in Omo National Park in southwestern Ethiopia. Found at the site were a number of bones including two partial skulls, four jaws, a leg bone, and about two hundred teeth. This discovery provided evidence of the first anatomically modern humans to appear in the fossil record about 195,000 years ago. This fits nicely within the time frame scientists claim for modern humans diverging from a common ancestor about 200,000 years ago. If the radiocarbon dating is correct, these fossils are the oldest known *Homo sapiens* remains, "making Ethiopia the cradle of *Homo sapiens*" (Leakey, 1969, 1132).

Ethiopia may be considered the cradle of *Homo sapiens*, but Mesopotamia, home of Sumer, is the cradle of *civilization*. The distinction is quite important. *Existing* and *civilization building* are two very different things. However, one could then reasonably ask, what about Göbekli Tepe? Evidence uncovered at Göbekli Tepe clearly indicates more than just simple existing was taking place. Considering that the settlement is at least 11,000 years old, it is much older than any found near Ur. Perhaps the enigmatic inhabitants of Göbekli Tepe should be considered the cradle of civilization, but the problem with this is how one defines *civilization*.

Some scholars adhere to the theory that Göbekli Tepe was a temple, but not all scholars agree. Archaeological evidence of day-to-day activities has led other scholars to believe that Göbekli Tepe was a multipurpose domestic settlement. Still, the general consensus is this was a hunter-gatherer site with the possibility of rudimentary agriculture. Does this constitute civilization? Perhaps it is the seed of civilization, but to date, no evidence of an advanced state of human society with a high level of culture, science, industry, and government has been found.

Regardless of the type of people living in and around Göbekli Tepe, one thing is certain: human beings were not simply created from the sands of the Earth a mere six thousand years ago, as some would interpret literally from the biblical Book of Genesis. Yet should we completely discount the Genesis story? Perhaps the truth has been hidden there in plain sight—a truth that would explain exactly what happened in the Garden those many years ago.

The Garden of Eden

There are many versions of the Garden of Eden story. However, one can be traced at least as far back as the third millennium BCE. This story was inscribed on clay tablets in Sumer and held as a matter of great importance, copied numerous times and stored in many libraries and personal royal collections. These sacred texts had been lost to the ravages of war and climate change until Sir Austen Henry Layard uncovered them in the Sumerian city of Nippur, one of the most important cities of ancient Mesopotamia. Mentioned first in the Sumerian King List, it became the sacred center of Mesopotamia, although it was never the capital. Nippur's significance was most likely due to its geographic location in southern Mesopotamia, which made it an ethnically and linguistically diverse gateway between two cultural groups:

the Sumerians in the south and the Akkadians in the north. In Nippur, the Mesopotamian kings received from the deity the confirmation of their right to the throne; royal power was not considered legitimate without its recognition in Nippur temples. Now, the ruins of the city are hidden under a group of huge hills, towering more than twenty meters above the surrounding plain.

After their discovery in the mid-nineteenth century, the ancient tablets were sent to the Museum of the University of Philadelphia, where they remained in the basement for decades. The public would have little to no knowledge of what was discovered until 1918, when George Barton published his translation called *Miscellaneous Babylonian Inscriptions*. It then took at least another four decades before Samuel Noah Kramer reexamined Barton's work.

The linguistic characteristics of the Sumerian script lend it a variety of possible interpretations, leaving it open to speculation, as we have seen. A fantastic example of this was provided by the late British scholar Christian Arthur Edgar O'Brien. O'Brien was a Cambridge-educated geologist and explorer who spent many years in Iran, which led him to assist in the excavation of the Tchoga Zambil Ziggurat in Southern Iran in 1936. O'Brien was deeply passionate about his work and devoted many years to studying prehistory, religious history, cuneiforms, archaeology, astronomy, and archaeoastronomy. In his research, O'Brien found that the ideogram for the Sumerian *li* had evolved from an originally vertical position depicting a plant in a pot (O'Brien, 1989). This phonetic sign had at least twenty-four meanings, but of the newest meanings, only one corresponded directly to the early pictogram, and that is *li*, meaning "cultivation" (O'Brien, 1989).

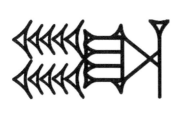 

On the left: Variable cuneiform symbol for li; on the right:
Earlier cuneiform symbol of li meaning "cultivation."
(Laszlovszky András at Hungarian Wikipedia [public domain])

In the Sumerian texts, Enlil is written as *dingir enlil li*. Modern scholars have traditionally accepted the newer Babylonian translation, which meant "God of the Wind," or as previously mentioned, "Lord Ghost." However, the older way of interpreting this term indicates the flower-pot sign was not *lil* but instead translated to the genitive "of." The word *dingir* was a title. It denoted a leadership role, similar to calling someone lord. Thus, O'Brien concluded from assessing the original Sumerian texts that *dingir enlil li* should be transliterated instead as *dingir en-ge-li*.

What does it mean and why does this matter? It means the true title of Enlil is "Lord of Cultivation." This matters, clearly, because it changes the entire way we read the Sumerian epics. Rather than telling us the tales of ethereal gods, this translation gives us a corporeal view of the Anunnaki. O'Brien also pointed out the name Enlil was spelled *Engeli*, but that the root of the word is NGL, which is the same as that in the Indo-Germanic term *angel* (O'Brien, 1989). Could the Anunnaki be equivalent to the angels of the Bible? It is important to note that even if this is so, it does not suggest that the biblical interpretation is the entire story, but rather that there is indeed a connection. This connection is a current that runs through many faiths, traditions, and cultures. Deeper etheric currents will be more closely examined in chapter 6, but for now, let's focus on the actual meaning of the Garden of Eden and its connection to the Anunnaki and origin of humankind.

The Truth Revealed

In Genesis 8:2, it says: "And the Lord God planted a garden eastward in Eden; and there he put the man whom he had formed" (KJV). An important consideration in this text is that Eden existed before man and the garden was planted in Eden. Further, even after cross-referencing all the translations for this verse, it is clear that there is a reason the text specifically says the Lord "formed" man. It is my belief that what we have here in the biblical story of the Garden of Eden is not the history of biological creation nor abiogenesis. It is not the story of the *birth* of the first human being. Again, what about Göbekli Tepe?

The narrative of the Garden of Eden is the story of the *formation* of man—with *formation* as in *civilizing*. We are looking at when the naked man of the wilderness was brought inside the walls of the first city, Eden. Enlil, the Lord of Cultivation, is Yahweh. In Genesis 2:5, we see that "the Lord God took the man and put him into the garden of Eden to dress it and to keep it" (KJV). Keep in mind that while the term *garden* may conjure images of a quaint Beatrix Potter plot of land able to yield a few bushels, this is not how it is meant in the ancient texts. The garden in Eden was an agricultural endeavor. Enlil had cultivated the land within the walls of Eden. This place of Eden appears in cuneiform and translates in Sumerian to "uncultivated plain."

The Hebrew *Adamah* translates to "ground" and the word *Adam* in Hebrew literally means "red," connecting Adam to the red soil of the uncultivated plain. While this connection has sometimes been recognized as a reference to humankind being created from clay, that is hotly debated in religious scholarship.

Thus, it is easy to surmise that Adamah, which the Anunnaki called "the black-headed people," was not the first name of a singular person but describes the first hunter-gatherer tribe civilized by the Anunnaki. These people were not only distinguishable by their black hair; they were also described as red. How could this be? It is my conclusion that they were considered red and associated with red earth because they used ocher, like many primitive people. There are many archaeological studies that have shown that the Natufians employed ocher, even potentially on their bodies. A discovery of particular interest was of adult cranial remains that show red pigmented areas. Fieldworkers reported that the "robust male had ochre pigment on his cranium, demonstrating that it was defleshed at the time of burial" (Garrard et al., 1991, 240). These traces are of great significance, as they are "one of the oldest occurrences of deliberately pigmented human remains in the Near East" (Bocquentin and Garrard, 2016, 11). Furthermore, many types of ocher fragments have been found in the Natufian layers of archaeological excavations. The same type of iron oxide veins occur in alluvial deposits in Mesopotamia. The ocher was most certainly used to extract or produce red hematite pigment, as these residues have been found on basalt pestles in the cave (Weinstein-Evron and Ilani, 1994). Archaeologists know without a doubt that the people who came before the Sumerian civilization was built routinely used hematite pigment. So it is not unreasonable to conclude that the Anunnaki associated the early Mesopotamian hunter-gatherers with the red pigment of the earthen soil that they used for body adornment both in life and to honor their dead in the afterlife, as the archaeological record shows.

Another important detail to consider is the concept of worshipping. The word *worship* comes from the original Hebrew *abad,* which means literally "to work for." With just the consideration of a few words, a clear connection can be seen. The leader of the Anunnaki subjugated primitive man, forcing him to work in agriculture. According to the Genesis account, God formed humankind from the Adamah, but before he did, the earth was barren of life because "there was not a man to till the ground."

> *And every plant of the field before it was in the earth, and every herb of the field before it grew: for the Lord God had not caused it to rain upon the earth, and there was not a man to till the ground (Genesis 2:5, KJV).*

Again, set aside traditional or even contemporary views of the Bible, and set aside the alternative views that have sprung out of the science fiction craze of the postwar era. Let's just look at the texts. Essentially, the ancients were telling us exactly what happened. Given the above, we could be saying the very same thing when we say something like:

> *Adam worshipped Yahweh, Lord of Angels, in the Garden of Eden*

and

> *The Adamah worked for Enlil, leader of the Anunnaki, in an agricultural settlement called Eden.*

In the Sumerian predecessor of the Adam and Eve story, *Enki and Ninhursag in Dilmun,* there is a link between the Sumerian word for rib (*ti*) and the goddess Ninti, whose name translates to "the lady of the rib." Likewise, according to the Genesis story, Eve is created from Adam's rib. There are so many parallels between the Sumerian and the Hebrew texts that are the foundation for contemporary interpretations of the story of the Garden of Eden. And this is the case with many, many Sumerian texts, including the Epic of Gilgamesh.

Civilizing the Wildman

The Epic of Gilgamesh, believed to be the oldest written story known on Earth, was passed down originally through an oral tradition. Thus, the initial author and its exact date of origin are not even known. The tablets of the Epic of Gilgamesh were found in Nineveh in the ruins of the Library of Ashurbanipal, the king of Assyria. In the story, the king of Uruk in 2700 BCE, Gilgamesh, was two-thirds god and one-third human. His people thought him so tyrannical that they sought help from the gods. The gods heard their cries and brought to them a being named Enkidu to challenge Gilgamesh. The tablets specify that, at first, Enkidu lived with the beasts of the forest and was wild:

> *born of Silence, endowed with strength by Ninurta.*
>
> *His whole body was shaggy with hair,*
>
> *he had a full head of hair like a woman,*
>
> *his locks billowed in profusion like Ashnan.*
>
> *He knew neither people nor settled living,*
>
> *but wore a garment like Sumukan.*
>
> *He ate grasses with the gazelles,*
>
> *and jostled at the watering hole with the animals;*
>
> *as with animals, his thirst was slaked with (mere) water.*
> *(Kovacs, 2004)*

As an archaeologist and historian, what I see in this text is the description of a primitive man. The line "He knew neither people nor settled living" says as much. Additionally, Enkidu was strong, bestial, and ate with the animals. The text specified he only drank water, differentiating between him and the civilized, who knew fermented beverages. One detail I find most interesting is that Enkidu was described as having shaggy hair all over his body. This does not sound like a modern man or *Homo sapiens sapiens*. This is not to suggest that Enkidu was somehow otherworldly, quite the contrary. There are a number of known and unknown species of hominids Enkidu could have been, everything from *Homo antecessor* or *Homo heidelbergensis* to perhaps some specimen yet to be discovered. Keep in mind, the missing evolutionary link bringing us from prehistory to modern humans has not been found. Instead, archaeologists have uncovered evidence that of many different types of hominids that have lived at one point, some likely overlapped periods and geography. This evidence includes skeletal remains, stone tools, campsites, and so on. What is not clear is whether or not any of these beings were particularly hairy.

The general public is led to believe that they were all "naked apes," linking them more closely to modern humans, because sculptors have provided museums and documentaries with their vision of how these beings may have looked. The public sees these images, and it just seeps into the subconscious as fact because it is part of such a scientific presentation. Yet, it is important to remember that any image you see of one of these early hominids comes from the mind of a sculptor, illustrator, painter, or otherwise. How can we know whether or not any of these hominids were covered with "shaggy hair," especially considering it was only recently that paleontologists accepted that dinosaurs had feathers and were related to birds, rather than reptiles? We all still tend to imagine dinosaurs with rough, green, reptilian skin, when, in fact, they very well may have had bright, colorful feathers like tropical birds! So, it is my interpretation that in the Epic of Gilgamesh Enkidu is from a separate hominid species.

In the story, a temple prostitute called Shamhat was sent to seduce Enkidu at the waterhole he shared with the animals. She was instructed to "perform for this primitive the task of womankind!" (Kovacs, 2004). Shamhat uses sex to entice him to Uruk to take on Gilgamesh. She goes on to tempt him with the visions of what life is like inside the city walls:

> *where the people show off in skirted finery,*
>
> *where every day is a day for some festival,*
>
> *where the lyre(?) and drum play continually,*
>
> *where harlots stand about prettily,*
>
> *exuding voluptuousness, full of laughter*
>
> *and on the couch of night the sheets are spread (!).*
>
> *Enkidu, you who do not know, how to live ... Kovacs, 2004*

Here, you can see that there is a stark contrast between life within the city and life outside. Once Enkidu is taken to Uruk, he is treated to a meal complete with beer. He is given the opportunity to bathe and groom himself with oil afterward, at which Shamhat exclaims: "He splashed his shaggy body with water, and rubbed himself with oil, and turned into a human!" (Kovacs, 2004). This final phrase is important. It makes it clear that Enkidu was not considered human until he partook in the cultural norms of urban life. It would be tempting to look at this text under a religious or mystical lens and somehow infer that Enkidu was physically transformed into a human being, as if either by magic or some advanced technology; however the context makes it clear that he was "turned into a human" simply at a cultural level.

One of the main themes of the Epic of Gilgamesh is taming the wild. Taming the wild in Gilgamesh is a way to express the desire for balance and deal with the discomfort of duality in the human experience. Balancing dualities crops up throughout the epic. For instance, Enkidu, though described as wild, was sent to tame the heart of the urban king Gilgamesh. Gilgamesh, though civilized, had been an unfair and imbalanced ruler. He needed a force to balance him to bring relief to the people of Uruk.

Not just anyone could accomplish this because in the beginning of the story it was well established that no one in town was comparable or equal to Gilgamesh. He was described as perfect. So, his counterweight had to be someone of an equal force. And this force was not just equal, but different and balanced, akin to different objects of similar weight on a scale. It became clear when Anu made Enkidu and said, "Let him be equal to Gilgamesh's stormy heart, let them be a match for each other so that Uruk may find peace" (Kovacs, 2004).

When comparing the two characters, a philosophical take on ecofacts and artifacts stands out. In archaeology, an *ecofact* is something created by nature, while an *artifact* is something created by humans. Enkidu's power came from nature, as he was large, wild, and strong like a beast. His power was an ecofact. Gilgamesh's power, on the other hand, came from his kingship. His power was an artifact created by culture. It took the ego of a man to become a king first, as well as the validation from other men to make it true to form.

Enkidu became wise "from other causes," or the act of human will. This is another notable take on the concept of balance, for Enkidu was brought in from the extremity of the wild nature by his opposite, a female. After sexual intercourse, "Enkidu was grown weak, for wisdom was in him. . . ." Wisdom, it turns out, is achieved through all of these balancing acts. While Gilgamesh is extreme in his approach to life, the balance he found through his relationship with Enkidu ultimately aided him in achieving wisdom as well. Once this primitive man had wisdom, he no longer settled for the limitations imposed upon him by his environment, geography, or even physical body. He set forth on a path of singularity with anything he imagined possible, transforming all that was natural and in the dominion of god into artifacts (e.g., stones into megaliths, metals into weapons, grains into bread, etc.).

Wisdom was also the result of Adam and Eve eating the fruit from the Tree of the Knowledge of Good and Evil. By understanding the duality of life through consuming the fruit, Adam and Eve were also led to wisdom. Interestingly, in some belief systems and early interpretations of the Genesis story, to "have knowledge" of something or someone meant that they have had sexual intercourse. In this way, the comparison between the two stories becomes more curious, as both accounts depict a female seductress transforming a male who had been made from the clay of the earth into a "man," with "knowledge" of duality.

In ancient literary traditions, this knowledge is typically gained in defiance of the natural order originally set forth by the gods. Adam and Eve showed hubris in rejecting the orders of their deity, thereby angering him. This led to the ultimate punishment of death. Is this to suggest that before Adam and Eve the world knew no death? If you were to interpret myths literally, then sure. However, myth is not a literal account of historical events, but rather, the constantly renewed narrative of archetypes and events from the collective that allows humans to fully experience their own consciousness.

So this death in the Genesis account may be the *realization* of the *concept of death* itself. In the Garden, man grasped his own mortality and named this concept. It was the realization that man would perish as well as the subsequent naming that made it so. Before eating of the forbidden fruit, man was in a state of blissful ignorance, like an animal. After, he was cursed with the foreknowledge that he and all whom he loved would eventually die. He could then look back and remember his previous state of innocence. He realized there were three states in him: his past state, his current state, and future state. This trinity shows up again and again in the mythology of ancient civilizations.

There could also be the interpretation of the "knowledge of good and evil" as the knowledge of inequality. If in the Garden the gods subjugated primitive man and had him engage in physical labor, perhaps the message from the serpent was the realization of this unfair treatment. Good and evil could be used as a metaphor for just and unjust. Perhaps Adam realized there was a duality that needed to be balanced. Maybe he began to covet the clothing and personal adornments of the "gods," as they represented social stratification, explaining that he "realized" he was naked. Professor David Melvin of Baylor University wrote that the "knowledge of good and evil" could refer to the secret knowledge of the workings of nature, the possession of which leads to the development of civilization, in particular (Melvin, 2010). He argues that the "knowledge" in Genesis 3:1–7 would correspond to instruction in the arts of civilization taught by the Mesopotamian Apkallu.

Aside from what the "knowledge of good and evil" could represent, this event itself could be seen as a turning point in human knowledge transfer. As Professor Melvin points out, the first humans did in fact achieve knowledge of good and evil and in doing so established that from the moment they were banished from Eden, so all subsequent cultural achievements in Genesis 4–11 are "human achievements, without divine intervention, although they are ultimately the result of humanity's reception of divine knowledge" (Melvin, 2010, 15). However, knowledge is thus linked to sin in Eden, which casts a shadow of evil over the notion of civilization itself or "humankind."

This dialectic is present in many of the most ancient accounts of the early world. Both the Epic of Gilgamesh and the Genesis account, as well as almost every story that followed, deal with the same themes: the fight for wisdom, godliness, or perfection through the restoration of balance between extreme dualities. Whether it is good vs. evil, light vs. dark, wild vs. civilized, Heaven vs. Earth, the list goes on. It echoed throughout the ages and usually reaches its acme through what Joseph Campbell referred to as the "Hero's Journey" or monomyth. The ability of these two myths, or any myth for that matter, to resonate with people for so many thousands of years shows that the themes presented are a natural and ongoing part of the human experience. Myths carry a universal truth that is lost when only examining a literal translation.

As an example of the dangers of literal readings, I often point to the English slang term *cool*. If someone were to find a text with this term, it would not be wrong to translate it to mean "at a fairly low temperature." However, it would not make sense in context. Imagine how difficult it might be for future archaeologists to understand that *cool* can also mean something socially and popularly admired. Just ponder the distance we have when we interpret ancient texts. While we may indeed get the translations correct, we are most assuredly missing the mark when it comes to accurately interpreting their meaning. In contemporary society, there are people that would question the meaning of *cool*, so just think about the chasm created not only by cultural difference, but also thousands of years. How can we be so sure that even with 100-percent-accurate translations, we are really getting the exact meaning behind ancient texts? We can't. We need many textual examples to cross-reference just to approach the truth. Due to the nature of history, we can never really know what was in the minds and hearts of the ancients. Nevertheless, we must continue to try to discern the greater messages locked within their words, which requires us to study a multitude of diverse ideas.

Antediluvian Sages

Secrecy has been a part of most religions, sects, and spiritual communities or even other groups in societies. To receive the secrets, many religions demand initiation rituals and additional mystical experiences from their followers. In ancient societies secret knowledge was an important strategy for securing power, status, or sometimes simply survival. Even the knowledge of writing was considered privileged information for some. Select groups called mystery cults attached particular importance to initiation, even constructing their social structures around different degrees of initiation. These levels of initiation created a distinction of ranks between adepts and masters or priests. Some of the best-known mystery cults of the ancient world are the Mysteries of Eleusis, the cult of Dionysus, the cult of Liber Pater in Rome and southern Italy, Mithraism, and the cult of Osiris.

Mystery cults survived through the ancient world and into Abrahamic traditions. Probably the most famous secret knowledge has been the pronunciation of the divine name יהוה (YHWH) in Judaism. The *nomina sacra* have been treated with the greatest respect in all religions because a name is credited with power. Behind it is the idea that whoever knows the name could dispose of the named person. YHWH was not translatable because it is not a name, a thought, a substance, or an existence. This points to the inexpressibility, inexplicability, and unfathomability of God. Out of awe and reverence for YHWH, his greatness and holiness, YHWH was no longer spoken by the Jews after the Babylonian captivity, instead, Adonay (my lord) and today Hashem (literally meaning "the name"). Later, the flow of Gnosticism, a second-century religious movement that offered salvation through gaining secret knowledge, affected Jewish mysticism leading to various sects such as Merkaba mysticism, Kabbalah, and Hasidism. Likewise, Christian mystic sects like the Manichaeans and Ebionites claimed secret knowledge. In Islam some groups of the Shia like the Alevis and Druze, as well as the syncretistic religions originating from the Shia, are attributed to Gnosis. Sometimes the Sufis, followers of Islamic mysticism, are counted among the Gnostics.

Many trace Gnostic traditions of secrecy, magic, and initiation to the ancient Egyptians. While the Egyptians did indeed embrace and cultivate this system, they did not originate it. The practice of keeping secret knowledge began in Sumer, the effects of which can be recognized in our modern academic system as what Michael Cremo calls "The Knowledge Filter" (Cremo and Thompson, 1993). This Knowledge Filter, which operates as a compartmentalized arm of the academic industrial complex, is still keeping the mysteries of Mesopotamia cloaked from public view.

The Knowledge Filter Began in Sumer

It's easy to credit modern thinkers with creating this Knowledge Filter. While terms like *new world order* and *global elites* have a place, using them to explain the knowledge filter would be a mistake. It reinforces the idea that modern powers preclude knowledge from reaching the public, when in fact, the Knowledge Filter began in Sumer. In ancient Sumer, elite scribal scholars claimed to be the exclusive bearers of secret knowledge from the gods, going so far as to claim they were the "heirs of the antediluvian sages," who were associated with Enki (Lenzi, 2013). Secrets of magic, healing, and celestial divination were hidden from outsiders by restricting access to tablets. To legitimize their claims to this secret knowledge, they maintained that their scribal ancestry gave them a special mechanism of communication to receive their secret writings from Enki by channeling the sages of antediluvian times. Theses scholars believed, or at least made others believe, that with their direct line to the antediluvian sages they should be the gatekeepers of knowledge.

Holding on to this position in society made them valuable not only to the public but also to royalty. As the conduit of otherworldly knowledge, these knowledge bearers had the ear of the king. They were the hidden hand in the king's decisions, a role that has been long since known from the evidence in the archaeological record from king lists, letters, and official texts, especially those in the Neo-Assyrian period (Lenzi, 2013). Historically, the ruling classes dominated by using opulent and excessive material commodities to create visible signs of wealth and social distinction. Elites throughout history have ruled by theater. As the great French historian and leader of the Annales School, Fernand Braudel, acknowledged, "there were two ways of living and facing the world: display or discretion" (Braudel, 1982). The elite used pomp and theater to dazzle the masses. They lived on display and tried to maintain and exploit the inequality in their social conditions. Secret knowledge was another display of power, becoming a symbolic asset for its keepers.

Sumerian education was a sophisticated system. Students began with mark-making and learning different words that they not only needed to be able to write correctly, but also to memorize and translate from Sumerian to Akkadian and back. After the initial training, which was not easily given to all, began the more complex subjects. As appears from the examination text recorded at the very end of Sumerian history, a graduate of the school had to have a good command of the language of secrets of Enki.

Scribal education followed a two-tier system. To become a scholar on up to an *ummânū*, students had to start at the bottom, the first tier at the temple school. The first tier trained students for institutional administration while the second prepared them for scholarly pursuits, especially *āšipūtu,* the practice of magic and exorcism (Gesche, 2000). It is important to keep in mind that exorcism in Mesopotamia was not the limited ritual we think of today. Sumerians believed specific demons caused specific diseases. If they could identify which demon by examining a patient and knowing the symptoms, the priests could prescribe the right treatment. These Sumerian exorcists were actually trained physicians and even held to ethical and legal standards similar to physicians today.

Students in the first tier of their education learned basic cuneiform. Then, they would move on to copying of literary texts. Additionally, the students would learn the basics of law, mathematics, land surveying, and other skills necessary for administrative activities (Gesche, 2000). For most students, the completion of this first level was the end of their scribal training. For a small number of students (only about 10 percent), study would continue on the second tier where they learned sacred texts like the *Enūma eliš, Ludlul bēl nēmeqi,* and those associated with *āšipūtu* (Gesche, 2000). To keep stages of knowledge separate for the first- and second-tier students, texts would include secrecy labels—located at the end of a tablet or sometimes the beginning—that warned lesser or non-scholars from reading secret texts. Labels denoting restricted texts are found spanning the late second millennium even into the Hellenistic and Parthian periods (Gesche, 2000). One such examples reads:

> *Original:*
> *AD.ḪAL DINGIR.MEŠ GAL.MEŠ ZU-u ZU-a li-kal-lim NU ZU-u aa IGI.LAL*
> *[NÍG].GIG DINGIR.MEŠ GAL.MEŠ . . .*

> *Translation:*
> *SECRET OF THE GREAT GODS. An expert may show an(other) expert. A non-expert may not see (it). A restriction of the great gods . . . (Lenzi, 2013)*

So what was the motivation for these select students to pursue higher education and initiation into the Mesopotamian Mysteries? The texts tell us exactly: *niṣirtu*, which translates to "the treasured secret of Enki." This treasured secret is the lost knowledge from before the flood that was saved by Utnapishtim, the forerunner to Noah in the flood story. The Standard Babylonian Epic of Gilgamesh indicates that Gilgamesh attained great knowledge from a time before the flood and then brought it to his people:

> *Original:*
> *[nap-ḫ]ar né-me-qi ša ka-la-mi ⌈i⌉-[ḫu-uz?]*
> *[ni]-ṣir-ta i-mur-ma ka-tim-ti ip-⌈tu⌉*
> *[u]b-la ṭè-e-ma ša la-am a-bu-b[i]*
> *Translation:*
> *He learned absolutely everything pertaining to wisdom.*
> *He saw what was secret, opened what was hidden,*
> *He brought back a message from before the flood (Lenzi, 2013).*

The texts point to the secret knowledge of Enki as the knowledge of a civilization before the flood, as well as the knowledge of medicinal plants. In the Epic, Gilgamesh visits Utnapishtim and brings back the secret antediluvian knowledge to civilization. Even Gilgamesh, as a powerful king, did not already have this knowledge. He needed to go to Utnapishtim, who had a direct line of communication with Enki in order to obtain these secrets.

The sacred texts reviewed by initiate scribes would be copied, translated, and studied by way of comparative analysis. For instance, there are multiple copies of the Epic of Gilgamesh. In some versions, there are redactions. It is similar to how the King James Version of the Bible does not include the same gospels as the Dead Sea Scrolls. The banned books of the Bible are Gnostic, usually considered to have sacred and secret wisdom. Here an example of a redacted paragraph from Tablet XI 196–197 that gives the first indication of this something more.

> *Enki says:*
> *a-na-ku ul ap-ta-a pi-riš-ti DINGIR.MEŠ GAL.MEŠ at-ra-ḫa-sis šu-na-ta ú-šab-ri-šum-ma pi-riš-ti DINGIR.MEŠ iš-me*
>
> *Translation:*
> *I did not disclose the secret of the great gods,*
>
> *I showed Atraḫasis (Utnapishtim/Noah flood hero figure) a dream, and thus he heard the secret of the gods (Lenzi, 2013).*

The texts make it clear that the secret knowledge of Enki is the knowledge of a civilization before the flood, as well as the knowledge of medicinal plants. It links Gilgamesh, and in turn the kingship, to this knowledge. However, it is Utnapishtim who survived the flood and gave Enki's secrets to Gilgamesh, forever establishing the power and importance of the priest class. Further, the flood story tells us that Utnapishtim was not the only survivor of the flood, meaning that there were others that carried the secrets of their antediluvian civilization:

> *Original:*
> *bu-ul EDI⸢N⸣ ⸢ú⸣-ma-am EDIN ⸢DUMU.MEŠ⸣ um-ma-a-ni ka-li-šúnu ú-še-li*
>
> *Translation:*
> *I made the animals of the steppe, the creatures of the steppe, and the members (lit. sons) of the ummânū hoard (the boat) (Lenzi, 2013).*

According to the text, Utnapishtim saved the *ummânū*. The *ummânū* translates to "chief scholar." These *ummânū* "were an elite group of scribes from before the flood" (Lenzi, 2013, 153) who survived with Utnapishtim and their animals where they resettled and shared the secrets of Enki with the kings and elites of Mesopotamia. In fact, it was Enki who defied the Anunnaki gods and warned Utnapishtim about the impending flood, a point we will revisit in more depth in chapter 6.

Genetic Engineering

What these texts appear to indicate is that the Garden of Eden is really the name of the world's first agricultural settlement, rather than the place where a single god created humans from dust and a rib six thousand years ago. It also seems that the Anunnaki were real flesh-and-blood beings who ate, made love, fought, and sometimes drank too much. What we can also tell from the Sumerian records is that these beings looked physically different from the locals who inhabited the area before civilization. Otherwise, why would they find it necessary to call the others the "black-headed ones"? Surely if they also had black hair, they would not find it helpful to differentiate in such a way. Further, statues depicting the gods had blue eyes, often picked out with lapis lazuli. In the region that is now Iraq, people with blue eyes can be found, though it is not a common trait. Since they were not a common feature, eventually the blue eye became a symbol of evil, and the ancients believed that people with blue eyes could curse you with a simple look. To protect themselves, the Assyrians would carry with them amulets made from blue-hued material like lapis lazuli or turquoise. Sumerian tablets containing ancient magical spells referenced those whose eyes were blue being filled with lapis lazuli (Kotzé, 2017). Even now in souvenir shops across the Middle East, you can purchase the nazar, a blue-colored glass amulet shaped like a droplet made to wear or hang from the rearview mirror of a car.

Archaeological reports suggest that the blue-eyed gene originated near the Black Sea due to a genetic mutation that occurred between six thousand and ten thousand years ago. According to Professor Hans Eiberg from the University of Copenhagen, all people originally had brown eyes but a mutation occurred in an individual that affected a gene called OCA2 and essentially turned off the ability to produce brown eyes (Eiberg et al., 2008). In the cross section of specimens he and his team examined, this mutation was seen in exactly the same spot in the DNA, indicating that all blue-eyed individuals are linked to the same ancestor (Eiberg et al., 2008). The geneticists believe that blue eyes originated from the Near East area or northwest in part of the Black Sea region, where the great agriculture migration to the northern part of Europe took place in the Neolithic periods about ten thousand years ago—perhaps in the northern part of Afghanistan, according to Eiberg (Eiberg et al., 2008).

It would take only one genetic mutation to make a difference.

Some theorists like Sitchin have asserted that the Anunnaki genetically engineered early humans. I would have to agree—with one important exception. In days of Sumer, only around six thousand years ago, this genetic manipulation was not done using lasers, lab coats, beakers, or even CRISPR, but rather old-fashioned selective breeding. While there is scientific evidence to suggest that primordial life was seeded, at the stage of life on Earth when the Anunnaki came on the scene, they treated the existing primitive hominids, including Neanderthals, as animals.

Here is how we know this. First, from the texts it is clear that the Anunnaki were against "mixing" with the lower races, the Adamah. They forbade this behavior, yet not all of the Anunnaki obeyed, leading to a hybrid race. Further, it is quite clear in the Epic of Gilgamesh that sex was used in the attempt to tame Enkidu. The Sumerian tablets are filled with sexually explicit accounts and a predominant narrative involving the idea of "seeding," which was associated with ejaculate fluid. This may explain the prevalence of incest in ancient royal families. This sort of selective breeding was practiced to keep bloodlines pure.

Imagine a time in human history when civilization was new and surrounding the walled city was a wild terrain that housed not only wild animals, but wild hominids. What if the displaced antediluvian sages also appeared differently, having lighter features or taller statures? Would they not appear as a different race? I believe these ancient texts all describe the scenario of urbanization and the inherent struggles it brought when people were no longer living together in smaller family groups, but instead in a cosmopolitan metropolis bustling with strangers with different languages, physical appearances, and cultures. For many years the mainstream narrative insisted that *Homo sapiens* and *Homo neanderthalensis* never interbred. In fact, even with hard genetic evidence to the contrary, there are still holdouts in academia who deny it.

CHAPTER 5

Watchers in the Sky

Right now, there could well be messages from the stars
flying right through this room. Through you and me.
And if we had the right receiver set up properly, we could
detect them. I still get chills thinking about it.
—FRANK DRAKE, American astronomer and astrophysicist

The Sumerian and Astronomy Connection: Astronomical Breakthroughs

Modern astronomy can trace its origins six thousand years ago to Sumer. The knowledge and technical advancements of the Sumerian astronomers were so groundbreaking that they were later adopted by the Akkadians, Babylonians, Assyrians, and even Greek scholars. Sumerian astronomy was both observational and mathematical. These ancient proto-scientists associated the planets and stars with gods and believed the study of celestial bodies made it possible to predict the will of these gods. The most important celestial bodies were the sun, moon, and Venus, which were monitored regularly by trained priests. The sun was given the name Utu; the moon, Nanna; and Venus,

Inanna, which the Babylonians would later call Shamash, Sin, and Ishtar, respectively. Close monitoring of the planets and stars was vitally important to the Sumerian way of life. The ancients believed that crops, fertility, the change of seasons, and even the fate of people still depended on the activity of celestial bodies and the deities they equated them with. Sumerian priests carefully tracked planetary movements across the night sky in order to calculate the time of harvest, the length of the year, and even to predict various events.

Through their disciplined observations, the Sumerians already knew at the beginning of third millennium BCE that the morning and evening star cast the same light: the illumination of Venus. At the end of the third millennium, a cuneiform text listed the Sumerian constellations. Amazingly, this text considered the planets as an independent category of heavenly bodies, different from fixed stars. These ancient astronomers also realized that unlike stars, these celestial bodies moved their positions.

Sacred temples were designed to allow the priests to carefully observe and record the activity in the night sky. These imposing ziggurats served as observatories with each level acting as a higher point of view until they could see the horizon line. The axis between the eastern and western corners of the ziggurats gives the direction of the equinox and the sides opened up an overview of the sunrise and sunset at both the summer and winter solstices. Using the naked eye, we presume, and their knowledge of mathematics, Sumerian astronomers could calculate the rising and setting of the celestial bodies against the Earth's horizon, in a method similar to what is employed today. They would then record the measurements in great detail onto clay tablets, some of which have survived to this day.

It was widely assumed that these ancient astronomers used basic arithmetic to predict the positions of celestial bodies. However, a 2016 study published in the journal *Nature* found that Babylonian astronomers were actually employing sophisticated geometric computational techniques to determine planetary positioning (Ossendrijver, 2016). These newly discovered methods clearly foreshadowed the development of calculus, which historians had thought could not have developed until the fourteenth century in Europe at the earliest. Astroarchaeologist Mathieu Ossendrijver of Humboldt University in Berlin examined tablets dating from 350 to 50 BCE that had not been studied until very recently. For fourteen years, this dedicated researcher toiled over these tablets in the British Museum's vast collection, trying to solve a mystery found in two dealing with astronomical calculations. The first peculiarity Ossendrijver noticed was that they provided instructions for making a trapezoidal figure. This seemed out of place to Ossendrijver, as it was not explicitly related to anything astronomical. He would go on to find two tablets that also discussed the drawing of a trapezoid, which made him wonder if he could make out a reference to Jupiter, since it was a favorite among the Babylonians, who equated it with Marduk.

After years of study, Ossendrijver received a visit from a retired Assyriologist named Hermann Hunger, who brought with him a cache of photos taken many years ago of an uncatalogued Babylonian tablet from the British Museum. This tablet described astronomical computations that Hunger thought might be of interest to Ossendrijver. After reviewing the old blurry photos, Ossendrijver had an epiphany. He found that the numbers on the uncatalogued tablet were identical to the trapezoid inscriptions he had been studying! This confirmed to him that the ancient astronomers of Mesopotamia had indeed discovered a complex computation that described the motion of Jupiter. The ancients were using a velocity versus time graph to track the motion of the planets. In a velocity versus time graph—as is taught now in any high school geometry or physics class—the principle is that the slope of the line can reveal useful information about the acceleration of the object, in this case Jupiter.

After this discovery, Ossendrijver began searching the British Museum for more ancient texts and found that the so-called trapezoid procedures belong to the corpus of Babylonian mathematical astronomy, which comprises about 450 tablets from Babylon and Uruk dating between 400 and 50 BCE, about 340 of which are tables with computed planetary or lunar data arranged in rows and columns (Ossendrijver, 2016). The remaining 110 tablets are procedural texts with computational instructions for calculating Jupiter's displacement each day along the ecliptic, the path that the sun appears to trace through the stars (Ossendrijver, 2016). The ancient computations recorded on the tablets covered a period of sixty days, beginning on a day when Jupiter first appeared in the night sky just before dawn. Thus, the ancient Mesopotamian astronomers were very interested in tracking the planet's movement across the night sky.

However, this was not all these trailblazing astronomers had discovered. They also found that in order to compute the time at which Jupiter would have moved halfway along its ecliptic path, they had to divide the sixty-day trapezoid in half. Basic thinking would have them conclude that the elliptical path would be thirty days. However, when they drew a straight vertical line down the different shapes of the trapezoids, they came up with slightly less than thirty days because of the different shapes of the trapezoids. This meant that the elliptical was actually slightly fewer than thirty days.

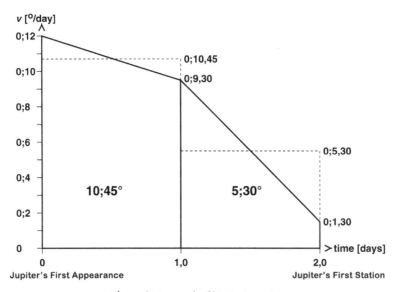

Time-velocity graph of Jupiter's motion.

This new information has major implications for the history of science. Long before ancient Greek astronomers such as Aristarchus of Samos and Claudius Ptolemy used geometrical methods, and much longer than the French and English philosophers and mathematicians in the late Middle Ages, the Mesopotamians had developed "abstract mathematical, geometrical ideas about the connection between motion, position and time that are so common to any modern physicist or mathematician" (Ossendrijver, 2016, 484). What's more, these ancient trapezoid techniques differ from those used by other advanced civilizations, such as the Greeks, in that the geometrical figures describe an abstract concept of space defined by time and velocity rather than actual physical form. Their ability to abstract using mathematical models puts them in a unique position among all other ancient astronomers, indicating that they did indeed have advanced knowledge beyond what is commonly recognized. In order to uncover this new information, it took the dedication of an expert with a side interest in history to push the boundaries of the accepted narrative and go beyond the museum's collection to study obscure texts that the general public does not readily have access to. Imagine what more we could discover if resources, associability, curiosity, and passion aligned on a daily basis!

Cylinder Seal VA 243

Modern research is now providing evidence that the ancients were far more advanced in their thinking and capabilities than archaeologists and historians had previously told us. So what then was the extent of Sumerian astronomical knowledge? In addition to information about the origin of the universe and indeed humanity itself, some researchers believe that the Sumerian texts reveal the development and structure of the solar system, including a list and characteristics of the planets. Researchers even claim that the Sumerians knew exactly how many planets there were and that they were heliocentric. Many will point to the cylinder seal VA 243, located in the Vorderasiatisches Museum in Berlin, an archaeological museum in the basement of the Pergamon Museum. Like most cylinder seals, the small stone was rolled onto unbaked clay to sign or authenticate administrative documents. This seal is believed to depict the sun in the center, surrounded by twelve planets. Experts dispute this claim, yet those who disagree do not provide an alternative explanation for the image. Is this specific image proof that the Sumerians believed they were in a heliocentric cosmological model surrounded by twelve planets?

Artist's sketch of VA 243.

I decided to take a closer look at VA 243 to see if there were any other details that could shed new light on this debate. What I discovered was not the evidence some would hope. Instead, I found a wholly new translation for this iconic Sumerian text.

According to many ancient astronaut theorists, the Sumerians believed the moon and sun to be planets, meaning that the eleven dots on the left side of the tablet along with the middle image as the sun would equal twelve planets. By today's standards, this is incorrect because there are eight (nine, if you include Pluto), in addition to the sun and our moon. In Sitchin's book, the *12th Planet*, he argued that the Sumerians knew of an exoplanet named Nibiru, which passes through our solar system every 3,600 years (Sitchin, 2016). This would mean that Nibiru was the tenth planet in our modern understanding of the solar system, so "Planet X" (Sitchin, 2016). On the cylinder seal VA 243, what Sitchin sees as the sun, mainstream scholars claim to be a star. As with most of the Sitchin vs. the mainstream debates, many readers and researchers are bounced back and forth between the two with no real option for an alternative perspective: if one is wrong, then the other must be right. Alternative explanations go unquestioned for so long that they become as dogmatic as the mainstream, thereby betraying their own principle of being alternative! Here is my own perspective, which does not rely on either argument.

In Sumerian art, there are great consistencies in celestial depictions. Suns have six or eight points. Stars are considered separate concepts from the sun, and they are often depicted simply as dots. One of the best examples of this is the Sumerian portrayal of the Pleiades. Often too, a dot will be placed in front of a figure to denote godhood. In a lot of images, you will find three signs associated with the specific celestial gods. The first is the sun god Uta, depicted as a small circle with four rays and with wavy lines between them and enclosed in a larger circle. Another common feature in Mesopotamian art is the depiction of the sun, moon, and star grouped together and clearly distinguished as such. Also, there is precedent for these dots to represent a constellation, in that it more closely resembles the seven-dot grouping used to depict the Pleiades. With this in mind, we can see that it is quite possible for this grouping of dots to represent a specific constellation, rather than a planetary system.

Using this theory, I went in search of Sumerian constellations with eleven stars recorded in the Babylonian star catalogue called the MUL.APIN. The only contender was the constellation Centaurus, or what the Babylonians called the Bison-man (MUL.GUD.ALIM) ("Mul-Apin 1"). Scholars believe the seal is dedicated to agriculture, especially since the seated god is seen giving a plow to the worker. The seal reads:

Original:

SI.GA D.IL.LA.TUR3 ARAD.SU

Translation:

"Dubsiga, Ili.il.laat[is] your servant" (Porada and Moortgat, 1941).

Depiction of soldiers loading chariots onto a boat from the reign of Ashurnasirpal II, 865–860 BCE, from Nimrud, Iraq, currently housed in the British Museum. (Osama Shukir Muhammed Amin FRCP(Glasg) [CC BY-SA 4.0, creativecommons.org])

So why do I think that the controversial image may be Centaurus? Why would these eleven stars of this constellation be surrounding the starlike image? I believe it could be depicting the myth of Centaurus, or Kusarikku, "Bison-Man." He is sometimes portrayed holding a *banduddû*, or what some have called "the handbag of the gods," or he has been depicted carrying a spade, both of which can be associated with agriculture. In the Sumerian myth the Enûma Eliš, the Bison-Man is one of Tiamat's offspring, who was defeated by Marduk. In *Ninurta's Return to Nippur*, the Bison-Man is "hung on the beam," as part of the story:

> *On his shining chariot, which inspires terrible awe, he hung his*
> *captured wild bulls on the axle and hung his captured cows on the*
> *cross-piece of the yoke. He hung the Six-headed wild ram on the*

*dust-guard. He hung the Warrior dragon on the seat. He hung
the Magilum boat on the . . . He hung the Bison on the beam
(Ninurta's Return to Nibru, 2018).*

Lines 64–69 go on to say, "Lord Ninurta stepped into his
battle-worthy chariot. Ud-ane, the all-seeing god, and Lugal-
anbara, the bearded (?) lord, went before him, and the awe-
some one of the mountains, Lugal-kur-dub, the . . . of Lord
Ninurta, followed behind him" (Ninurta's Return to Nibru,
2018). The story tells of the Bison-Man being hung on the
beam, which meant the spokes of a chariot. Take a look at the
way chariot wheels are depicted in Sumerian art. They have six
spokes attached to a rather large ball in the center.

If you remove the wheel itself and instead imagine that the
"Bison-Man" is wrapped around the beam, you may get what
appears to be the six-spoked image in the sky surrounded by
the eleven stars of the constellation originally known as the
Bison-Man, Centaurus, in the VA 243 seal. Thus, it could be
that the mysterious constellation-like image depicted in VA
243 is Centaurus as described in the story of *Ninurta's Return to
Nippur.* This is by no means definitive proof; however, I think it is
just as good as any other explanation offered so far. Some who
read this may feel one of a few different emotions at my analysis. First, if they are inclined to only agree with Sitchin, they
will discount this alternative as merely an attempt at debunking. In other words, how dare I question Sitchin? The second
feeling may be that I have offered an alternative explanation
that is unconvincing and perhaps pseudoscientific since, while
I am a trained historian and archaeologist, I am not specifically an Assyriologist. In other words, I should "stay in my
lane." What I hope is that, instead, readers will take a third
view, one that recognizes the importance of always questioning
ideas no matter how entrenched they may be in one's frame of

reference. I believe it is vitally important to stay curious and always encourage inquiry.

I once took a course in archaeoastronomy at the Politecnico di Milano where the professor, well-known and -respected Italian astrophysicist/archaeoastronomer Giulio Magli, was asked a question by one of my classmates. The student questioned Professor Magli about an exhibition that was going on in the British Museum about the Scythians. He posted a link to a picture of a panther plaque and mused about whether the three central studs on the plaque could be representative of Orion's Belt. Professor Magli responded, "Nice joke . . . the same can be played with three post-lamps in the street, and even with three suitable mountains on a map (not to say, three pyramids in Egypt). . . ." The student responded by clarifying that he did not mean this as a joke and that he genuinely wondered about the possibility that this plaque depicted Orion's Belt. There was radio silence. The student was ignored. While the Politecnico di Milano is a very well-respected university and Professor Magli a top professional in the field, it makes it even worse to think that this student was essentially discouraged and even potentially ridiculed for simply daring to posit an Orion connection. It is absurd because the class was on archaeoastronomy, a field in which you analyze and question how the ancients viewed the relationship between their culture, religion, and folklore and the sky.

Secrets of the Constellations

We can clearly see that the ancients knew quite a lot about astronomy and had the ability, as evidenced by the academic research, to think in a complex and abstract way. Anyone who has visited the Great Pyramid at Giza, Megalithic sites, or places like the Nazca Lines will tell you that the ancients knew far more about the cosmos than most scholars give them credit for. One researcher in particular can attest to the sophisticated understanding ancient people had and that is my friend and colleague Gary David. After following Gary's work in college, I met him some years back in Indiana at a conference on ancient mysteries. Gary is an author and independent researcher with a master's degree in English literature from the University of Colorado. He has studied Southwestern archaeological ruins and rock art for nearly thirty years and has written numerous books about the Hopi and other Ancestral Puebloan cultures of Arizona and New Mexico, including *The Orion Zone: Ancient Star Cities of the American Southwest* and *Eye of the Phoenix: Mysterious Visions and Secrets in the American Southwest*. While researching this book, I contacted Gary to ask his thoughts on the mythological significance of the constellations to the Sumerians. He explained his analysis of the constellation of Eridanus and its important relationship to ancient cultures, including the Sumerians.

ERIDANUS—
Sky-River to the Underworld
BY GARY A. DAVID

Spiral Stargate

The spiral, the whirlpool, the vortex . . . This icon was used in cultures around the world to signify an inter-dimensional portal, a transition between worlds, or a gateway between one reality and another. It is the doorway through which the shaman begins his or her ecstatic quest along the World Tree (*axis mundi*) from the physical to the spiritual plane. In essence, it is a stargate—but not the metal ring on terra firma seen in the movie and TV series of the same name. It is instead a divine tunnel located in the sky through which the soul achieves transcendence.

Egyptian Wadjet (Ujat), "whole one," the all-seeing Eye of Horus superimposed on Orion and Eridanus. (Gary David)

Next to the left foot of Orion is the swirling source of a great sidereal stream named Eridanus. Esoteric author E. Raymond Capt has called it "the River of the Judge" (Capt, 1973). Encompassing the largest area of any constellation, it meanders from the celestial deity whom the ancient Egyptians identified as the god Osiris, judge of the Underworld, toward the southern realms. Hermes

Trismegistos, the Greek name for the Egyptian god Thoth, associated this eddy in the sky with death and transition.

In their classic book *Hamlet's Mill,* scholars Giorgio de Santillana and Hertha von Dechend write: "That there is a whirlpool in the sky is well known; it is most probably the essential one, and it is precisely placed. It is a group of stars so named (*zalos*) at the foot of Orion, close to Rigel (beta Orionis, Rigel being the Arabic word for 'foot'), the degree of which was called 'death,' according to Hermes Trismegistos . . ." (Santillana and Von Dechend, 1998).

The Greek word *zalos*, also spelled *salos*, means "tossing of the sea in a tempest; agitation, rolling"—a swelling, swirling, or roaring of waves, i.e., a maelstrom. However, the same word also carries the sense of either "fool" or "holy folly." The Hebrew name for Orion is *Kesil* (or *cesîl*), which signifies "'Foolish,' 'Impious,' 'Inconstant,' or 'Self-confident'" (Krueger, 1996).

At the head of the River is the star Cursa, which is called "the Footstool" of Rigel, located 3° to the northwest of Orion's left foot (if the front of Orion is conceptualized as facing us). Located eighty-nine light-years away and having a size and mass about three times that of our sun, it is one of about two dozen stars that suddenly and inexplicably produce huge flashes, perhaps related to a magnetic shift. In 1985, for instance, it increased in luminance by an amazing three magnitudes (or a factor of fifteen) and stayed that bright for over two hours until it faded back to normal brilliance

(Kaler, n.d.). Perhaps this relatively quick burst of light was the result of some interdimensional travelers passing through the whirlpool portal near the star Cursa.

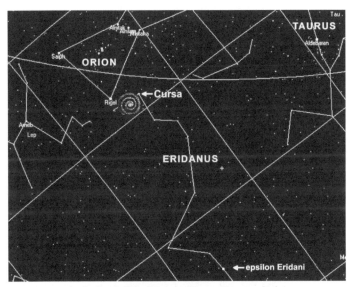

At the head of the River is the star Cursa, which is called "the Footstool" of Rigel. (Gary David)

End of the World, End of the River

The constellation Eridanus was once conceptualized as a place of calamity. In this area of the sky, for instance, the impetuous Greek youth named Phaethon crashed and burned after he took the chariot of his father Helios for a joyride. Plato's *Timaeus* interprets this not as a cautionary tale of a callow youth but as a mythological description of an historic event—that is, one of many cyclic destructions of the world (Cornford, 1955).

The name *Eridanus* may have been derived from the Sumerian city of Eridu, which literally means "mouth (or confluence) of rivers." This proto-urban center once located in the marshland near the Persian Gulf signified not death but birth—the birthplace of civilization, in fact (Eridanus [constellation], 2019). One of the earliest Sumerian periods was the Ubaid, which stretched from about 6500 BC to 3800 BC (Ubaid Period, 2019). Archaeologists have found odd clay statuettes dated from this period that depict lizard-like creatures with elongated heads, slit eyes, and spindly limbs.

Zecharia Sitchin in his book *The Cosmic Code* translates ERIDU as "Home in the Faraway" or "Home away from home" (Sitchin, 2007). The first home was apparently among the stars. A text called the Sumerian King List states: "After the kingship descended from heaven, the kingship was in Eridu." This was basically the spot where the gods called the Anunnaki descended from the heavens to the Earth. The first king named Alulim supposedly ruled for 28,800 years (*Livius.org*). The names Eridanus and Eridu may also be related to the name of planet Earth.

Eridu was ruled by the earth/water god Enki. (*En-* means "lord" and *ki* means "earth.") Enki was also known by three names: "Lord of Sweet Waters in the Earth" (fresh water), "Lord of Deep Waters" (salt water), and "Lord of the Abyss" (netherworld). His primary symbols included the goat and the fish, which were combined in the zodiac constellation of Capricornus. Both Eridanus and Capricornus are water-related constellations (Capricornus; Eridanus, 2019).

Journey to the Underworld

Like the marshes of the Nile delta in Egypt and the Euphrates delta in Iraq, the "End of the River" Eridanus is probably imbued with the spiritual power of the reed (David, 2008). In heaven its harbor is Achernar, a bright star with a magnitude of 0.5. On earth the Great Pyramid and the ruins of the city of Eridu are located on approximately the same latitude—29° 58' 47" N and 30° 49' 01" N, respectively. In fact, they are less than one degree (or about fifty-eight miles) apart, although Giza is nearly nine hundred miles west of Eridu. However, the sky-view is similar. Achernar was seen from both places as early as 22,000 BC and disappeared below the horizon in 8500 BC. Thus, it was visible above the southern horizon for about 13,500 years—one-half of a Great Year (26,920 years). This period clearly spans what the ancient Egyptians called the *Zep Tepi*, or "First Time," when the *Shemsu Hor*, or "Followers of Horus," reigned as demigods.

Author Graham Hancock describes this initial world cycle: "Here is what the Ancient Egyptians said about the First Time, Zep Tepi, when the gods ruled in their country: they said it was a golden age during which the waters of the abyss receded, the primordial darkness was banished, and humanity, emerging into the light, was offered the gifts of civilization" (Hancock, 1995). This great swath of early time resonates with the Sumerian King List previously mentioned. At both Giza and Eridu, however, the star has returned, hovering just above the southern horizon for the last few centuries. *Zep Tepi redux?*

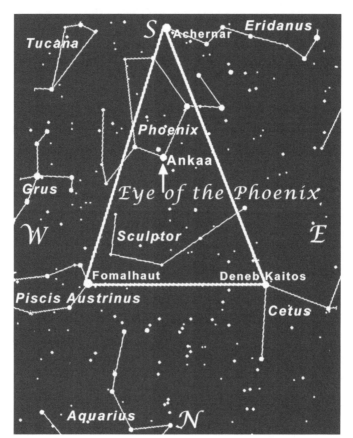

Eridanus with Achernar at the top (south), Aquarius in the zodiac at the bottom (north), and Phoenix with Ankaa at the center of the celestial pyramid. (Gary David)

The constellation Phoenix rests where Eridanus empties into the cosmic ocean. *Benu* is the Egyptian name for the legendary phoenix. This bird is customarily perched atop an obelisk, a pyramidion (apex of a pyramid), or a benben stone. The last was sculpted to mimic a cone or rough pyramid of meteoric iron naturally formed by its fall to earth (Budge, 1960). The Egyptian word *ben* denotes both the nominative "seed" or "semen" and the infinitive "to copulate" or "to impregnate"—all particularly apropos of the phallic obelisk (Bauval and Gilbert, 1994). In addition, the cognate *ben-t* means "cincture, belt, girdle" (Budge, 1960) and might refer obliquely to Orion's belt. Alnitak, the most eastern star of the belt (corresponding to the Great Pyramid, or Khufu, in the Orion Correlation Theory) literally means "the Girdle," while Mintaka, the most western star (corresponding to Menkaure), is called "the Belt" (Allen, 1899). As with every example of truly divine omnipotence, the positive aspects are counterbalanced with the negative. Hence the word *ben* also means "evil, wickedness," and the words *ben-t* or *benut* can also refer to pustule, boil, abscess, or pus (Budge, 1960).

The stars comprising Phoenix, in addition to their aviary connotation, can be conceptualized as a barque. Metaphorically identified in *The Egyptian Book of the Dead* as "The Boat of Millions of Years," thus signifying its journey across the vast reaches of deep space-time, this tiny craft carries the soul to its destiny in the afterlife:

"Let it be granted to me [Ani] to pass on to the holy princes, for indeed, I have done away all the evil which I committed, from the time when this earth came into being from Nu, when it sprang from the watery abyss even as it was in the days of old. I am Fate and Osiris, I have made my transformations into the likeness of diverse serpents. Man knoweth not, and the gods cannot behold the two-fold beauty which I have made for Osiris, the greatest of the gods. I have given unto him the region of the dead. And, verily, his son Horus is seated upon the throne of the Dweller in the fiery Lake [of Neserser], as his heir. I have made him to have his throne in the Boat of Millions of Years" (Budge, 2003).

The most brilliant star in the constellation is Ankaa, or Al-Anqa, which literally means "head of the phoenix." But its other Arabic name, Na'ir al Zaurak, denotes "Bright One in the Boat." Located seventy-seven light-years away, this yellow giant is spectral type K with a magnitude of 2.4—not a particularly bright star from our perspective. But in relation to the sun, it has four times the mass, sixteen times the diameter, and eighty times the luminosity (Phoenix [constellation], 2019).

A pyramid rises from three major stars in the region. Its base is formed by Fomalhaut (magnitude 1.2) in Piscis Austrinus, or the Southern Fish, and Deneb Kaitos (magnitude 2.0) in the tail of the sea monster Cetus. Pointing southward toward the underworld realm of the dead, its apex is formed by Achernar, where the River ends. The constellation of the Sculptor is enclosed within the pyramid near its base, perhaps fashioning or adorning its inner *sanctum sanctorum*.

Fixed Stars, Fixed Fates

Although we ultimately control our fate, many people believe that the stars exert some influence over our earthly existence. For millennia the intuitive science of astrology has studied the unique effects of a given planet or fixed star on our lives. Let's take a look at our pyramid of stars.

Fomalhaut, for instance, is traditionally associated with idealism, mysticism, and lofty visions. Success, immortal fame, and spirituality are the benefits of this star culminating in one's natal chart. It is one of the four Royal Stars of Persia, known as the "Watcher of the South." The others are: Regulus in Leo (the "Watcher of the North"), Aldebaran in Taurus (the "Watcher of the East"), and Antares in Scorpio (the "Watcher of the West"). The Watchers, of course, were also known as the Anunnaki, as previously mentioned.

The other point forming the pyramid's base, Deneb Kaitos in the whale constellation Cetus, is linked with the devouring aspect of the collective unconscious. It facilitates the unexpected eruption of chaos or mayhem into our lives—the emergence of a juggernaut. In general the constellation emphasizes the ability to command and make war.

The apex of the pyramid, Achernar, is connected to natural disasters, including floods and fires. The former element makes sense in terms of this turbulent star's position at the end of the Eridanus, the latter by virtue of its location near the conflagration of the phoenix.

Ankaa (Alpha Phoenicis) at the heart of the constellation Phoenix is understandably related to transformation, transfiguration, or transcendence. Astrologist Bernadette Brady comments on one modern scholar who exerted a global influence: "Joseph Campbell, the famous mythologist and author, has Ankaa culminating with his sun, indicating that the star was connected to his life work, his career, his mark in the world. Joseph

Campbell raised our collective consciousness to a higher level with his understanding, teachings, and writings about the importance of myths" (Brady, 1998).

The name Ankaa echoes the Egyptian word *ankh*, the icon of life everlasting. The related Egyptian word *anqa* means "cordage, tackle of a boat," thus harkening back to the Phoenix as a vessel used to cross the ocean of time. In addition, Anku is the god that binds the foes of Osiris, god of the underworld.

Looking at the Sumerian lexicon, we find that the word *an* refers to "heavenly" and *ka* means "gateway." Thus, the Sumerians probably knew Ankaa (*an-ka*) as a sky portal.

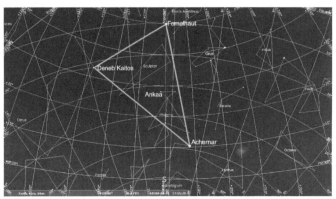

Sky-view looking south in 10,500 BCE from Giza, in a period that the ancient Egyptians called Zep Tepi, or "First Time." (Gary David)

As a vessel sailing toward immortality, the constellation Phoenix has Ankaa for its boatman at the rudder. As the fabulous firebird, Ankaa becomes the all-seeing

Eye of the Phoenix. As the temple for both mythological versions, the sidereal pyramid becomes the pyre upon which the Eye of Providence blazes, envisaging the eternal fields of bliss beyond all temporal cycles. The source of celestial River Eridanus begins in the material realm near the left foot of Orion and flows southward, bringing the soul to the "land down under," not Australia of course but the mythical—that is, *spiritual*—underworld.

The Solar Bird

As Gary points out, we find the Sumerians may have seen the Ankaa (an-ka) as a sky portal. The name Ankaa can be traced to the Arabic العنقاء *al-ʿanqāʾ* "the phoenix" (Kunitzsch and Smart, 2006). Hence, the association of this star system and the Phoenix is steeped in many traditions, as is the symbol of the phoenix itself. The phoenix, the benu, the falcon, the eagle—indeed, all of these birds of prey represent a continuity of ideas in the ancient world creation story. As Robert Bauval postulates in his article "Investigation on the Origins of the Benben Stone: Was It an Iron Meteorite?" from the journal *Discussions in Egyptology*, the benben stone the Egyptians worshipped in the Mansion of the Phoenix might have been a meteorite (Bauval, 1989). The Egyptians may have seen the meteorite as a star that came down to the Earth, giving rise to the myth of the "seed" or sperm of Ra-Atum, the father of the gods.

However, since the stone is conical in shape, Bauval ponders the connection of the benben with the sun because it would not appear to fit in with how solar symbols are normally depicted as a disc. He goes on to suggest that while the phoenix represented the sun god's self-creating power, its cosmic identification was not limited to the sun (Bauval, 1989). He states that in the Middle Kingdom, the phoenix was also said to be the moon or sometimes Venus and that his power of self-creation symbolized the rebirth of celestial bodies or gods. Yet it is difficult as historians to look back at the intentions of the ancients, as we unintentionally wear a biased lens of our own cultural framework. There are indeed many possible ways to try to understand the meanings behind these ancient texts. To broaden our understanding, I would like to introduce to the discussion another important mythical bird, the Ziz of Jewish mythology.

The Ziz was a very large bird of prey whose wingspan was said to be so big it could block out the sun. Rabbis have said that the Ziz is comparable to the Persian Simurgh, while some scholars compare the Ziz to the Sumerian Anzû and the ancient Greek phoenix (Wazana, 2009). The Bible also mentions the Ziz in Psalms 50:11 (KJV), stating: "I know all the birds of the mountains and Zīz śāday is mine". In Enoch, the phoenix appeared as a companion to the chariot of the sun, along with another very large bird that together, "pull the chariot" and were "crimson like the rainbow." The description goes on to say the birds "carry dew and heat, descend to earth, and ascend from it with the sun's rays according to God's orders" (Enoch 6:6–7). Likewise, in the Jewish pseudepigraphical text, *2 Baruch*, written soon after the destruction of the Temple of Solomon in 70 CE, there is a passage that emphasized the mystical importance of birds as messengers and their connection to divine wisdom. The author, Baruch, says: "Nevertheless, as you said unto me, I will write also unto your brethren in Babylon, and I will send by means of men, and I will write in like manner to the nine tribes and a half, and send by means of a bird" (Baruch 77:17). Baruch went on to explain how he wrote two epistles: one "sent by an eagle to the nine and a half tribes" and the other "sent to those that were at Babylon by means of three men." (Baruch 77:17). He declares that he called the eagle and spoke these words unto it:

> *The Most High hath made you that you should be higher than all birds. And now go and tarry not in (any) place, nor enter a nest, nor settle upon any tree, till you have passed over the breadth of the many waters of the river Euphrates, and have gone to the people that dwell there, and cast down to them this epistle. Remember, moreover, that, at the time of the deluge, Noah received from a dove the fruit of the olive, when he sent it forth from the ark. Yea, also the ravens ministered to Elijah, bearing him food, as they had been commanded. Solomon also, in the time of his kingdom, whithersoever he wished to send or seek for anything, commanded a bird (to go thither), and it obeyed him as he commanded it (Baruch 77:17).*

The Anzû, Ziz, and phoenix were cosmic birds, not necessarily solar birds, although they showed connections to the sun. These great birds were sometime represented in anthropomorphic forms like the Mesopotamian Apkallu.

This brings me back to Buvaul's point about the benben stone. While this stone is conical, it is related to the phoenix myth, which, as he states, was also said to refer to a few different celestial bodies in the Middle Kingdom. I cannot help but wonder whether these cosmic birds represent meteors. In the Greek-Slavonic Apocalypse of Baruch, the author writes: "In the site from where the sun goes forth Baruch sees a bird of huge dimensions circling the sun. The angel identifies it as the Phoenix, explaining that the bird is guarding the earth—by flying alongside the sun and spreading its wings, thus receiving the sun's fiery rays" (Kulik, 2009). It continues: "as the sun shines behind the Phoenix, it spreads out its wings, gradually gaining full measure. At dusk, the sun's rays are defiled from

Wall relief of an eagle-headed winged Apkallu from Nimrud. (Osama Shukir Muhammed Amin FRCP(Glasg) [CC BY-SA 4.0, creativecommons.org*])*

the lawlessness and unrighteousness of men it has seen all day, and the Phoenix likewise contracts its wings, exhausted from having restrained the burning heat and fire of the sun from

140

scorching all living creatures" (Kulik, 2009, 227). This description clearly separates the solar bird motif from the sun alone and puts it in a position of service to the sun. It carries a sort of "heat and fire" it derives from the sun. It is a destructive force, as well as giving new life and rebirth. It was also believed that this bird would vocalize a warning to other birds before it appeared loud enough to scatter its fellows.

In my reading of these texts and others, I could not help but think that what is being described is a comet. Rather than associate the solar bird motif with the sun alone, it could seem that what the ancient texts are describing is a connection between a comet and a great bird. On February 15, 2013, a superbolide (an extremely bright meteor that explodes in the atmosphere) known as the Chelyabinsk Meteor blasted into Earth's atmosphere. It was caused by a sixty-six-foot near-Earth asteroid with a speed of 40,000–42,900 mph (Popova et al., 2013). It was visible over the skies of Russia and captured on multiple dashcams. Judging by the duration of the flight, atmospheric entry occurred at a very acute angle. Seconds after that, the celestial body collapsed, causing a destructive propagation of shock waves. The shock waves caused extensive damage and injured hundreds of people. According to NASA estimates, it is the largest known celestial body to fall to Earth since the Tunguska meteorite in 1908 (Brumfiel, 2013).

There are still many videos available online that captured this occurrence from different angles and locations. The footage shows just how awe-inspiring such a celestial event can be. It also shows how the ancient motif of the phoenix may have been associated with a comet. Just before the meteor appears, the birds, as if forewarned, scatter. As the meteor enters the atmosphere, it looks like a star, falling from the sky, but as it picks up speed, it appears to fly, glinting with light radiating outwardly like the wings of a great bird. The smoke trails of particulate matter paint the sky behind it as it finally blocks the sun. The meteor breaks apart in the atmosphere, so there is not a single impact site, but rather deposits of dark stones seed the landscape. Could this be similar to what the ancients may have seen, leading them to embrace this type of solar bird iconography? Both ancient Mesopotamians and Egyptians revered the falcon, both sharing a similar and intriguing connection between this holy bird and the concept of the divine wisdom.

The Egyptian Temple of Horus at Edfu contains references to birdlike figures similar to those in Mesopotamian texts. The god Horus was himself often depicted as a falcon or a man with the head of a falcon, extraordinarily similar to the Apkallus, or sages of Mesopotamia. According to E. A. E. Reymond's translation of the building texts in the Edfu temple, the temple was constructed by mortal beings called "Builder Gods" (Reymond, 1969, 26). They received the plans to construct the temple as well as for all future temples from the Seven Sages. These great teachers were identical to the Seven Sages, or Apkallus, in Mesopotamian texts, who taught antediluvian wisdom to humanity. According to a scholar from the University of Tartu, the Apkallus were demonized in Genesis and later, in the Book of Enoch, appear as Watchers and giants, illegitimate teachers of humankind before the flood (Annus, 2010). Enoch's work, according to the scholar, "reconciles these two different adaptations by making Enoch in every respect superior to the Watchers" (Annus, 2010, 231).

Further, the Apkallus were at times viewed negatively within Mesopotamian literature as demons or evil beings capable of witchcraft. Thus, Jewish scholars were not single-handedly responsible for this inversion of Mesopotamian traditions; the tendency toward inversion of antediluvian teachers of human-kind from benevolent to malevolent was already beginning in Mesopotamia (Annus, 2010,). This is also apparent in collections of Mesopotamian exorcism and demonology texts.

The Edfu texts, in addition to many other Egyptian texts, give clues to a connection between the Mesopotamian Apkallus and what Reymond translated as the "Seven Sages" (Reymond, 1969, 28). These texts also make clear that there is a difference between the "Seven Sages," and the "Builder Gods," who performed "the actual work of building" (Reymond, 1969, 41). These Seven Sages of ancient Egypt were connected to Thoth, the god of wisdom. The Apkallus were similarly connected to Enki, the Mesopotamian god of wisdom. The texts paint a picture of a world in which mysterious Sages, believed to be divine beings and creators of knowledge, disseminated high culture such as the architecture of sacred places (Reymond, 1969). Yet, these divine Sages could only pass on this knowledge to initiates, who could not invent something wholly original or new (Reymond, 1969).

The Edfu texts illustrate remarkable similarities between Mesopotamian and Egyptian ideas. These stories could very well represent real accounts of the arrival of human survivors of a lost civilization who were somehow inspired or influenced by a mysterious divine spark of higher wisdom. These antediluvian men of reason, wisdom, and practical building capabilities were by all accounts human. Yet the Sages were depicted as divine originators of this sacred knowledge who handed it down to the Builders. Later, it would seem that they would all be lumped together and considered gods under a more loose definition of the term, as was often the case with religious syncretism in the ancient world. These deified beings would collectively come to be known as the Watchers.

The Watchers

In reading Gary David's essay, it would appear that there are a number of constellations referred to as "Watchers," such as the four Royal Stars of Persia known as the "Watcher of the South"; Regulus in Leo, the "Watcher of the North"; etc. Because these constellations are in the sky appearing to always look down on the earthbound spectator from above, it makes sense that they be thought of as "Watchers." But what connection might these constellations have to the Anunnaki?

While some researchers may disagree, after careful research I believe that the Watchers in the Books of Enoch and Jubilees are indeed the Anunnaki. These gods were celestialized and only after they had died were worshipped in the theocratic way. Scholars such as Christian O'Brien have argued that the temple at Nippur was not initially intended to be a temple but rather the house of Enlil (O'Brien, 1989). Further to the point, there is evidence to suggest that before any outside influence, the Sumerians had no shrines or temples. It was not until three centuries after the Anunnaki had left Sumer that the structure became a temple in the religious sense. Moreover, *the Watchers* is also a term used in the texts to refer to the Apkallus. Therefore, the Apkallus are Anunnaki as well. Here is a careful distinction, however: while all Apkallus are Anunnaki, not all Anunnaki are Apkallus. Allow me to explain. First, let's looks at the references to the Watchers in the ancient Hebrew texts. In the Book of Jubilees, it says:

> *And in the second week of the tenth jubilee Mahalalel took unto him to wife Dinah, the daughter of Barakiel, the daughter of his father's brother, and she bare him a son in the third week in the sixth year, and he called his name Jared, for in his days the angels of the Lord descended on the earth, those who are named the*

Watchers, that they should instruct the children of men, and that they should do judgment and uprightness on the earth. (Jubilees, 4:15)

And it came to pass when the children of men began to multiply on the face of the earth and daughters were born unto them, that the angels (Watchers) of God saw them on a certain year of this jubilee, that they were beautiful to look upon; and they took themselves wives of all whom they chose, and they bare unto them sons and they were giants (Jubilees, 5:1).

In the Book of Enoch, a lot of attention is devoted to the story of the Watchers, but the term *watchers* is too common to include all of the mentions in this study. While the Books of Enoch and Jubilees are the most commonly referenced pseudographs on the Watchers, there are others, including one by author Philo of Byblos, born in the first century in Lebanon. In his work *Sanchuniathon* he mentions beings called Zophasemin, which in Hebrew meant "Watchers of Heaven" (Charlesworth, 2010). The Watcher theme is frequently seen in a wide variety of these ancient texts and often associated with the stars. The Mesopotamian hymn to Nusku outlines a method to receive a good dream, with an address to the dream god Anzagar (Butler, 1998). The tablet outlines a prayer to personified "Watchers of the Night," which reads:

May the evening watch, the midnight watch, the morning watch, may night bring me (a dream), let me sound your praises. O[An]zagar, Anzagar, who brings (dreams) to humankind, messenger of prince Marduk, O Nightfall, awesomeness of the nighttime, O three watches of the night, who are wakeful, watchful, alert, and non-sleeping, you will grant a verdict to wakeful and sleeping, you will full your responsibility, you will look out all night until the morning watch. (Foster, 2005, 718).

It seems that the ancient Mesopotamians saw their deities as having a place among the stars that would allow them to watch over man and to some extent interfere with man's affairs. The potential meanings of some of these early constellations demonstrate, in my opinion, the significance the ancients placed on the cosmos as it related to life on Earth. They seemed to view the heavens as a separate plane of existence, not only in a material sense but also in an etheric sense. As Gary David wonderfully articulated, the ancients likely perceived a "divine tunnel located in the sky through which the soul achieves transcendence." This is different from a stargate in the material sense; however, the implications are no less meaningful.

In the context of spirit travel, the constellations can be seen as star maps. Many ancient sites all over the world were built aligned to them. Some of these sites were temples and had ritual purposes we may never fully understand. Stonehenge, for instance was a part of this ancient human knowledge system of the stars, serving as a template to help orient us to the cosmos. Ancient sites like this and Göbekli Tepe encourage us to ponder the relationship between the cosmos and human consciousness. The question remains: What might happen when human beings are in correct alignment with both the celestial bodies and consciousness?

THE WATCHERS AS TEACHERS

In Egypt, Osiris brought to the people gifts of civilization and gave the Egyptians their first set of laws. He is remembered primarily as a benefactor of humanity, enlightener, and great civilizer—in particular with regard to agriculture. In addition, he organized a number of large-scale construction and hydro-technical works. Osiris also taught humanity how to cultivate grapes for wine and grow wheat and barley so that people could enjoy what he thought of as a more noble way of living. Similarly, the ancient Egyptians remembered and revered

Thoth as the inventor of mathematics, astronomy, and technology. They also believed that it was Thoth's will and energy that kept the strength of Heaven and Earth in balance. His great knowledge of celestial mechanics, geometry, healing, and botany earned him a reputation as a great lord of magic and the bringer of all fields of knowledge, both human and divine. The ancient Egyptians prescribed their well-recognized wisdom and knowledge of celestial affairs to the teachings of Thoth, which they zealously stored in their temples and passed from generation to generation in the form of forty-two volumes of instructions. Moreover, Thoth was considered a deity who understood the mysteries of all that is concealed beneath the celestial vault. Tradition holds that he recorded his knowledge in secret books hidden in different places on Earth in the hope that they would be sought by future generations—but that only those worthy of this sacred knowledge would find them and use their discoveries to benefit humankind.

In Peru, local legends claim that roads and sophisticated architecture were the fruit of the works of pale red-haired people who lived thousands of years before. The bearded red-haired god Viracocha was accompanied by two shining loyal warriors, whose task was to convey the god's message to every part of the world. These messengers walked on the sea as easily as they could walk on land. Viracocha was also a teacher of science and magic and the owner of a terrible weapon that appeared in times of chaos to bring order to the world. He taught people how to live. He was a scientist, architect, sculptor, teacher, healer, and engineer.

Before his arrival, legends say that people lived in utter mess and many went naked like savages. They did not have houses or other dwellings except caves and roamed around in search of something edible. Viracocha, however, changed all this and marked the beginning of the Golden Age. This mysterious god arranged terraces, fields, and walls and crafted irrigation canals. He treated the sick and returned eyesight to the blind. He introduced advances such as medicine, metallurgy, agriculture, animal husbandry, and the fundamentals of engineering and construction in Peru.

The legends of the Chimú culture tell that another strange deity came from the north, from the seaside, and then rose to Lake Titicaca. The humanizing of Viracocha is most clearly manifested in those legends, where he is credited with various purely earthly qualities—calling him clever, cunning, kind, but at the same time the son of the sun. Many legends report that he sailed on reed boats to the shores of Lake Titicaca and created the megalithic city of Tiwanaku. From there, he sent bearded ambassadors to the ends of Peru so that they would teach people high culture and proclaim that he was their creator. He would eventually become dissatisfied with the behavior of the local inhabitants, so he decided to leave their land. He and his people set out for the Pacific coast and headed west into the setting sun.

The Aztecs attributed their whole system of knowledge to the god-king Quetzalcoatl and his companions, who were also the first inhabitants of the land and initially sowed the seeds of humankind. He was also believed to be an enigmatic light man with a beard, of strong stature with a high forehead and big eyes, who arrived from behind the sea in a boat that floated without oars. Quetzalcoatl was thought of as the god of the world. This bearded man taught people how to use fire for cooking. He also built houses and taught families how to live together as husband and wife. It is Quetzalcoatl that is credited with the invention of the improved calendar. He brought to Mexico all the crafts and sciences necessary for the transition to civilized life, which ensured the advent of the new Golden Age.

As a brilliant builder, he revealed the secrets of masonry and architecture. He was the father of mathematics, metallurgy, and astronomy and was said to have measured the earth. Likewise, as teacher of agricultural science, Quetzalcoatl introduced corn, a staple crop in these ancient lands. The great healer, he was the patron of physicians and sorcerers and taught the people how to use medicinal plants. Additionally, he was revered as a giver of law and patron of technology and high culture. His cult was filled with mysteries related to life after death. It was also believed that Quetzalcoatl himself had traveled to that light and returned to tell people about it.

Like the people who would become the Sumerians, many scholars believe that the Maya also migrated from other areas. Mayan legends tell that their ancestors came twice: first in a large migration from the ocean and then in a second smaller group that came from the west. This second group became the Q'eqchi' people of Guatemala. From their sacred book the Popol Vuh, we learn that their people were also familiar with a mysterious wanderer who had passed through the land. The Q'eqchi' called him Q'uq'umatz. Q'uq'umatz was associated with the feathered serpent and, like Enki, closely linked to water. He was considered a great organizer, the founder of cities, and the author of laws and the calendar.

In the mountains of Colombia, north of the Inca state, lived another mysterious people known as the Muisca. Their legends also contain information about a bearded teacher who came from the east whom they called Bochica. The description is the same as that of the Incas. To the east of the Muisca region, in Venezuela and neighboring areas, scientists again came upon the evidence of the mysterious wanderer's stay. There he was

149

called Tsuma, and it was said that he had taught them agricultural science. According to one of the legends, he told all people to gather around a high cliff where he stood on top and gave them the laws and instructions.

Westward from the Yucatán in the jungle of Tabasco, local legends tell of folk heroes who caused many inventions, as in the myth of Pacal Votan, the greatest ruler of the city of Palenque, a Maya city-state in the south. The tomb of Pacal Votan was discovered in 1952 during excavations. According to the legend, Pacal Votan left his homeland and founded Palenque. Pacal Votan was considered an avatar for the new incarnation of Quetzalcoatl, sent by the gods to divide the people into villages and teach cultivation and a hieroglyphic script, the samples of which remained on the walls of their temples.

Even as far off as Easter Island, legends about the arrival of sages there resemble the Edfu texts. In both, the native island was destroyed by a terrible storm and flooding, the impacts of which were so powerful that the sacred land was obliterated, resulting in the death of its divine inhabitants. In both cases, the gods of the former homeland escaped by boat and eventually sailed to the country where they settled, bringing with them great knowledge. Additionally, both accounts tell that the path taken by the scribes, architects, and astronomers was revealed by the gods.

In these and other cultures, these teachers were revered as gods. However, there are clear indications that these were human beings. Yet these human teachers do not obscure their belief that the original source of their advanced wisdom was from "the gods." So if the builders of the ancient world, including the Anunnaki, were indeed human beings, as the Edfu texts make very clear, who or *what* were their gods?

Terrestrial Gods?

In the tablet *Enki and the World Order*, Enlil collected a set of instructions intended for humans in various cities. He handed them over to Enki so that he might distribute them. These instructions were called *mes*. The *mes* were official decrees of the gods that would be the foundations to all attributes of a higher civilization. A *me* was a law, or set of holy instructions that guided technologies, religious and ceremonial practices, etiquette, and social institutions. Think of them as legally binding cultural blueprints. *Me(s)*, as in the word *Mesopotamia*, which means "between two rivers," literally meant *between*. These doctrines were binding because they came straight from the gods themselves and were agreements *between* the gods and humankind. They were the first covenants.

Originally, *mes* were collected by Enlil, the spirit, then given to Enki, lord of the earthly realm, who could materialize them. Enki would then broker the *mes* to the selected rulers at Sumerian administrative centers, starting with the city of Eridu, and on to Ur, as *Enki and the World Order* detailed. Just as with the Tablet of Destinies, there are no specific physical descriptions of these *mes*. We do know, however, that in one tablet, the goddess Inanna displays them to the people of Uruk upon her arrival in "the boat of heaven." In this account, the *mes* are not only represented as tablets, but also functional tools and artifacts, such as musical instruments.

Just when the myths have us thinking we know what these *mes* are, however, we come to find that not all of them were actually tangible—some were conceptual. How these *mes* were displayed is still a mystery. Not only were they conceptual or abstract, some were also negative. Some *mes* would come to represent all that is evil and destructive in humanity.

Sumerian gods dictated to and instructed the first kings, who were installed at city centers to "destroy other cities" (Kramer, 1963). They encouraged "falsehood," yet taught the functions of "victory" as heroism, meaning evil and sin were also divinely decreed and royally enforced (Kramer, 1963). Another important aspect of this legend is that Enki appeared in the physical realm, so he needed a medium to channel the other gods. To communicate with the others, he would sometimes summon the bird Anzû (Imdugud), as his messenger.

According to the account given by Samuel Noah Kramer in his important work *The Sumerians: Their History, Culture, and Character*, nearly one hundred separate *mes* appear on tablet fragments. He lists some as:

- Kingship
- Weapons
- Law
- Art
- Music
- Power
- Enmity
- Falsehood
- Metalworking
- Scribeship
- Craft of the builder
- Terror
- Peace
- Judgment

These *mes* are important to our understanding of human development and the role the Sumerians played. This is the first time in history we see such a highly advanced system of rule in place, a system that was divinely decreed. They were inspired ("through the spirit came") by Enlil, which possessed Enki to take action here on Earth. Enki was the earthly, biological mediator. Though the Sumerian accounts have him eating, drinking, and colluding with humans on the earthly plane, he held his position still higher than those he called the black-headed ones. He was their lord. To maintain this balance of power, Enki lived high in the mountains and had gatekeepers. These were the world's first human kings, and their bloodlines were carefully recorded. Evidence of this can be traced to the Sumerian King Lists.

In this tradition, kingship was handed down directly by the gods. If the human king moved to another city, his kingship would be transferred from one city to another, which gave the perception of intrinsic authority. No one would necessarily question this authority. This divided people, making the original 99 percent against 1 percent. This 1 percent was the select few kings of Enki, who ruled over cities and people. Through the generations, this closed group that carefully guarded their lineage developed their own parallel set of cultural symbols and practices. These symbols can be traced from the Sumerians to the ruling elites of today. The most ancient and, to some extent, most important is the bird Anzû.

Depictions of Anzû can be traced back thousands of years. This double-headed bird dates as far back as far as 3800 BCE and was the Sumerian symbol for Ninurta, the god of Lagash, who would slay Anzû in a fight for the Tablet of Destinies. Some biblical scholars believe that this is the original personification of Nimrod. An interesting and telling depiction of

Anzû is on a silver and copper vase dedicated by Entemena, king of Lagash, to Ninurta from 2400 BCE. The vase shows Enlil bringing down an "extract" from the constellation Leo to create Ninurta and Entemena, both depicted as lions.

The astronomical alignments of Leo, Taurus, and Sirius were very important to the Sumerians, particularly the elites. So, depicted on this vase, we have the two sons of Enki, symbolized as and created from extracts of the constellation Leo. What you'll see next is that the same process was used in the creation of the third brother king, Gudea, who was born under the sign of Taurus. Gudea was called the "architect" of the House of Ningirsu.

There are many statues of Gudea, many made from rare diorite. However, the oldest ever known—in fact, the oldest ever statue of a known king from Mesopotamia—was stolen from the Iraqi Museum. Clearly, this and artifacts like it are of great interest to looters. These symbols have been important to the elites since the beginning of human civilization. They continue to be revered, coveted, and used as a means of communicating their message of authority over humanity to this very day. There are some who believe that there are modern elites who seek out these artifacts as trophies. They share the feeling that these symbols rightfully belong to them and should be in *their* possession only. They have a sense of entitlement because they believe they can trace their lineage to the very first kings of Sumer, making them part of the original ruling class.

The double-headed eagle from the myth of the Anzû can also be found in Anatolia, and later Babylon. In fact, examples of this symbol are found all around the world. Over a period of about a thousand years, it spread throughout Asia, India, and Europe.

The cult of Ninurta developed as a new center of worship, as the adoration of Anu, Enlil, and Enki moved northwest from Sumer in the third millennium BCE in yet another example of syncretism. Thus, Ninurta became Nimrod, the builder of the tower of Babel. Remember, it was Nimrod who rebelled against God by building the tower, much like Ninurta's rebellion. Many are familiar with the Freemasons' reverence for King Solomon. However, in the fifteenth and sixteenth centuries, it was Nimrod, not Solomon, who was touted as being the first Freemason. This connected the origins of Masonry to the Tower of Babel, rather than the Temple of Jerusalem.

To many in Abrahamic traditions, Nimrod is the original founder of a one-world totalitarian government, a New World Order. He was the great unifier and master builder. In light of this, the Scottish rite uses Ninurta's symbol to represent its thirty-second and thirty-third degrees. Moving forward, this symbol would be used on everything from family crests to military, government, royalty, and large global corporate symbols—and even in the Third Reich. The eagle, known for its superior eyesight, can see in both directions when it has two heads. Henceforth, this creature was associated with the all-seeing eye of the elite bloodlines sanctioned by the Anunnaki gods to rule over and enslave humanity.

This desire to unify the world under a totalitarian regime has been bubbling under the surface like an oil seep throughout all of history since the days of the Sumerian kings. And that brings us to the question, why would oil companies have an interest in these excavations? Are they, too, looking for the Tablet of Destinies? While there are no descriptions available of the Tablet of Destinies or its contents, we know from Enûma Eliš that Tiamat gave this tablet to Kingu, which put him in charge of her army of "star-beings," as some have translated. Then, Marduk goes on to battle Tiamat and her army. Taking the Tablet of Destinies from Kingu's breast, he sealed it with his own seal and put it on. This leads us to believe the Tablet could be worn. In the poem *Ninurta and the Turtle*, it is Enki who had possession of the Tablet, which would later be stolen by the bird Anzû. This tablet was the original weapon of mass destruction, as its installation brought about the very shift in humanity that turned us from peaceful, spiritual, natural, and egalitarian hunter-gatherers to the controlled, oppressed, enslaved, "us versus them," bureaucratic dystopia we see throughout the historic record.

So often, people ask if the weapons archaeologists are looking for beneath the desert sands in the Middle East are those for physical warfare. Are they nuclear weapons? Ancient chemical weapons? Or perhaps something technologically advanced, yet unfamiliar to us in modernity? While I believe there is a great chance that we may one day find amazingly advanced technology far surpassing what we believe the ancients were capable of, this is not what they are searching for now. As we examined in the beginning of the book, Sumerian inventions improved the day-to-day lives of the ancients and eventually our own. By contrast, they are also the very mechanisms that threaten to destroy it. The invention of complex governmental, financial, and bureaucratic systems comprises the real weapon of mass destruction.

Too often, we do all think of weapons in a purely physical form, but the weapons of culture are often the most dangerous. By confining the masses to a narrowly defined set of parameters, those interested in maintaining complete control can easily do so. For as long as humans maintain a corporeal existence, we need some form of worldly order. Laws, institutions, arithmetic, record keeping, speaking—these are all necessities. These are also markers of civilization and what made the Sumerians, as well as us, different from the earlier hunter-gatherer settlements like Göbekli Tepe. However, barriers that limit our expression of free will are weapons of control. These barriers often arise from a power struggle between our will and the will of opposing forces.

The world order forever changed the way life was lived on Earth. In the Enûma Eliš, the creation of the universe is explained. In *Ninurta and the Turtle*, the shift in power is outlined. However, in *Enki and the World Order*, a form, function, and purpose are created on the planet Earth. The corporeal realm was formed, building the walls of both stone and culture. Enki, the lord of the Earth, is described as a "craftsman." Such descriptions have led some to associate Enki with Lucifer. According to the legend, whoever possessed the Tablet of Destinies would have the divine right of kings. This would allow them to be the ruler of the universe, but that's not all. The tablet also granted the power of all past, present, and future knowledge. With this tablet, anyone can be a Watcher, for they would have the ability to "see" in all directions, just like the symbolic double-headed eagle.

For much of this book we have posited that the Anunnaki were, in most every sense, real. They were the kings and influencers of the ancient world whose followers revered them for their novel ideas and amazing aptitude for technology. This reverence was also due in part to the willingness of these beings to share their advanced technology with the local people, in effect, much improving the locals' lives. While this very terrestrial narrative seems to be the most likely, it still leaves questions unanswered. Understandably, there will be readers who will feel that while I have made the case for an earthly explanation of the Anunnaki, I have not properly addressed seemingly otherworldly aspects of the Anunnaki. In the next chapter, I will do just that, but full disclosure: the information in the chapters that follow may test the openness of your mind and push the boundaries of what you are comfortable exploring. This will be either because they do not directly support the postwar rocket technology framework of our understanding of extraterrestrials, as Sitchin documented, or because they rely on the suspension of all previously held beliefs on the nature of the universe itself. If you are a staunchly unquestioning supporter of any of the authors I have referenced thus far in this book and do not wish to entertain an alternative to the alternative, I would suggest that you close this book now and walk away with your beliefs intact. If you are ready to venture down a path of inquiry that takes into account modern science and the mysteries of mind, space, and time, keep reading.

CHAPTER 6

Higher Dimensions

There could be shadow galaxies, shadow stars,
and even shadow people.
—STEPHEN HAWKING,
British theoretical physicist

I n my work and research, I have found that things are not always as they seem. I have also found there to be another, possibly otherworldly aspect to the Anunnaki: the question of where the antediluvian visitors acquired their higher information. One could ask, where do any of the great thinkers like Nikola Tesla or Sir Isaac Newton get their insights for that matter? Could they have all come from a similar, perhaps universal source? Could this source have been otherworldly? The confluence of ancient shamanism and modern science points to this possibility.

In a number of fields such as metaphysics, psychology, biology, and quantum theory, we find the idea of a repository of information outside of ourselves that can potentially be accessed. This is sometimes called the collective unconscious or universal consciousness, depending on whom you ask. Regardless of the name, theories point to an interconnectedness between all living things and even possibly a collective memory. There are many examples in the archaeological record of shared beliefs and experiences of people from very different backgrounds. While the archaeological record also shows plenty of examples of diffusion, migration, trade, and expansion, these still do not fully explain the consistency in certain mystical experiences. Even if stripped of cultural identity, there seem to be core similarities in the experiences of the ancients, particularly those of the shamans and priests.

Jung believed we experience the unconscious through symbols such as art, music, and language, both written and oral. When considering the astonishing consistency in the underlying themes of these symbols, it would indeed seem that there is a collective mind or alternate plane of reality. This is especially true with archetypal symbols, which are mysteriously transmitted throughout history and even up to today. While such symbols offer a glimpse into this continuity of message, they are only scratching the surface of a much bigger unified experience. If there is a universal consciousness filled with infinite data, perhaps organisms, unique in design and function, are wired in such a way that they can tap into it. Perhaps these organisms can even send and retrieve data.

I think of this like modern digital devices. Our devices sync with other digital devices and services. The transmission of data between them all can seem magical. If someone were to observe the sharing of data between two smartphones and not know anything about the technology behind it, the devices could appear to independently communicate with one another for reasons we would infer either correctly or incorrectly. We are limited by our senses. Likewise, humans do travel, communicate, and spread ideas as well as symbols. However, these ideas are derivatives of each other; is there ever really completely original information? By looking at the archaeological and historical records, it appears that there are times when people seem to have had a spark; something radical enough to constitute a complete paradigm shift.

An astonishing number of ancient civilizations—the Harappa, Sumerian, Egyptian, and Mesoamerican—appeared on our planet almost simultaneously near the end of 3000 BCE. The theory of the single center from which culture migrated to all regions of the Earth has not been ruled out. Nevertheless, Sumer, being the historical cradle of culture, surpassed in its development the entire population of the planet and was the focal point of urbanization. It served as home to the Anunnaki, who passed special knowledge to certain people for several hundred years. Indeed, history tells the story of many different cultures sharing a shamanistic element. They also shared beliefs in nature spirits, demons, and possession. They valued the messages in dreams, trances, and even psychedelics. What these ancient high priests and initiates knew then is the same as what high priests and initiates of our modern world know and believe and have tapped into.

We can find answers in Silicon Valley, where an increasing number of tech elites are discovering that there is a thin veil between this reality and another. When you pierce the veil, you can make contact with strange entities that are to this day not well understood. This is the secret teaching that has been hidden and passed down only from the mystery schools to the initiates. This was the wisdom first discovered in the early Neolithic caves when the shaman would go into a trance-like state and experience things, and with this Prometheus-like quality, the first technology the beings gave us was fire. Fire was like capturing the sun with its warmth, safety, and power. That's why fire is associated with knowledge and images of torches and lamps are often used as logos for universities. It was not until we were able tap into the alternative dimension, this other plane, that we could begin to receive their messages.

The Shaman

Shamanism is likely the oldest religion. And even today, its practice is quite widespread throughout the world. Anthropologists attribute the emergence of shamanism to the Stone Age, when the first man was able to make fire and was interested in the forces of nature because he was directly dependent on them. It must be said that at that time people were more open to nature and communication with it, and shamanism served as a method of merging with nature. The shaman's view of reality was comprised of three levels: the upper world or heaven, the middle world or Earth, and the underworld or the lower world. This three-world concept is not only spatial; it is also symbolic. Spirit beings, deceased ancestors, and the gods dwell in the upper world. They offered wisdom and insight to the visiting shaman. The middle world concerns the earthly and is comprised only of matter. The lower world consists of animalistic power and of the dead who have not traveled to the higher world.

In addition to this three-part cosmos, shamans see that everything has life, not just humans and animals, but also stones, plants, and even the stars. To them, everything has a soul, which opens them to a multidimensional world of connection. Everything and everyone are interrelated. Shamans travel through the three worlds in search of knowledge, strength, and a better understanding of reality—a reality where the body, soul, and spirit are different but united as one. Nature and the spiritual world are inextricably linked to this unity. To the shaman, spirits are conscious, intelligent, and communicative beings who roam freely through the different dimensional planes but are invisible to ordinary people. The shaman has guarded the space between the natural world, of which humans are a part, and the supernatural. The shaman could make contact with the world of spirits and cross the boundary between Heaven and Earth as well as the past and the future. These ancient wise men became mediators between the spirits of nature or spirits of deceased ancestors and the mundane world. Often special rituals were needed to facilitate this communication with spirits.

Usually, for shamans to ensure that they could enter a different state of mind, altered consciousness, or trance, they would transform into something else, dressing in animal skins and performing certain dances and sounds. Theoretically, in this state, shamans could travel to various dimensions and receive answers to questions asked of them by the people of their community or an individual. These answers could be general guidance, cures, how to make the weather favorable for the harvest, or even technological advances. Shamans were also known to use mind-altering substances such as psychedelics to access this higher dimension. Whichever methods they used, the knowledge of how to attain these altered states was passed down from generation to generation by word of mouth.

In our current age, this is sometimes called mediumship, and a person who can communicate with spirits is a medium. It can also be referred to as channeling. Some modern-day practitioners have claimed that in their trances, they have made contact with wise beings from a higher plane of existence. This belief has found its way out of the forests of the backcountry and into centers of government and commerce, most notably Silicon

Valley. Can shamans, both ancient and modern, really cross over to some other plane of existence? If so, could this alternative dimension be the source of the Seven Sages of antiquity?

The Anunnaki Now

It is believed across many faiths that there was a time when the gods were with us, but at some point, they left. This can be better understood if you use a different framework. Assuming that the Anunnaki and all other beings inhabiting a past physical plane were in fact humans, then they would have left because they died. With this death there should also have been an end to the rapid advancement and great changes in social structures of ancient civilizations. However, that was not the case. The passing of the gods did not leave such a vacuum. Civilization continued to advance, leading us eventually to smartphones, the internet, and self-driving cars. We still experience technological advances, and we still have elite individuals at the top of our social hierarchies who, in effect, "run the show." If the Anunnaki were simply humans with great creative and leadership capacities, then they do indeed still dwell among us. What then is the difference between a leader in the general sense and an Anunnaki? It is the same thing that differentiated ancient rulers and kings from those seen as Anunnaki: their ability to connect with off-world advisors, or sages, and ascend to the position of Anunnaki. An otherworldly connection and subsequent ascension made gods of men.

Off-World Entities

Ancient texts of all sorts tell of great earthly kings communicating with off-world entities in order to have their questions answered. This was done through dreaming, meditation, prayer, trance, or even the consumption of medicinal plants. During their 1959/1960 excavation season, German archaeologists found a Sumerian text in the Seleucid era temple of Anu in Bit Res unlike any they had previously seen. It became known as the Uruk List of Kings and Sages. A text different from other known Sumerian King Lists, this accounting consisted of seven kings and their associated sages, followed by a note on the "Deluge," followed by eight more king/sage pairs (Lenzi, 2008). The text is also very special in that it was among the few tablets actually uncovered in situ—according to the archaeologists, it had not been disturbed by looters who had previously littered the area with other tablets and fragments (Lenzi, 2008). This text has become the basis for scholarly theories that propose that Mesopotamian scholars, *ummânū*, traced their professional ancestry to the sages and subsequently to the god Ea. If we look at the most recent translation of this text, there are some very interesting details that emerge:

> *During the reign of Ayalu, the king, Adapa was sage.*
>
> *During the reign of Alalgar, the king, Uanduga was sage.*
>
> *During the reign of Ameluana, the king, Enmeduga was sage.*
>
> *During the reign of Amegalana, the king, Enmegalama was sage.*
>
> *During the reign of Enmeusumgalana, the king, Enmebuluga was sage.*
>
> *During the reign of Dumuzi, the shepherd, the king, Anenlilda was sage.*
>
> *During the reign of Enmeduranki, the king, Utuabzu was sage.*
>
> *After the flood, during the reign of Enmerkar, the king, Nungalpirigal was sage, whom Istar brought down from heaven to Eana. He made the bronze lyre, whose ... (were) lapis lazuli, according to*

the technique of Ninagal. The lyre was placed before Anu . . .
the dwelling of (his) personal god.

During the reign of Gilgamesh, the king, Sin-leqi-unnini was
scholar.

During the reign of Ibbi-Sin, the king, Kabti-ili-Marduk was
scholar.

During the reign of Isbi-Erra, the king, Sidu, aka Enlil-ibni, was
scholar.

During the reign of Abi-esu, the king, Gimil-Gula and TaqisGula
were the scholars.

During the reign of . . ., the king, Esagil-kin-apli was scholar.

During the reign of Adad-apla-iddina, the king, Esagil-kin-ubba
was scholar.

During the reign of Nebuchadnezzar, the king, Esagil-kin-ubba
was scholar.

During the reign of Esarhaddon, the king, Aba-Enlil-dari was
scholar, whom the Arameans call Ahiqar (Lenzi, 2008, 142-143).

The Mesopotamian scribes made a clear connection between the seven sages and their human counterparts. The text also references the tradition of having a "personal god." There is a similar pattern in the Mesopotamian Bìt mèseri more often cited as a source of the Seven Sages myth. This text gives the same names of the seven sages as the Uruk List of Kings and Sages, but they are described as the fishmen or Oannes:

They are the seven brilliant puràdu-fish, puràdu-fish from the sea,

the seven sages, who were created in the river,

who ensure the correct execution of the plans of heaven and earth
(Lenzi, 2008, 145).

166

In the Bìt mèseri text, the Seven Sages are treated as humans and as seen in the Oannes figure dressed as fish. While this image has prevailed, the fact remains that this is a later interpretation of a more ancient myth. Berossus, the Hellenistic-era Babylonian writer and priest of Bel Marduk, discusses the Seven Sages in *Babyloniaca*. Berossus's writing is, of course, many years removed from the events, as he wrote in the third century BCE. The Bìt mèseri text is also a newer document and a retold version of the older Uruk List of Kings and Sages, where the Seven Sages were first depicted as specifically nonhuman entities. Scholars believe that the names of the sages do not originate from the more commonly cited Bìt mèseri but from another text, possibly a chronicle that was later adapted. Based on the lack of ritual instructions associated with the Bìt mèseri incantation, as well as textual clues found by Lenzi, it is most likely that the humanization of the Seven Sages occurred much later (Lenzi, 2008). Moreover, there are other medical texts, spells, and rituals that call upon the Seven Sages as supernatural beings. The texts make it clear that the *ummânū*, the scribal scholars who served as counselors to the kings and in society as ritual experts, as well as authors of important cuneiform tablets, were human. Even so, there are still some Bible literalist scholars who try to resolve these inconsistencies by simply calling the Apkallu half divine, a third divine, or some part divine, but also part human. Nevertheless, the text makes it very clear that the human courtly advisors received their knowledge from the sages who were fully nonhuman, or, as some may say, divine.

What the original texts are telling us is that the kings of Sumer had very learned scribal advisors who would transmit the knowledge they received from supernatural beings to the ruler so he could be the actual "builder" of his kingdom. Using these supernatural plans, Sumerian rulers were able to accomplish remarkable feats of engineering, planning, technology, and cultural advancement, leading to all of the progress seen throughout the ancient world. While this may sound absurd, it is certainly not the first time this framework has been seen in the history of the ruling class and technological advancement. We find the very same methods employed at the dawn of the European Renaissance.

Enochian Magic

As discussed earlier, the Book of Enoch contains many references to the Watchers. This cryptic text would play a key part in the work of renowned sixteenth-century English mathematician, astrologer, scholar, and fellow of Trinity College, Cambridge, John Dee. Dee was the author of forty-nine books on scientific subjects, but his pursuits in the occult brought him a dubious reputation.

Born in London July 13, 1527, Dee descended from a noble Welsh family, the Dees of Nant y Groes in Radnorshire and ancestor of Roderick the Great, Prince of Wales (Shepard, 1982). Dee's father, having been a gentleman server at the court of Henry VIII, afforded Dee a good education at Cambridge University (Shepard, 1982). After he completed his studies in 1547, he became interested in astronomy and traveled to Belgium, Luxembourg, the Netherlands, and France. He would eventually return to England in 1551, where he would end up accused of trying to murder the new Queen Mary in 1553 through magic. He was imprisoned at Hampton Court, but later released.

This stint tarnished his reputation and people looked at him with suspicion. He would later write that people saw him as "a companion of the hellhounds, a caller and a conjuror of wicked and damned spirits" (Shepard, 1982, 389). His luck would change during the reign of Queen Elizabeth I, however. In 1572, astronomers located a new star in the sky and, five years later, spotted a mysterious comet. Because of his knowledge of astronomy, many people flocked to Dee to learn what these celestial anomalies could be—including Queen Elizabeth. After years of studying subjects such as astronomy, alchemy, divination, Rosicrucian theories, and Talmudic mysteries, to name but a few of his interests, Dee eventually found himself advisor to the queen.

A defining event in Dee's life occurred in November of 1582. While praying, Dee had a vision that the light from the west window of his laboratory shone brightly and revealed the angel Uriel, rendering him speechless. Uriel smiled and gave him a piece of convex crystal and instructed him to use this crystal to communicate with the beings of another world. If he gazed into this crystal, these beings would appear and show him the mysteries of the future. In his work with the crystal, Dee hired an assistant named Edward Kelley, a mysterious man rumored to have had his ears cut off after being convicted of counterfeiting coins.

Kelley saw seven entities he called Madini, Gabriel, Uriel, Nalvage, Il, Morvorgran, and Jubanladace. He believed these beings to be angels, and they offered occult instructions on how to make the elixir of life, spells, incantations, and how to ask the entities for advice. They were also said to have given Kelley a secret language called Enochian. This language was the same Sumerian-type language that the Watchers spoke in the Garden, which was believed to have been corrupted into Hebrew after Adam was banished. He predicted scientific technologies far ahead of his time, like the telescope, solar power, lasers, the speed of light, and multiple dimensions.

Dee and Kelley continued to used techniques including meditation to contact otherworldly entities and acquire technology that would change the course of human history, including the science behind cutting-edge navigation and cartography tools that would eventually advance the discovery of the New World. Dee believed these entities were angelic, but Kelley grew afraid and came to consider them demonic.

Dee led a long life of magic and advising. He was a scholar and scribe who counseled many nobles in addition to the queen. His Enochian Magic established rituals that were later revived by the magical Hermetic Order of the Golden Dawn, with some being adapted by Anton LaVey and the Church of Satan. Without laboring the point further, I would direct you to the work of my dear friend Dr. John DeSalvo, a biophysicist and researcher into ancient mysteries and the paranormal for over thirty years, who has published numerous books on Enochian Magic. Certainly consult Dr. DeSalvo's work if you would like to learn more about the lives and adventures of Dee and Kelley. There are some fascinating details and history certainly worth a second look, which is why I contacted him to ask about his views on the possible science behind how such a thing as Enochian Magic could work.

As a former college professor and a scientist and expert in Enochian Magic, his views are unique. He said that while Enochian Magic works, it is not the result of the imagination working overtime or the wishful thinking or subconscious activity of the magician. Instead, he believes that Enochian Magic is real, and the Aethyrs, or spiritual realms, and angels are real worlds and real beings. His theory as to why and how it works is that our brains—most likely our cortical areas, which are responsible for our higher brain functioning and the interpretation of our sensory inputs like sight, sound, touch, taste, and smell—are also responsible for receiving psychic information. Dr. DeSalvo points out that while it is believed that we use less than 10 percent of our entire brain, no one knows for sure exactly what this percentage is, postulating that perhaps some part of this unused part of our brain is employed for psychic transmission and reception.

He believes that there are undiscovered cortical regions that code for and are receptors of psychic phenomena that work in the same way as our retinas, enabling us to see by functioning as receptors of light rays. He says we are capable of entering each Aethyr when that brain area becomes activated as a result of reciting a Call. In so doing, we also become aware of the angels residing in that region. The pineal gland, which is a structure in the direct center of our brain that many cultures claim is a psychic center, may also house psychic reception centers.

Dr. DeSalvo goes on to point out that in Eastern meditation, a verbal mantra is employed as part of the practice. It's a resonating sound, which causes changes in the nervous system. He explains that this is the reason a meditating individual relaxes and enters a deep trance and an altered state of consciousness. He says this is also true of the Enochian Calls—they are like long mantras, which stimulate specific areas of the brain responsible for the awareness of each of the thirty Aethyrs and their angels.

As a person who practices meditation and yoga, I found this explanation fascinating. Since Dr. DeSalvo is a credentialed scientist and former professor, I asked him whether he believed his theory could be tested. He said he hoped that the theory would eventually be tested by measuring activity in the cortical areas of the meditator's brain while he or she is experiencing an Enochian Meditation and entering the Aethyrs. He says that such a clinical study would indeed show whether or not specific regions of the brain are activated with each Call, adding that if these areas can be identified and mapped, we certainly would have some interesting neurophysiological verification of Enochian Magic and how it works. Dr. DeSalvo says this exciting neurophysiologic research could also produce incredible breakthroughs involving altered states of consciousness, but warns that until we can demonstrate that Enochian Magic has a scientific basis, we are only left with what we can experience. He believes, however, that the specific technique he teaches in his books has the greatest potential for opening up these dormant centers in the brain so that his students can explore these Heavens or Aethyrs for themselves (Lynn-DeSalvo interview, 2019).

While this may all sound far removed from the Anunnaki, I believe that with the information I have presented thus far, you can start to see connections. How interesting it is that since written history, we have distinct accounts of rulers using scholars and scribes who claim to have made contact with off-world entities from different planes of existence. These entities offer amazing new technologies that secure the power and prestige of a ruler and spur cultural progress as seen in the Agricultural Revolution, Age of Exploration, and the Renaissance. Has this practice died? Is it relegated to a mystical and often romanticized picture of history that lives on only in fable?

Gateway to the Stars

Silicon Valley in the San Francisco Bay Area serves as a global center for high technology and home to many global technology companies including Apple, Facebook, and Google. This is a global nexus of innovation and technological progress. It is also a place where the very wealthy tech elite have taken to a new obsession: hallucinogenic drugs. One of the favored is dimethyltryptamine or N,N-dimethyltryptamine, also known as DMT. DMT is endogenous—meaning it is produced in small quantities by the human body in the process of normal metabolism. It is synthesized during REM sleep but can also be taken in certain psychedelic substances as it is also an alkaloid of many plants. The chemical structure of DMT is similar to serotonin, one of the important neurotransmitters in the mammalian brain. Once inside the human nervous system, DMT acts as an agonist of 5-HT2A serotonin receptors. DMT is a powerful psychedelic that causes an altered state of consciousness with a religio-mystical experience with intense visual and auditory hallucinations and changes in the perception of time and reality.

DMT is found in nature in many plants, often used by shamans of South America in their practices. Ayahuasca is a drink, entheogen, and hallucinogen traditionally produced by the shamans of the native tribes of the Amazon basin and used by the locals to communicate with the spirits in order to obtain practical knowledge of the environment and the human body to achieve healing abilities. It contains DMT.

People who have experienced a DMT trip often say that it is so different from anything known to man and almost impossible to describe or express in words. Perhaps the strangest and most notable aspect of the DMT experience is that many people will share remarkably similar visions. In studies conducted in 1990–95 by a psychiatrist Rick Strassman at the University of New Mexico, many of his volunteers experienced what they felt was an extraterrestrial presence, whom they characterized as "elves," "aliens," "guides," and "helpers" (Pickover, 2005). At the same time, visually some of these creatures resembled clowns, reptiles, praying mantises, bees, spiders, cacti, gnomes, and figures made from sticks. In general, all research participants reported that these creatures were residents of a parallel, independent reality (Strassman, 2001).

Terence McKenna, ethnobotanist, mystic, psychonaut, and one of the most prolific authors and lecturers on DMT, described his own experience where he had a meeting with beings he referred to as "self-transforming machine-elves" (Strassman, 2001, 187). McKenna believed DMT could be used as a tool to connect with creatures from other worlds. Similar reports are also given by other users who have experienced DMT trips. These individuals also often reported meetings with intelligent beings who were trying to figure out information about our reality.

Clearly there is a long history of humans using plants, mushrooms, and even animals like frogs and snakes in order to experience their psychedelic effects. McKenna has suggested that our apelike ancestors imitated other animals by eating things that caused unusual behavior. In this way, they discovered the earliest mind-altering substances (Strassman, 2001). There is a plethora of archaeological evidence indicating that many ancient cultures used psychedelics to alter their consciousness. As Strassman points out, archaeologists have found ancient African images of mushrooms sprouting from a human body as well as prehistoric northern European rock art that suggests the influence of psychedelically altered consciousness (Strassman, 2001). In the Book of Enoch, it states that the Watchers taught early man "charms and enchantments, and the cutting of roots, and made them acquainted with plants" (Charles, 1917). To "make them acquainted with plants" could mean that the Watchers taught early humans which plants could be used to alter their perception of reality. In fact, some researchers have proposed that language developed out of psychedelically enhanced appreciation of and associations with early hominid mouth sounds. Others suggest that psychedelic states formed the basis of humans' earliest awareness of religious experience.

This may not be too far-fetched. Some anthropologists will suggest that there was no real moment of change; that humans have evolved slowly as a result of natural adaptation to their environment. Others have suggested that this shift in consciousness may have happened as a result of changes in the diet of early hominids, even suggesting that cooking habits may have provoked physiological changes in the brain. In the late 1990s, Harvard University primatologist Richard Wrangham theorized that a change accelerating the rate of brain growth occurred in human ancestors about 1.6–1.8 million years ago, when *Homo erectus* learned how to roast meat and tubers over a fire (Wrangham, 2010). Wrangham argued that it was the act of cooking that essentially predigested food, making it easier and more efficient for our ancestors to gain nutrients. This increase in caloric efficiency theoretically allowed human ancestors to spend less time foraging, chewing, and digesting, eventually leading to the development of a smaller, more efficient digestive tract (Wrangham, 2010). This reduction in the size of the digestive tract freed up energy to enable denser brain growth. Humans have more neurons than any other primate, leading the brain to use at least 20 percent of our body's energy when resting. This has left the question: where did our ancestors get that extra energy to expand their minds? Wrangham has set out to find the answer by proving his "digestion theory." In his lab, he and his colleagues have studied what happens to rodents and pythons when they eat cooked meat instead of raw meat. His published reports show that these animals grow up bigger and faster and take less energy to digest the cooked meat.

Wrangham's studies are ongoing and not without their critics. For instance, there is very little archaeological evidence to prove that this was a pattern for *Homo erectus*. In fact, most archaeologists will point to evidence showing that an increase in meat was due to the scavenging habits of early man and the important role of the female in tuber gathering in labor division. While the cooking idea is fascinating and may have certainly contributed to human brain development, it does not appear to be what caused such a rapid shift in consciousness. Most researchers will agree, however, that there was some sort of event that initiated a chain of consciousness events. Some have even named this mysterious event "The Big Brain Bang," while others have called it simply "The Leap." Could this monumental event in the structure of the human brain have been the discovery and ingestion of mind-expanding substances?

It is not unreasonable to think that ancient man, at the very least, found and ate psychedelic mushrooms. Scientists have referred to mushrooms as "aliens from another world." The fact is that they are very significantly different from all other types of terrestrial vegetation. When mushrooms are deprived of chlorophyll, they can still grow in complete darkness and, unlike all other plants, absorb oxygen.

It is a fact that shamans used hallucinogenic mushrooms to enter into trances in which they communicated with the spirits of the dead and their deities and learned about the future. It is known that in the North, shamans also used toadstools. There is evidence that suggest the Vikings used *Amanita muscaria*, commonly known as the fly agaric or fly amanita, before battles, after which they had no fear and would rush into the fray. The ancients were amazed by the ability of fungi to grow without seeds, as if from nowhere. It had been suggested that they appeared after lightning strikes, as a result of exposure to dew or some miraculous forces. Some even believed that divine powers were involved in the appearance of the mushrooms. However, much more common in the Middle Ages was the idea that mushrooms were derived from the influence of evil forces.

It is not exactly known when ancient people became familiar with the psychedelic properties of mushrooms, but the first rock carvings of mushrooms date back several thousand years. It is believed that the most ancient written records of mushrooms were made by Euripides (480–406 BC), although, no doubt, there were more ancient written sources, because most would have been lost during wars, fires like those at the Library of Alexandria, or just simple decay over time.

While we do not know exactly when humans discovered mushrooms, it is safe to say that they did make an impact—although to what extent is controversial. Perhaps one of the most inflammatory claims about humankind's illustrious history with magic mushrooms was made in 1970 by Dead Sea Scrolls researcher John Marco Allegro. Allegro published a series of articles in the *Sunday Mirror*, which preceded the publication of the book *Sacred Mushroom and the Cross,* in which he argued that Christianity was a fertility cult associated with psychedelic mushrooms and Jesus was nothing more than a mushroom himself.

According to Allegro, primitive man living in the sun-scorched, often deserted lands of the Near and Middle East was almost completely dependent on rain. Rain caused plant growth and so ancient man came to believe that a mighty phallus existed high in the sky and the rain was his seed, which poured out to fertilize the womb that was earth (Allegro, 1970). This simple explanation, he described, is how all the religions of the Fertile Crescent were born—the ancient cults of the Hellenes and Persians, Judaism, Christianity, and even Islam were all are descended from primitive faith based on the heavenly phallus. Having created their theory of the divine rain, people came to revere rain and water for their life-giving powers.

In Allegro's research he believed that the ancient Meso-potamians found a tool they thought could move them from this world to heaven (Allegro, 1970). This discovery did not become public, as their god was jealous of this power and allowed this magical glimpse of paradise to be seen only by a select few. Thus, a priesthood appeared with secret preparation and ceremonies during which the initiates took the drugs as a way to give themselves greater powers than the others. Very rarely, only by virtue of great need, were these secrets some-times recorded. Instead, they were transmitted from priest to initiate by verbal instruction. Allegro further proposed that the only reason these mushroom mysteries would have been written down would have been in a time of persecution or when there was a danger of losing the thread of the tradition during a war (Allegro, 1970). Even in those instances, there was a need to put down the names of substances, instruc-tions on how to use them, and all other important details in a hidden code, which Allegro believed to be the true meanings behind the books of the New Testament.

No matter how plausible Allegro's theory may or may not be, his work does show that there was a deep fascination with and appreciation for the mushroom in many religions of the ancient world. This means that it is more than likely that the Sumerians had access to and regularly used some form of psy-chedelic substance for their religious ceremonies. It is known by archaeologists that the Sumerians used opiates and ancient narcotics derived from *Cannabis sativa* (hemp), *Mandragora* spp. (mandrake), *Lolium temulentum* (darnel), and *Papaver somniferum* (opium) (Teal, 2014). There is also evidence that opium poppies were present in Sumer by 3000 BCE, but they were used only by priests in healing temples, as well as in conjunction with the hemlock that the Sumerians used for euthanasia (Teal, 2014). The pharmacopeia of Mesopotamia was detailed and elaborate. They employed plants and minerals such as sodium chloride and potassium nitrate, as well as snakeskin, turtle shell, cassia, myrtle, asafetida, thyme, willow, pear, fig, fir, and dates (ibid.). Considering their most likely use of mind-altering substances, it is quite possible Sumerian priests employed these drugs to contact the Seven Sages, much in the way that Dee and Kelley applied meditation to accomplish the same goal and in the same way that the most ancient shamans had done before them.

These ancient techniques for contacting off-world entities are still being used today. People in powerful positions are experimenting with DMT, meditation, and a host of strange medical procedures in the pursuit of "higher wisdom," "tech innovation," "expanded consciousness," and "ascension." These experiences are said to be life-changing for people and their interactions with the so-called "machine elves" so profound that they have left people feeling blessed with cosmic wisdom and infinite love. Are these seemingly benevolent beings real? Are they only here to help, or could there be a darker side to this occult practice?

As we have discussed earlier, there is good scientific evidence to suggest that life was seeded here on Earth by way of a meteor that brought in primitive life that may have originally formed somewhere else in the universe. Microbe spores may have been propelled through space by radiation emitted by stars, along with extraterrestrial retroviruses that drove the Cambrian explosion. If so, it is possible, according to ethnopharmacologist, research pharmacognosist, and brother of Terence McKenna Dr. Dennis McKenna, that in an "act of genomic surgery on a biospheric scale," tryptophan and its neurotransmitter messengers like DMT and serotonin were also seeded into the biosphere in the Archean Eon (McKenna, 2017). McKenna speculates further on this point, asking whether a biotechnologically advanced civilization, able to travel through space, could seed these molecular messengers to "function as a selective evolutionary pressure enabling the eventual appearance of complex nervous systems and intelligence" (McKenna, 2017, 3). As far-fetched a theory as it may sound, it is not outside the realm of possibility.

With science it is possible to understand the precise ways an extraterrestrial civilization could have indeed manipulated the genetics of primitive humans both directly through retroviruses and indirectly through targeted evolutionary pressures that would steer humanity toward the "Great Leap" of the human mind. This is a far more advanced and sophisticated way of achieving the goal of genetic manipulation than the idea of an anthropomorphized alien being hopping into a 1950s rocket ship and coming to Earth to collect primitive resources such as minerals and stones. Surely a race of advanced beings would not need such things and, to suggest so, limits our perception of the vastness of the universe and the possibilities it holds.

More often than not, the Sumerian texts are very clear that their priests used medicines and incantations to receive telepathic information from beings they believed to be divine. They were very specific in their descriptions, and when you begin to research tablets outside of the few that past researchers like Sitchin studied, you will find that there is a great deal of information provided. It is not necessary to fill in the gaps when the Sumerians often did this for us already, as they were meticulous record keepers and very practical in most aspects of their life. After years of studying Sumerian texts that are not commonly cited, I can only conclude that the Anunnaki—the real human technocratic elites of ancient Mesopotamia—were in direct contact with an extraterrestrial source they believed to be sages. These sages are the same off-world entities that many other civilizations found ways to contact to also receive technology. These are the same beings that John Dee and Edward Kelley contacted. These beings have been the real hidden hands behind our progress since humankind's beginnings in the Garden and have been at the helm steering the technical progress of many groups including the Sumerians, ancient Indians, Egyptians, Greeks, Romans, Aztecs, and even the Germans during World War II, and now the tech elites in Silicon Valley. Who are these "machine elves" and what is their interest in humanity?

Machine Elves

Machine elves is, as mentioned, a term coined by Terence McKenna to describe the beings he experienced while using DMT. Notably the machine elves have been experienced in similar ways by a diverse cross section of people, some even having experiences at the same time of the same beings. Why are these beings seen by people on psychedelic drugs? During a DMT experience, these entities have come to and telepathically spoken to the ingesters. They have been known to delight in showing people visions, tricks, the past, the present, the future—sometimes all at once, as if to bend space-time. They also give advice and teach about technology. Modern geniuses have often credited their creativity to dreams or meditations—including Nikola Tesla who regularly conducted realistic "dream experiments" in his lab to run complex visualizations of his inventions.

The Nazis also believed they were in touch with interdimensional beings who would give them engineering plans and technologies. These channeling activities took place in the Vril Society, whose founding members were four female mediums who allegedly received channeling from the vicinity of the star Aldebaran. They translated messages from an alien language that seemed to be a sort of proto-Sumerian, very reminiscent of Enochian. The beings they channeled outlined the schemes of advanced aircraft, which were then modified by Nazi scientists. The Vril Society was named after the ancient Sumerian word *Vri-Il*, meaning "godlike." They used Sumerian symbols and venerated the Sumerian god Ilu, who, according to Sumerian mythology, was the first god, creator, and demiurge who came from the stars and created people on Earth. The members of the Vril believed that they could use telepathy to communicate with these beings and give the Nazis a technological advantage over their opponents. Could the Nazis have tapped into an extra-, or maybe supradimensional intelligence that, until then, only shamans and ancient priests of the mystery cults could? What I soon found out while researching these and other questions was that this tradition is still very much active in our modern geopolitical landscape.

The Whistleblower

A reader who asked to go by the name RedViking_45 contacted me to share his personal story about his encounter with entities he believed he contacted through spiritual practices. He claimed to have information on a Secret Contact Program within a fringe element of the government funded by the Rockefellers and with the mission of turning everyone into soulless avatars or empty vessels for off-world entities to inhabit. He likened it to the 1997 science fiction film *Contact*, because according to the documents, these beings were instructing humans on how to build machines to make contact. Unlike the film, however, the machines the entities are wanting us to build are the result of a transhumanist agenda where man and machine unite. He provided me with documents to support his claims and asked that I keep them until he and his family have resettled somewhere in Southeast Asia. These documents, known as the *Contact Papers*, will be made available once I am given permission by RedViking_45.

Dear Dr. Lynn,

I am writing today to tell you in greater detail about an experience I had, what I know, and how I got the Contact Papers. About five years ago, I attended a local "New Age" fair with my cousin who was into Reiki. The fair featured a variety of vendors selling things like books, jewelry, and art. I bought a few books on natural health and healing, but that was about all I really came for. My cousin was really into everything there, so she ended up in some workshop on "past life regression," leaving me alone and bored. I am generally not into all this woo. I served two tours in Afghanistan and stopped believing in religion and god after that.

I must have looked lonely or lost, so some dude came over and started talking to me about the upcoming presidential election. I explained to him that I was a registered Independent and really didn't have time for either political party, as he started to come across as a radical. He surprised me by saying that he was also an Independent but only because he knew that all good world leaders were "on the same team." He went on to explain how ever since ancient times, a set of spiritual teachings referred to as the "Ageless Wisdom" has been handed down from each generation by a group of unseen beings. He claimed that there is a systematic account of the evolution of consciousness in man that describes how the universe came to exist, its nature, and its future.

I was a little taken aback by how blunt he was. I went on to ask how he knows this, and he told me that he was also in contact with these beings. I asked him how. Before he could answer, my cousin interrupted saying that we had to leave because she didn't want to pay for any more parking. I think the man could tell that he had piqued my interest so he stuffed my SWAG bag with some brochures and flyers, but then he made it a point to place a picture in my hand. He held it there for what seemed like too long, and I awkwardly pulled my hand back and shoved the picture in my tote bag. The man stared into my eyes, smiled, and told me that I had just touched the hand of the Maitreya.

Later that night, I looked through my tote bag and found the picture. It was a black and white photo of a slender hand, fingerprints and all. I wondered what he meant when he said I had touched the hand of Maitreya. Who was this person? I found the answers in the literature he gave me. According to the organization this man was promoting at the New Age fair, the Maitreya is the World Teacher that will appear to unite all religions in peace. The arrival of this being, whom some call an avatar, messiah, or Christ, who would lead the Earth of the Age of Pisces into the utopian Aquarius era. Jesus, as typically symbolized as the fish, ruled over the Age of Pisces. He also chose fishermen as his disciples. This Christ was the Maitreya for the Age of Pisces, as every era would have its own "world teacher." Jesus would be replaced by a new world teacher in the Aquarius era. The image of the hand on the picture was that of the Maitreya himself.

These claims were amazing. I had never read or heard anything like it before. I read that the hand was a personal "calling card" of the Maitreya and that the image of his hand had started to appear in several locations around the world. The most notable example was photographed by a lady in Barcelona, Spain. Upon entering the guest bathroom of her house, she noticed a hand print on the mirror and went to clean it off. A few days later, she saw the same handprint appear in her own bathroom. Rather than wipe it off, she called her son who worked for a local nonprofit. He came over and took a picture of it and sent it to the leader of the group that claimed to be in touch with the Maitreya. They were able to confirm that the handprint was that of the Maitreya himself. Ever since, they have distributed pictures of the handprint because it is said to have healing powers and mysterious physical properties like those of the Shroud of Turin.

At first, I thought the healing powers of the Maitreya's hand were dumb, but I kept the picture in the drawer of my nightstand. Months went by and I hadn't given the hand picture or the story of the Maitreya much thought. It wasn't until I started working with two friends I met through the Facebook group of an organization that helped people meditate. In the group, I learned how to meditate at various times in the lunar cycle. The goal was to help bring about world peace. I found the whole thing relaxing and rewarding. One evening in April, I was deep into my meditation when all of the sudden, I saw a strange light. Well, let me back that up. I didn't actually see the light with my eyes, it was more like I saw it in my head and felt it in my eyes. I know it sounds strange, but I can assure you that to experience it was even stranger!

The light got brighter and brighter before it finally pulsated with alternating colors. It went from purple to electric blue, to red, and then back to purple. It looked like a purplish fire in my mind's eye. I was enthralled by the whole colorful display until I suddenly realized that the pulsating colors were taking the shape of a human hand. I instantly knew that this was the hand of the Maitreya! Then, I heard a voice. The voice sounded male but was not particularly deep. I tried to speak but could not utter a word. Instead, I received a flood of information, almost like it was being downloaded into my consciousness. Then, the pulsating light became dimmer before finally fading into nothing, but weird little specks of blue and red flashed intermittently.

I opened my eyes and cannot explain how I felt. There really are no words. I knew enough to hurry over to my kitchen junk drawer, get out a pad and a little broken pencil, and write down what I had "heard." After purging this information as fast as I could, I looked down to see what I had written. The message read:

"The gates shall soon be opened. From the center of the planet they shall emerge, and I will take my rightful place at the helm of this great vehicle. The seven tricksters will dance across the heavens in celebration of my return. I will reclaim the remnants of my kingdom. The sons and daughters of Enki will be lifted up by the knowledge of their true nature as encoded in the essence of life."

I was freaked out. I had no idea what it meant. I knew it was important because I could feel it. I have since tried to get more messages, but I have not experienced any else like this no matter how much I try to meditate. It has gotten to the point where now when I even just try to meditate, I fall asleep. I am not certain, but I believe that the only explanation for what I experienced was that I somehow channeled a being when meditating. I believe that the being I channeled was an Anunnaki. While I have no way to prove this, I feel it in my bones, and I believe that it is important for the world to know the message that I was told. This is the first time I have ever shared the message. Some may call it a prophecy. Others may call it a dream. I am not sure.

After this happened to me, I started to read a lot online and found information on channeling. I came across an organization that claimed to be able to train people how to contact entities on behalf of World Goodwill and Peace. This sounded really cool because the ways things are going in the world today I think we need peace. This was when it was all revealed to me, not all at once, but eventually I found out the truth. So I joined the group that will have to remain nameless. I cannot say their name to you because I signed an oath that I am afraid to break. They have all of my information and even photos of my family for identification purposes. I hope you can understand. I guess this makes me some sort of whistleblower, I don't know. All I know is that I cannot live with this burden anymore and the world needs to know the truth about what is happening at the highest levels of government.

I started participating in what they referred to as the "Work." This included monthly meditations during the full moon, which I know sounds hokey for a grown-ass man, but there was something to it. I got almost addicted. Over a lot of months I met up with a group of what they called "co-workers," and we did a group meditation. During this meditation, we summoned some sort of being. This being came into existence from an orb of light that appeared like a speck of dust. It started to grow and get brighter until it was so bright that I could feel its heat. The being started speaking but only in a way that I could feel and see what it was saying. It was telling us to unite the world's religions and complete the plan so that it will have an avatar ready for its appearance on earth. Still at this point, I thought I had just found religion. I didn't think it would go beyond that.

It wasn't until May of 2018 that I came across information about the group that I joined that made me regret everything. The group has a reading room and library filled with occult books. I made a pilgrimage there and started exploring what they had. There was no one around, so I spent a lot of time just looking and that's when I saw a bunch of papers and folders on the information desk. I went over there to take a look and stopped dead in my tracks when I saw a paper with a photo of a UFO like the kind you see in old movies. It was an old picture, but it was out of place enough to get me to stop and take a closer look. It was then that I saw more documents that looked like they had Sumerian writing. I heard someone talking in the hall, and I don't know what I was thinking but I grabbed up a bunch of the documents and left before the lady who let me in got back from her break. These are the documents that I sent you copies and pictures of. Please do not share them yet. I will let you know when it is safe to put them out publicly if you want to. You can see by what they said why.

These documents show that in the depths of the governments of some countries are working in secret to study UFO technology and even contact representatives of extraterrestrial civilizations. All these documents indicate the fact that there is a policy of secrecy around the UFO unprecedented in its scope and significance. Everything connected with it is downplayed in media and television, especially in the U.S., despite the obvious commercial appeal of this subject. Have you ever noticed how there have been no Anunnaki movies? With the exception of a little nod in Ridley Scott's Prometheus, there has been no media interest in the Anunnaki. Instead, people are stuffed with low-grade fiction and fake occultism about bird people, which in no way adds real awareness of the truth.

The entire known history of humankind is permeated by data on the existence of certain "secret societies" among people. The fact that they existed in the past is in no doubt even among the most skeptical researchers and historians. Naturally, secret societies exist even now, and according to some data they have always been around, though I'm sure you would know about this. Basically, anyone who is at a certain evolutionary level, either by intelligence, talent, or psychic awareness, gets recruited to become members of secret associations. In view of the activities of secret societies, there has always been a two-tier science on our planet: elite and consumers. Because of this consumer demand for toys and distraction, science and technology acquired by secret chan- neling activities of secret societies, according to some estimates, were at least eighty years or more behind. So who knows how long we have had things like radio or AI? If you look up the patent for the Sensorama Machine, it's a virtual reality device that was designed in the 1950s but just like what we have now. People are working all over to develop free energy and antigravity.

The financial rationale for hiding the latest discoveries is obvious: money is made on what is continuously bought. So according to infor- mation, one of the companies producing electrical equipment bought and froze a patent for eternal electric bulbs invented at the end of the last century. This is the same reason all information about the signif- icant inventions of Nikola Tesla, in particular about the "solid state converter" which converted the energy penetrating space into electric- ity, was taken out of circulation. A device the size of a can of pop was tested for a week, providing a completely free-of-charge electric power for driving a car. That was something to worry the oil companies and manufacturers of electricity. It is logical to assume that there are other motives for secret societies to hold on to some of their scientific and technical achievements. It is possible that many of those who for a long time systematically withdrew or destroyed books and manuscripts with secret knowledge have done so for very understandable human considerations.

Secret societies are extremely interested in owning advanced knowledge and high technology. This is why people go missing. You'll see promising researchers disappear without a trace, their works taken from libraries by someone, their names disappearing from the books. You never hear from them again. They say there is a whole list of scien- tific and technical areas like remote viewing and psychological optics, transmutation of chemical elements at simple temperatures, wireless transmission of energy at a distance, antigravity, space-time management, some aspects of genetic engineering and parapsychology. This also includes information about UFOs, but between the secret societies there has always been a hidden competition since the beginning of the twentieth century. They believe that the beings they interface with want them to unify people and bring about a global system.

The main outlines of this government start to come together at the start of the twentieth century. The secret societies of the Illuminati enlightened in Great Britain and the United States combined their own efforts in a structure called the Round Table in 1919. Organizations like the Council on Foreign Relations and the Bilderberg Group all are in on this.

In the 1950s, President Eisenhower signed the secret Executive Memorandum of the NSC 5410 to create a committee called "Majority-12" to supervise and control all secret activities regarding extraterrestrial civilizations—Allen Welsh Dulles, director of the CIA; John Foster Dulles, secretary of state; Charles Wilson, secretary of defense; Admiral Arthur Redford, chief of the Joint High Command; Edgar Guve, director of the FBI: title "Wise Men." These six were members of a secret society of researchers, which is called The Jason Society.

The guys were key figures of the Council on Foreign Relations. These included twelve people, including six in government positions at Majority-12. For many years, this group consisted of senior officers and leaders of the Council on Foreign Relations, and later the Tripartite Commission. Among them were Gordon Dean, George Bush, Zbigniew Brzezinski. There are so many others that these documents list. They are referred to collectively as the "New Group of World Servers." When I was in this organization, we had to write reports on the activities of these people. We were also supposed to support their work through prayer and meditation. This isn't new, though, as we previously talked about.

For thousands of years, organizations have played the role of conscious mediators between humanity and other space civilizations. The shadow government was provided with a whole range of technologies foreshadowing it in an effort to dominate the world in exchange for ensuring the secrecy of the civilization of these beings they believe come from the Zeta Reticuli star system and noninterference in their affairs on Earth.

What I am telling you is all in the document I have provided. They also have drawings and plans for strange devices and what look to be craft, but I cannot say for sure. All I know is that this might sound like a lot of YouTube video stuff, but you saw the pictures. They had Sumerian all over them. There were also pictures of artifacts and things from Iraq. What I am telling you, Dr. Lynn, and hopefully showing you with these documents, is that the Rockefellers were funding UFO research at the same time and through the same organizations as they were funding spiritual and occult research. They want to recruit as many people as possible through their meditation groups because they believe that these alien beings are light beings that need energy to manifest through people because people according to these papers "are telepathic electro chemical antennae that can connect to different dimensions." They believe that this planet is a third dimension which is the primal sea between the lower and upper dimensions. The elites are looking for psychically available people who can interface with other dimensions. These entities are like some sort of weird parasite. When I was involved in this group trying to summon the new world teacher, or Maitreya, what I didn't realize at the time was that I was summoning Archons, who I now know after studying are biological androids. You asked me about DMT. All I can say is that, yes, part of this meditation group was encouraged

191

to try DMT so that we could contact these beings. I didn't do it, but I know that before doing it they would have you sign up with your "guide," who was a licensed psychologist. They would record the session, and after you came off your high, they debriefed you and kept that in a file and were required to write reports and send them to a place only referred to as "Headquarters." All I ever knew about Headquarters was that they had a location in New York, the City of London, and Geneva.

I really want to get this information out, so I am starting with you. The public needs to know what these groups are planning. They are essentially a death cult and are looking forward to ushering in Armageddon. This is one of their group meditation mantras. They try to invoke who Christians refer to as the "Anti-Christ." They believe that this anti-Christ will take the form of a UFO. I have had to take a real hard look at the part I played in this and all that I put my family through. After having time to really deal with all of these things, I am convinced that these entities that some call the Anunnaki are not aliens but demons.

After speaking with and reading the account of RedViking_45, I recognized a lot of familiar themes. I started thinking about all of the cultures that say they have contacted teacher beings from alternate realms. All indeed claimed to have received technological advancements from these beings and would go on to establish great cities and structures. However, it seems that there would always be a price. Eventually, these otherworldly beings would demand payment for their gifts of civilization, and that payment would sometimes be the blood of the people. This was certainly the case in Mesopotamia, after advancing to an extraordinary degree, the likes of which the ancient world had not seen. This can also be seen in Babylon and Carthage, both of which sacrificed their children. It happened again with the Aztecs, who became infamous for their mass killings and sacrifice of their own people. Even in the case of the Nazis, it is clear how things ended: the deaths of millions of Jews. How will our modern civilization fare when it comes to paying the price for our technological advances? Is this bloody collapse something modern civilization will eventually face? What does our future look like?

CHAPTER 7

Nibiru and Armageddon

*The end of the human race will be that it
will eventually die of civilization.*
—RALPH WALDO EMERSON,
American poet and philosopher

Nibiru

What is our fate? It seems as though we have struck a critical point in our development as a species. Some say we are
doomed, citing the Nibiru Cataclysm as our ultimate demise.

The references to Nibiru in the Mesopotamian tablets are
fragmentary at best, often related to the epithets of the god
Marduk, which gives rise to different interpretations. Astronomical associations are complicated by the fact that because
of the anticipation of the equinoxes, the arrangement of stars
in the sky was different from the modern one. In particular,
in ancient Mesopotamia, the polar star was Thuban, of the
constellation Draco, associated with Tiamat. Another nuance
is that in the ancient world the Earth was considered flat.
While the tablets available now do not appear to suggest the

contrary, I do suspect that it will not be long until we will find the Sumerians knew better. Nibiru was said to be washed by the ocean (Sea of Tiamat), in particular the so-interpreted concept of "two heavenly gates" along the sides of the horizon which would appear to leave the stars at sunset and go to the underworld on the rise. According to the hypothesis that *Nibiru* can best be translated as a "crossing point," which divides not the horizon but the celestial equator—Tiamat is the Milky Way, or the dark stripe in its middle, and Nibiru is located on the Milky Way.

If we consider Nibiru to be an astronomical body, the other difficulty is that there are reconstructed lists of stars revered in Sumerian-Akkadian culture. So celestial objects that may be similar in a number of theories to Nibiru are already mentioned in these lists as separate objects. The ancients also divided the sky into several "paths" associated with the main gods. Nibiru was located on the path of the god Anu and associated with the planet Jupiter several times (there is once a mention of it being associated with Mercury). Some researchers consider Nibiru to have been Jupiter, although this is contrary to the lists. There is a hypothesis pointing to the Orion belt, but Betelgeuse is not visible in the month of Adar, or the Hebrew twelfth month, March, by the Gregorian calendar and so does not align with the texts. There is also a hypothesis connecting Nibiru with the star Sirius—the brightest star of the night sky. In one instance, Nibiru is described separately from the planets and stars, and this description has Nibiru fixed in the center of the "twelve starry months," which allows the concept to be interpreted as a fixed point on the axis of the world or the axis of the ecliptic of the celestial sphere.

The relatedness of the myths of the ancient world about the dragon Tiamat, killed by Marduk, is clear. In particular, we can look at the Greek myth, which called the constellation "Dragon." This dragon was killed by neighboring constellation Heracles during Titanomachy, the ten-year series of battles fought between the Titans and the Olympians. In a similar Indian myth, the god of thunder Indra kills and dismembers the body of the serpent Vritra. In Indian mythology, Indra is dedicated to the constellation Aries. Further, in the neighboring Persian lands, the name of the planet Mars (astrologically corresponding to Aries) was "Verethragna," which means "the killer of Vritra." According to this information, it is unlikely that Mars is a candidate for Nibiru since it is already mentioned by the Sumerians. Aries also has a very bright star, Hamal, which could be a marker of the vernal equinox and, therefore, could be the star of Marduk or Nibiru. Other researchers believe Nibiru is any visible astronomical object that marks the equinox that occurred at the end of the month of March, or the celestial point that could mark the equinox. This could mean that the Sumerians considered Aldebaran to be Nibiru.

These explanations, however, are not typically ones that come to mind when hearing of Nibiru. Nibiru is now viewed as Planet X, whose orbit, according to Sitchin, crosses the solar system between Mars and Jupiter once every 3,600 years. Sitchin, as we discussed, claimed that Nibiru was described in Sumerian texts as the twelfth planet, for which he named his book. This is the planet where Sitchin believed the Anunnaki once lived, theorizing that the rogue Nibiru will zoom past the Earth, causing a great catastrophe due to its gravitational pull. This is reminiscent of Velikovsky's planetary collision framework.

However, astrophysicists refute the possibility of the existence of Nibiru, citing that nothing with that mass and orbit exists. They also argue that the Anunnaki could not have lived on such a planet because the supposed location of Nibiru would put it out in the Kuiper belt and the Oort Cloud where there is no sunlight, making the temperature far too cold to support life as we know it. Further, there are no Sumerian tablets currently known that name the planet Nibiru nor its connection with the Anunnaki. The only Sumerian cylinder seal often cited as evidence is VA 243, which we discussed earlier. While my own speculation on what VA 243 depicts may not be correct, it at least shows there are many ways to interpret these tablets. If you choose to accept Sitchin's hypothesis, it still makes it the only tablet to show any connection to another planet. Even then, it does not include references to this planet's name, nor does it discuss this as being the ancestral home of the Anunnaki.

In the Sumerian texts, the word *Nibiru*, spelled *Neberu*, is superscripted with the cuneiform sign for "god," meaning that, if anything, Nibiru was a god. Alternatively, or perhaps in conjunction with this fact, there are also instances when the word *Nibiru* is superscripted with the cuneiform sign for "star." This is not unusual because, as we saw in chapter 5, ancient Mesopotamian astronomers associated celestial bodies with deities. Again, note how there is an alternate spelling for Nibiru. When considering this, I looked more deeply into cuneiform dictionaries, and I am of the mind that Nibiru was most certainly not a rogue planet but perhaps a comet.

If you examine the newer Akkadian spelling *Neberu*, meaning "to cross over," or sometimes it is *Neberi*, meaning "a Ferryman"— as in one you may need if you were "crossing over"—when you break the word apart, you can read the original spelling for Nibiru as separate parts to be: *Ne-Be-Ru/Ri*. According to the older translations, *Ne* meant a "brazier," or a container for hot coals. *Ne* also meant "strength" or "force" ("The Pennsylvania

Sumerian Dictionary"). *Be* meant "to diminish" or "receive" (McKenna, 2017). Finally, *Ri* meant to "lay down," "cast," or "throw down" (McKenna, 2017). Thus, you may easily interpret *Nibiru* to mean "a forceful brazier diminishing as it is being thrown down." Considering the association made to both stars and deities, it would seem reasonable to understand Nibiru to be a comet. If you put yourself in the position of an ancient Sumerian, a brazier or container to hold hot coals could be a sensible and accurate way to describe a comet. Moreover, to think of the actions of this celestial brazier as being cast down to Earth, or at times simply crossing over it, appears to match a general description of the movement of a comet.

For the sake of argument, let's say that rogue comets are to blame for catastrophes rather than rogue planets, especially considering that astrophysicists agree that a rogue planet is not a likely scenario. This would actually make more sense when applying Sitchin's 3,600-year calculation because it gives more wiggle room for possible candidates with so many comets out there. It would also seem to fit more with past forecasts and doomsday predictions.

Just like the gods from many other cultures, it is predicted that the Anunnaki will return to Earth one day. According to Sitchin, we can expect Nibiru and the Anunnaki sometime after the year 2900 CE, since the initial pass of Nibiru happened in 556 BCE. However, Turkish writer and researcher Burak Eldem later calculated that Nibiru would return in the year 2012, inspired by the Mayan calendar. Nibiru initially appeared to be a mythological invention from an ancient civilization with no specific relevance for the year 2012, but the existence of the planet appeared to be confirmed by NASA on December 31, 1983. With the Infrared Astronomy Satellite (IRAS), a large infrared telescope, a new celestial body was discovered: a planet as big as Jupiter and so close to the Earth that it could be part of our solar system. The object was at that time on the western edge of the Orion constellation, was particularly cold, and possibly moved toward the Earth. It would later be stated that no distant planet, but a distant galaxy was observed.

Despite this correction, the theory of an approaching planet was elaborated in 1995 by Nancy Lieder, founder of the ZetaTalk website. She claimed to be in contact with aliens from the Zeta Reticuli galaxy through an implant in her brain, and she was chosen to warn humanity. Planet X, an object four times the size of Earth, would make its way through our solar system in May 2003 and cause a polar shift in the process and wipe out most of humanity. In April of that year, the planet would become visible to everyone on Earth as a red cross in the sky.

The coming and going of 2003 has shown that this prophecy was incorrect. Lieder stated afterward that she had deliberately announced an incorrect date, with the aim of testing whether national governments would take steps to inform and protect citizens. She would only present the real date if the object was so close that no errors could be made in the calculation of the course and it was impossible that those in power would misuse this information at the expense of others. Lieder also referred to her object as Planet X, but Sitchin has emphatically denied a connection between "his" Nibiru and her apocalyptic doomsday scenario that would have taken place around 2012. Nevertheless both were successful at attracting many followers.

It was then predicted that on May 15, 2009, Nibiru or Planet X would be visible for the first time, from the southern hemisphere, with a small telescope or even with the naked eye as a faint, red object. After a few months the planet could also be observed by the rest of the world. As that date has passed, this prophecy can also be checked, and it seems that it did not come true. That NASA did not mention Nibiru could be explained by conspiracy theories that citizens are kept ignorant to prevent global unrest, but there are also no convincing photos or videos from independent amateur astronomers on the internet. They have often captured a glittering object close to the sun just before or after sunset, but that shimmer can often be explained well by lens flare—the reflection and scattering of light due to irregularities in the material of the lens. There are no known photos with an unknown object that could only be explained by acknowledging the proximity of Nibiru.

In May 2009 and the months that followed, amateur astronomers were unable to present convincing images of Nibiru. However, something that could be Nibiru does appear to have been photographed in January 2008 by the Amundsen-Scott South Pole Station telescope in Antarctica. These photos can be found on YouTube and include a red star, including the shadow of a planet or moon that revolves around it, amid a number of other celestial bodies. The visual material would have been made by aiming the telescope at a location in the sky that is defined by the coordinates 5h 53m 27s, -6°10'58".

But anyone who uses these coordinates to check Google Sky with their own eyes for a reddish object that could be identified as Nibiru will be disappointed. Google Sky shows only a black surface in the constellation Orion. NASA's explanation is that there is a "technical glitch": the dataset is made up of a large collection of images from the Sloan Digital Survey, and when the photos were Photoshopped, something must have gone wrong. There has been a promise for some two years to repair the defect with the next update, but so far this has not happened.

Some still question that if Nibiru does not exist, why is the exact part of the starry sky where the object would be obscured? On the other hand, if Google Sky and the government organizations involved really wanted to hide a celestial body from the general public, why didn't they proceed more subtly? If only the few pixels had been removed from the object itself, everyone could have seen with their own eyes that Nibiru was not there. The black area, on the other hand, feeds the conspiracy theories, making it unlikely that Google Sky would try to hide a planet, comet, or star in this way.

Moreover, the evidence that Nibiru should be hiding behind a dark area is not very convincing. The only source that links these coordinates to the location of the planet is a video posted on YouTube in early 2008 but since removed. Google Sky has been around since August 2007. The person who added the coordinates to the so-called photos of Nibiru could therefore know they referred to a hidden location in a black area. It is possible that Google Sky keeps ordinary people ignorant to prevent global unrest and deliberately hides a planet behind a black surface, but it is also possible that Nibiru supporters have searched for a black surface in which to place their planet and so maintain the myth.

It is important to note that NASA emphatically denies the existence of Nibiru and lists a series of arguments on its website to support that conclusion. They contend that a large planet, brown dwarf, or other large celestial body in our solar system would not escape the notice of astronomers. The object would influence other planets through its gravity and be visible with infrared telescopes. NASA has been scanning the sky since the early 1980s, but it says it has found no trace of Nibiru. Moreover, there are no indications from the orbits of the inner planets that a large, heavy celestial body would pass through our solar system every 3,600 years.

Nevertheless, astronomers still seem to cover themselves in the event that soon a red object suddenly appears in the sky. Astronomer Brad Carter, affiliated with the University of Southern Queensland, stated that Betelgeuse (alpha Orionis), a red supergiant in the constellation Orion, is at the end of her life and is about to become a supernova (Praetorius, 2011). If that happens, a second, red "sun" will be visible for weeks, about the same size and possibly many times brighter than the yellow-white we are used to (Praetorius, 2011). The supernova is not expected to have any adverse consequences for life on Earth. According to Carter, the exploding of Betelgeuse will take place sometime in the next 10,000 years (Praetorius, 2011).

Do astronomers think it is necessary to explain in advance a suddenly emerging red celestial body in the constellation Orion? This also feeds the conspiracy theories. If the prophecy is right, then Nibiru should have been visible to everyone in 2012, yet it was not. NASA can still silence those who believe that the prophecy is being fulfilled by claiming that they are not looking at an approaching planet, but there will still be those will prefer the explanation of a scientific institute such as NASA to mythological prophecy.

The concept of a planet that is in the vicinity of the Earth once every 3,600 years cannot be proven. Whether this story is based on truth or not, it cannot be determined using science. In fact, much of the science available seems to discredit the idea. As with any other ancient story, a number of elements are undoubtedly possible and others are even probable, but there is no conclusive evidence. Moreover, there is no consensus about the correct interpretation of the Sumerian texts and the data mentioned therein.

After NASA reported a new, large celestial body on the edge of our solar system in 1983 and withdrew this claim a little later, Nancy Lieder announced the proximity of Planet X and the approaching apocalypse. Her claim to be in contact with extraterrestrial beings should not be a reason to believe her prediction in advance (Lieder, 2003). Many previous predictions about Nibiru or Planet X have not come true. Although the basis of the prophecy does not seem stable, it is not very strange that supporters still believe in Nibiru. Most of them will not have studied astronomy or have a telescope at their disposal, and if they suspect NASA of withholding information and misleading the general public, they cannot single-handedly disprove their theory of an approaching planet even if they want. The black area in Google Sky at the location on the starry sky where Nibiru should be makes further self-study impossible and fosters conspiracy thinking.

Moreover, from the recent announcement of supernova of Betelgeuse it could be deduced that NASA is anticipating the possibility that a large, red celestial body will actually emerge. The description of the supernova and that of Nibiru do not differ much from each other: both will be visible as a red object in the constellation Orion, as large as and possibly even brighter than the sun. Only the expected effects of the celestial bodies differ. According to NASA, the supernova will hardly have any influence on earthly life, while Nibiru is predicted to cause large-scale natural disasters. It is not impossible that NASA anticipates the arrival of Nibiru and is trying to prevent mass hysteria by already stating that the bright red object is a harmless natural phenomenon. Such a diversion maneuver fits into conspiracy thinking, because supporters of doomsday prophecies expect that world leaders will leave the people in the dark for as long as possible in the face of an inevitable apocalypse. The existence of Nibiru as a rogue planet seems unlikely, but even if the planet appears to exist, it may turn out to be a supernova or even a comet.

The Return of the Anunnaki

According to many, including Sitchin, the Anunnaki are going to return to Earth. Whether this is on a planet that is defying the laws of physics or a metallic 1950s spaceship I'm sure will continue to be debated. Let us assume that they will come back, which is also to assume they ever left. According to whistleblowers I have spoken with and supported by follow-up research, the real risk of the return of these beings will not be from a cataclysmic event. Rather, it will be when the stars align just right and the Earth is aligned with the group consciousness that is literally trying to summon these beings. The individuals may just open a Pandora's box that they can never close; perhaps that is the point. The threat does not come in the physical form in the beginning; it will be a spiritual battle. Keep in mind when I say *spiritual*, I do not mean religious. These matters transcend religion and speak to a universal cosmic truth that humanity has yet to fully comprehend.

A surprising number of ancient cultures have legends about portals to other worlds or portals to parallel worlds and space-time holes. The alignment of celestial bodies has a lot to do with these. Many cultures also have an axis mundi believed to connect the physical to the spiritual plane. This is the stargate, as Gary David calls it: "a divine tunnel located in the sky through which the soul achieves transcendence." Shamans and priests of the mystery schools gathered at these sites. They performed rituals while gazing at the sky, hoping to make contact with off-world intelligences. But as we have already discussed, this practice is not limited to the ancient world. The goal of some of the wealthiest and most powerful individuals in our modern world involves similar activities, and some are actively pursuing locations for possible stargates. In fact, some believe that the search for these stargates has led to secret archaeological excavations all around the world.

In my own work, I have met a number of people who insist that the war in Iraq had nothing to do with the search for Saddam Hussein's weapons of mass destruction or even Middle East oil fields. The real reason has been rumored to be supposedly ancient secrets and technologies that the United States wanted to take over. There is a strange connection to this theory and the looting of the Iraq National Museum, which we will examine further in the next chapter, but for now, I would like to point you to the work of Dr. Michael Salla, former assistant professor in the School of International Service, American University. When the war in Iraq began in 2003, Dr. Salla published a story telling that before the invasion of Iraq, the Bush administration learned of an ancient stargate hidden in central Iraq (Salla, 2003). Dr. Salla asserts that:

> *competing clandestine government organizations are struggling through proxy means to take control of ancient extraterrestrial (ET) technology that exists in Iraq, in order to prepare for an impending series of events corresponding to the "prophesied return" of an advanced race of ETs (Salla, 2003).*

Dr. Salla points out that a very important part of the Sumerian accounts of the Anunnaki involves the beings leaving this planet between 1800 and 1700 BCE (Salla, 2003). He bases much of his information on Sitchin's work, as well as von Däni-ken. He argues that there are a number of sources that describe the present era as near the prophesized return of the Anun-naki. He contends, again using Sitchin's ancient astronaut the-oretical framework, that these beings may physically return to rule over human beings and enslave us all again (Salla, 2003). Thus, if the Anunnaki are about to return, the supposed star-gates would first have to open to let them in.

However, in the documents I was given by RedViking_45, there is a reference to an invocation used by initiates of modern occult groups that calls upon the opening of a stargate. This invocation states: "From that which we call the gate of Gaia, let the Plan of Order and Light commence, and may it open the gates where the Wise Ones wander" (Contact Papers, per RedViking_45). If perhaps there are reasons beyond what we are told about our involvement in the Middle East, I suspect that there is more of an unseen or spiritual focus at play. Nev-ertheless, a wide range of ancient texts seems to make clear that there will be a coming event that will alter the course of history. Will this be a violent, catastrophic attack or impact? We will have to wait and see; the evidence we have so far does not make it clear. At any given moment, prophecy or not, our planet could be hit by any number of meteors.

Again, this doomsday scenario is easy to imagine because it fits well with our encultured expectations of what a cata-clysmic event would look like. It reinforces our primal fears of violence and bloodshed and is further reinforced by science fiction movies. To challenge this very specific interpretation of anthropomorphic aliens blasting in like a spaceship or a celes-tial body ripping into the Earth, I would remind you of what was discussed closer to the beginning of this book with regards to meteors bringing extraterrestrial life to Earth.

Imagine for a moment a different, more insidious dooms-day scenario—one that comes in quietly. If perhaps Nibiru is a meteor, then it may not have to be very big to create an extinction-level event or even carry extraterrestrial life. It could enter our world in such a quiet way that it might go completely undetected. If a meteor came into Earth's atmosphere and even just exploded at the upper levels, it could still deposit an extraterrestrial virus that could completely wipe out humanity. Since it would be extraterrestrial, it would be difficult for us to accurately predict what its outcomes would be, so it is easy to just assume it would want to harm us, at the very least, or even kill us. Yet this may not be accurate. If the beings in this hypo-thetical "Soft Armageddon" scenario were the Archons of the Gnostics and the Watchers we have been examining, then their reasons for invading could be more complicated.

Some believe that these entities, or the mechanical elves, are looking for avatars so that they may experience life in the ways that humans do. They want to live in this dimension. It may be the case that rather than kill us, the extraterrestrial virus will make us all zombie avatars so that these off-world entities can inhabit and use us for their own purposes. If the Anunnaki Sages are divine beings that dwell in different planes of reality, as the Sumerian texts indicate, then this scenario offers them the opportunity to return and manifest in a corporeal sense. They would become lords of this world, and we would be but a shell of our former selves until there would be no need for us at all. Again, this is basing the connection to the Anunnaki and the end of the world on the works of Sitchin and Lieder. Otherwise, who is to say that these beings ever really left us to begin with? It would seem that looking at a cross-comparative analysis of the literature, they may have never gone away but have been hiding in the darkness waiting for us to summon them using certain meditative practices or even hallucinogenic substances.

I am frequently asked whose theories are correct. What I say is that I hope you will consider the points I have made and do your own research. Just remember, even the alternatives need alternatives if there is to be a genuine discussion and effort to reach the truth. Truth is above ego, and the cult of personality starting to take over so many aspects of the alternative research community is tearing us apart. It is important for us to enter into an idea with an element of healthy skepticism. As philosopher and scientist René Descartes said: "Doubt is the origin of wisdom."

CHAPTER 8

The Cover-Up

History is nothing but a pack of tricks
that we play upon the dead.
—VOLTAIRE, French historian
and philosopher

A s on many trips down the rabbit hole, we can emerge with just as many, if not more, questions as answers. I have learned a lot in my quest for the truth about the past, including how interested the global power elites are in finding and concealing certain elements of what has come before. History is an important tool in shaping reality. It may come as a surprise to some, but history is not a set of facts, places, people, or events. These are merely historical data points. It is the act of connecting these points that creates history. History is a weaving of the thread through these fixed points. Archaeology, as the acquisition and systematic analysis of evidence of the past, can provide more measurable and observable data points; still, even these artifacts are not history in themselves. This is why the historian is needed.

Napoleon once lamented: "What is history, but a fable agreed upon?" To understand the cover-up, it is important to grasp the origin of historical thought and the era in which the concept of history began to be formalized. Historians of Greek and Roman antiquity had a great appreciation for, and an understanding of, the importance of recording past events, but both their purpose and methods were different. For example, Herodotus combed over Greek literature, trying to rationalize hero myths to build a narrative account of history. His work was expansive and ambitious, leading to a greater need for a chronology. This resulted in improvisation on his part. Herodotus placed a particular importance on the individual's role in history, rather than the roles of the elites.

Unlike those who favored wide-ranging, poetic histories, Thucydides referenced specific points on a historic timeline, such as the beginning of the Peloponnesian War, to create a chronological framework for the Greek past. The Greeks saw war as an important force in what they considered their destiny; therefore, they paid special attention to the fate of states in the context of wars. Even so, they still understood the role of the individual in history. Even though the Greeks considered the concept of destiny when writing history, that did not necessarily imply a divine causation, as Greek historiography addressed only events, people, and institutions, rather than philosophical matters, looking only for human causations. Greek historiographers showed less concern over philosophy and more for the general accounting of provable events—if not by firsthand accounts, at least by reason. Due to the fragmentary nature of Greek city-states, this was difficult to achieve.

By contrast, Roman historians tried to form a more cohesive narrative, putting a stamp of "Romanitas" on historical events, including adaptations of Greek histories (Breisach, 2007). For example, Polybius used the chronological system of Olympiad years, making strides in unifying the Roman historical narrative. This chronology was an accomplishment; however, he lacked the comprehensiveness seen in the work of Greek writers such as Herodotus. Rather than writing about myths and legends in trying to build a logical history, Polybius focused on more recent accounts of history, believing that firsthand witnesses were the most reliable. He was so pragmatic that historian Ernst Breisach asserts: "[Polybius] angrily rejected the purpose of writing history for entertainment or for the satisfaction of antiquarian or local curiosity" (Breisach, 2007, 49). The goal of Roman historians in putting down their histories was teaching lessons about life, encouraging those in the public sphere to apply those lessons to the present. By contrast, the Greeks did not concern themselves with producing civic behavior; rather, they felt history should "tell a story of the past, that would above all inspire, teach and occasionally it may entertain" (Breisach, 2007).

Modern historians are very careful when evaluating sources, and although sources were not analyzed similarly by Greek historians, they did consider them, often preferring firsthand accounts. Also, modern historians often try to organize events in chronological order. Regarding renowned historian, Kurt von Fritz's position, both the Greeks and Romans tried to arrange things in "real" order. But reality is subjective, so reality to the Romans may not be considered real to the Greeks. Modern historians' definition of *the real* may seem unreal to future historians. Even if the chronology of the Greeks and Romans is not completely accurate, based on their understanding, it was real and accurate to the people of the time. However, history "should make visible the living forces which are working in the progress of history" (Fritz, 1936, 315). Greek and Roman historians both valued the role of the individual in history to certain extents. Also, although they both tried to find human causations for historical events, the difference was their purpose: to the Greeks, it was entertainment, while for the Romans, it was teaching lessons to shape policymakers. Ultimately, the state of history now is more sophisticated in its methodology. Yet, its Greek and Roman roots are apparent. This, paired with the declining state of public education, has created a climate of boredom and disengagement in the classrooms of today's schools. Things change at the university level, though not necessarily for the better.

When people find out that I am a historian, I usually get one of two reactions: "Wow! That must be so cool! I've always loved history!" or "Wow . . . that must be so boring. I always hated history in school." Oddly enough, even I hated history in school. Don't get me wrong. I have always had an interest in ancient civilizations and archaeology. (My first excavation took place in my backyard, much to my mother's dismay!) Yet history was something that I liked to learn about on my own. I did not enjoy it in an institutional context, at least not in elementary or high school. Today, history relies on memorization and repetition, but history is not something that can be effectively taught in this manner. It is not like mathematical equations or multiplication tables.

To deal with history this way suggests a sense of absoluteness. There is no question that history is comprised of certain absolutes since to study history is to study an actual series of events that once occurred (Linenthal, 1994). However, to claim that history *is* absolute circumvents the question of ontology, a branch of inquiry and complex philosophical issues that question the nature of being. Doing so would not account for the importance of historical lenses, memories, and varied ways of interpreting past events. Thus, history is also relative and "always changing in response to the increase or refinement of knowledge" (Linenthal, 1994, 987).

What Is History?

In 1961, the great historian E. H. Carr asked the question, "What is history?" to which he concluded that "the really important part of a historian's work lay in the edifice of explanation and interpretation which was erected on this foundation" (Carr, 1932, 200). He did not minimize the importance of the absoluteness of history, but rather conceded that history is, in part, relative. In his career-defining article "Everyman His Own Historian," historian Carl Becker agrees that there is a duality to history, stating, "There are two histories" (Becker, 1932, 222). Becker went on to describe the first history as being "absolute and unchanged—it was what it was whatever we do or say about it," while the second he said "is relative" (Becker, 1932). Becker accepts that there is a relativity to history but emphasizes its absoluteness by promoting a more practical view: "history is, for us and for the time being, what we know it to be" (Becker, 1932).

Although not explicitly addressed, academic Edward Linenthal, specialist in religious and American studies and sacred spaces, agreed with Becker's dual definition of history in his article "Committing History in Public." However, he added that there are, indeed, two histories: academic and popular. He laments that many academic historians feel estranged from public history even with a growing interest among the general population, as evident in the increase of historical television programs, engagement in historical reenactments, visits to historic sites and museums, and concern for the preservation of historic sites.

For example, upon visiting the Little Bighorn Battlefield National Monument, Linenthal learned how the National Park Service removed a plaque praising the Native Americans who fought in the battle placed there by protestors. Instead of disposing of the plaque, the Park Service was displaying it in the visitor center with an explanation of the viewpoint of the Native Americans. To Linenthal, this gesture made the "visitors a part of that history, helping them understand that their presence and reaction were a continuing part of the history of the site" (Linenthal, 1994, 987). In this way, he emphasizes the relativity and fluidity of history.

The primary difference between both scholars' analysis of what history is, or should be, is that while Linenthal argued to enhance history through public involvement, Becker wanted to "reduce [history] to its lowest terms" (Becker, 1932, 222). For historians to present history to the public in its lowest terms, they risk losing public interest since people's memories and experiences are so diverse and unique. Arguably, the more simplified the interpretation, the less people can relate because reduction means taking something away. Therefore, historians can reach people better by expanding, not reducing the narrative. As a result of expanding the historical narrative, historians can close the gap between the academy and the general public, offering a more inclusive and fair historical landscape—something from which researchers like Sitchin and others considered "fringe" would have benefited. By making certain theories or authors taboo, it only makes them more appealing.

When I was a freshman in college, I was so excited to attend my first archaeology class. On the very first day, I eagerly looked down at my large, glossy, hardcover edition of my over-priced textbook. Considering how much I had anticipated this class, combined with the fact the textbook was so expensive, especially to a broke college student, I wanted to believe every word in it. It was a no-brainer. I felt as though I were holding the keys to human knowledge. I had set the stage for confirmation bias, making me more vulnerable to the suggestions in this book because of the value I had placed on it as well as the class in general. This is dangerous territory, especially for a young mind.

After the professor passed out the syllabus, he went over his attendance policy, grading scale, etc., and proceeded to tell us our very first assignment. With pen in hand, I hung on his every word. Our very first assignment was to choose from a list of "pseudoarchaeologists" provided by the professor. Once we made our selection, our task would be debunking them. As my eyes worked over the list, my exuberance gave way to embarrassment. I recognized some of the names as researchers and authors who had been an inspiration to me. While I didn't subscribe to all of their theories individually, there were a few authors with whom I did agree. I did not know what to do or whom to pick. I selected an author I didn't recognize. I did the best I could considering my surprise, and I was still excited to see how this would develop. After all, college is supposed to be about challenging your thinking, right?

The next day, we went over our work, and for the next week, we continued to debunk fringe theorists. At one point, someone in the course complained because they wanted to get right to learning excavation methods. The professor told them that they always start new archaeologists' training by teaching them how to debunk first. What came as a shock to me, however, was not so much the exercise in debate or critical thinking, but rather the reason he gave for this teaching method. The professor clarified his position by stating that if professional archaeologists do not make it a point to consistently debunk "amateur" or "armchair" archaeologists, then they put their own jobs at risk. He likened it to a labor union or guild, stating that we must all stick together for the good of the industry, explaining that this is why we use "academese" when writing.

Have you ever wondered why academic papers are so dry and, dare I say, boring? It is by design. Academese is a way to separate us (the academics) from you (the general public). According to the dictionary definition of *academese*, "it is the learned and often dry style and diction of an academic or scholar. It is pedantic, pretentious, and often confusing academic jargon" (*Dictionary.com*). The example given is "Chieftaincy as a sanctional source, a symbolic referent, an integrational integer, and for ethnic and sub-ethnic definition, represents an orientational base for the charismatic." How engaging is that sentence? Not very, I'm afraid. I won't dare insult your intelligence and presume that the average reader cannot understand academese, because this is not true. You can take a report written in this style word by word, study it closely, and understand what it is communicating. That is not the point. The point is that it is not *engaging*. A lack of engagement creates a barrier to interest and therefore accessibility.

This is how earth-shattering scientific information can be published without the public knowing. It is all hidden in plain sight. Some of the other barriers to public access to historical and scientific information are in the publication distribution itself. In order to access many of the important scholarly articles available, you have to be able to get on at least one of many academic databases, which are subscription-based and very expensive. Academics, students, and alumni have access to these databases through their university affiliation. This takes published information out of reach for many people. The good news is that you can get on some of these exclusive databases at your local public library, but not everyone knows this. How would they? Where is it advertised? It's not. Academics working in the educational industrial complex want you to trust them and no one else. They actively try to dissuade their students from exploring innovative ideas.

My personal experience in that first archaeology class was indeed eye-opening. It motivated me to keep pursuing alternative theories, likely because of how taboo they were. (I've always been a renegade.) There were times throughout my academic journey when I inevitably became discouraged, wondering what it was all for. One of these times, I decided to contact one of my favorite alternative researchers, Michael Cremo, author of the book *Forbidden Archaeology*, whom I previously mentioned with regard to the Knowledge Filter. I was pleasantly surprised when he responded to my question. I had explained some of my experiences to him and asked if I should just drop out and pursue alternative research instead. His response set me on the course I am currently charting. His sage advice was that I had two paths before me. If I stayed in academia, I could make an impact by pushing the envelope, but it would only be little by little. If I left, I could reach more people, but I would lose credibility and still not change the academic landscape. He encouraged me not to give up.

After this, I decided to remain in college as a renegade and sort of a double agent. I vowed that I would learn all that I could and then apply the methods to my independent study. I am forever grateful to Michael Cremo. I had the pleasure of meeting him for lunch when we were at a conference together some years ago. It was like coming full circle. I owe a lot to this great forbidden archaeologist and researcher, a man whose name was listed on my old professor's class syllabus as a "pseudoarchaeologist." It wouldn't be long after leaving the academy that I would discover the Anunnaki connection and how deep the cover-up went. This discovery led me down the path of my own initiation; from naive greenhorn to battle-hardened soldier in the war to save history.

Sumer, Suppressed

In March of 2013, I received an email from a gentleman claiming to have knowledge of a new discovery near the ancient Mesopotamian city of Ur. After confirming the story, I found that there indeed were new excavations underway in a lesser-known site called Tell Khaiber. This was an amazing prospect, considering that the area has been off limits to researchers because of the political climate in modern-day Iraq. Until recently, archaeologists have avoided Ur and the surrounding sites for security reasons. Only a handful of groups like the Global Heritage Fund (GHF), an NGO based in California, have traveled to the area. Over the past thirty years, the region has succumbed to wars and violence. After the 1950s revolution that toppled Iraq's monarchy, a military air base was installed nearby, taking the site off limits to foreign archaeologists for sixty years.

While the U.S. invasion in 2003 removed Saddam Hussein from power, Baghdad's struggling government and economy

were forced to deal with greater priorities than funding archaeological excavations. Iraqis had to focus on rebuilding their
current cities, rather than resurrecting cities from their past.
Thus, the new excavations were both surprising and exciting. These were the first foreign excavations in southern Iraq
since the 1930s, when a British and American team, led by Sir
Charles Leonard Woolley, son of George Herbert Woolley,
excavated Ur in the 1920s and '30s. Woolley's work resulted
in some of the most important discoveries of modern time, as
we've discussed in the previous chapter.

With the importance of Ur, and the understanding of how
limited further research has been, it is easy to see why when
satellite images showed the presence of a large templelike
structure in the area, researchers jumped at the opportunity.
The excavation of the site officially broke ground in March
of 2013, as a joint collaboration between British and Iraqi
teams. A six-member British team worked with four Iraqis to
dig in the southern province of Thi Qar, some two hundred
miles south of Baghdad and more than ten miles from Ur.
This site is the first major archaeological discovery so close to
the city's center.

Three weeks of work on location confirmed the presence of
at least one monumental building. Satellite images showed it
to be square and to measure at least 250 feet on a side. There
are rows of rooms encircling a grand courtyard. The rooms
excavated along the eastern side of the building have solid
pavements of regular mud bricks. The walls are nine feet thick,
indicating that whatever was behind them was of immense
importance. One large hall has a series of beautifully decorated
floors further pointing to this being a sacred site.

Such a monumental complex is an uncommon discovery.
It is extremely unusual to find complexes this old on such a

massive scale. Early theories were that it was a temple, palace, or "administrative center," dating back at least four thousand years. The structure isn't the only interesting discovery here, though. Some of the early artifacts reported were a 3½-inch clay plaque depicting a worshipper dressed in a long-fringed robe along with assorted pottery shards. Fragments of vessels made from stone and also a piece of ivory were excavated as well, along with various tools of copper and stone. The archaeologists found a rim fragment from a once-magnificent alabaster bowl and not one, but two molded clay plaques showing a male worshipper and a female figure, respectively. Perhaps shockingly, human remains were found, too. The shallow grave of an infant buried just under the surface was uncovered. Its body had been placed in a pottery jar, which was then laid on its side.

Among the discoveries, tablets were also unearthed, some just lying right on what had been the ground. This is rather astonishing, since unbaked clay is very fragile. The tablets were sent for analysis, but early hints of what they said were a partial list of men's names, along with their father's names, which indicates a record of patriarchal lineage and, possibly, elite bloodlines. Perhaps this is another King List? Amazingly, one small piece of a tablet mentions orchards and gardens, like those in the Garden of Eden. Another tablet fragment referenced the city's governor, leading us to theorize that the settlement at Tell Khaiber was at least significant enough to have a governor. The administrative center idea has emerged as the leading theory.

In addition to the pottery, tablets, and bodies, a mysterious item made from rare and expensive diorite was uncovered, baffling archaeologists. Diorite is a gray rock that is relatively rare and extremely hard, making it notoriously difficult to work with. It is so hard that ancient civilizations used diorite balls to work granite. The use of diorite in art was important in Mesopotamian empires as well as both the Inca and Mayan civilizations, which utilized diorite in their fortress walls and weaponry—a testament to its strength. Theories for what this artifact is have ranged from a recycled chip from a larger relic to a game piece. No one knows for sure. Other objects include a diverse variety of tools, such as large grindstones, spindles, flint sickle fragments, pounders and grinders made from imported stone, and copper weapons. This shows that numerous economic activities took place in this administrative center, leading to great wealth.

Perhaps one of the more interesting discoveries is a statue depicting the Mesopotamian goddess of healing, Gula, also known as Ninkarrak. Could this mean that the administrative center is actually a healing center? Before we can begin to answer this question, it is important for us to first look at who the goddess Ninkarrak was, and why she was so important.

Like most ancient gods, Ninkarrak was known by many different names through different periods of rulership: Gula, Ninisinna, Bau, or Baba. Much later, she would be syncretized with Ishtar. In addition to having different names, Ninkarrak held different titles, including "The Lady Who Makes the Broken Up Whole Again," "The Great Healer of the Black-headed Ones," "Herb Grower," and "Creates Life in the Land." All these titles are indicative of a vegetation goddess with regenerative power. In fact, she is credited as having "breathed life" back into humankind after the Great Flood. Ninkarrak not only represented healing, gardens, and the creation of life, she also represented gateways. As the protector of boundaries, her image was frequently depicted on *kudurrus*, or boundary stones.

Ninkarrak was the daughter of Anu and wife of the warrior god Pabilsag (in Isin), Ninurta (in Nippur), and Ningirsu (in Lagaš), and mother of three other healing deities: Damu, Ninazu, and Gunurra. This revered healing goddess had many cult centers, including Nippur, Umma, Lagaš, Larsa, Uruk, Borsippa, Babylon, and Assur, but the most prominent cult center was Isin, where her temple was named "Dog Temple." In her temple in Isin, there were over thirty dog burials discovered, as well as many dog figurines. Although different theories abound, archaeologists are still unsure of why she was associated with the dog. My personal thoughts on this is that it somehow relates to the star Sirius, also known as "The Dog Star."

Considering how Ninkarrak would eventually be seen as Ishtar—who would later be associated with Isis by the Egyptians—a comparative analysis of their iconography yields interesting connections. Firstly, Ishtar's main icons are the lion and the bull, or the constellations Leo and Taurus. In Babylonian creation myths, the constellation Leo was not known as a feline, but rather "The Big Dog." Just as gods were syncretized, often so were zodiacal symbols.

Moreover, ancient Sumerian texts sometimes refer to the lion as *Mul Ur-Gu-la*, which translated means "a great carnivore" (Gula, the goddess, also means "great"). This term is broad and has been used interchangeably to mean lion, dog, wolf, etc. Lastly, the bright star in Leo's chest was known by the Babylonians as Regulus, meaning "royal star." It was believed the elites born under this star would have victory and ultimate power over the people on Earth.

Every year there is an important alignment of Sirius and Leo, leading some to consider this a time of spiritual healing wherein souls are initiated into higher realms of consciousness. Historically, the Dog Star and Leo are calendrically combined, as they rise together and are intrinsically linked (Malina and Pilch, 2000).

Reverence of certain astronomical alignments of Leo, Taurus, and Sirius did not end with the Sumerians. Researchers in the field of alternative archaeology Graham Hancock and Robert Bauval have proposed an idea about the relationship between both Leo and Taurus and the design of the Giza Plateau. They postulate that the Great Pyramid has concavity to its faces. This concavity causes the north face of the pyramid to reflect sunlight in between two specific areas during the year when the sun is over the Great Pyramid at noon. These two points of light correspond with the position of the sun in the signs Leo and Taurus in the tropical Zodiac (Hancock and Bauval, 1997).

After excavating some of the site, the archaeologists used a gradiometer to measure the site's magnetic field. A gradiometer is a special type of magnetometer with multiple sensors: one closer to the ground to collect magnetic data about the surface and the other above the first sensor to collect information about the Earth's magnetic field. An archaeologist would then subtract one reading from the other, essentially filtering out the noise from the Earth's magnetic field and allowing subtle features of archaeological interest to be detected. In theory, the gradiometer could record magnetic differences between the walls and rooms of the complex without disturbing the deposits underneath. This way, they could locate any other possible buildings. As of 2013, the site's magnetic field is actively being researched and recorded.

Excavations resumed at Tell Khaiber on January 12, 2014, with a larger team than before. This time, eleven British archaeologists worked in the field for nearly three months. As they continued to excavate the primary structure, they learned just how significant this discovery is, describing it as having remarkable symmetry and "a ground plan with no known parallels" (Campbell, Killick, and Moon, 2014). Thus, it will come as even more of a surprise to learn that when they went back, they found a second building just a short distance away from the administrative center. Although little is yet known about this new building, one thing looks to be true; this area has the potential to become the Sumerian version of the Giza Plateau.

Along with this newly discovered building, fourteen clay tablets were excavated with more still in situ. Many of these tablets are administrative documents like receipts and records of sales, most of which discuss grains. Some are short notes, while others are much longer and more complex ledgers. These financial records were housed in one designated room of the building. Another room contained numerous models made from clay. These models depicted unidentified wheeled vehicles, human figures, and mysterious three-dimensionally shaped objects. As if these weren't strange enough, in the north section of the building, the archaeologists were surprised to find an eye, made from what they believe to be an early form of glass.

Artifacts were not the only things uncovered. Just as in 2013, a body was found buried in pottery. This time, it was not of an infant, but rather a woman in her late twenties. She was placed in a pair of large pottery jars and then buried in the corner of a room. Around her neck dangled a magnificent necklace comprised of more than fifty imported semiprecious stones. She also wore two beautifully fashioned pins, denoting her relative wealth and status. Who was this woman, and why was she buried in the corner? The mystery remains unsolved. Samples of collagen were taken and sent to the University of Liverpool for DNA analysis. Perhaps more will be revealed after the results come in. If so, they will assuredly be buried in the AP newswire. Aside from additional pottery, statues, and tablets, one artifact stood out, as it had the archaeologists "completely stumped" (URAP Report, 2013). It is a cylindrical piece made from pottery, standing about 17¾ inches high. The piece is sealed at both ends. However, it has three little circular notches in descending order around the middle section of one side.

Only a select few of these unique discoveries were mentioned in a standard press release. Upon learning the details, I immediately contacted the university involved with questions. After the project director granted me an interview, I was later given the cold shoulder and was unable to maintain meaningful contact moving forward. As a result, I decided to investigate the financial supporters of this excavation. This led me to discover a tangled web of big oil, global banks, elite industrialist families, secret societies, U.S. presidents, and Nazis—yes, Nazis. As they say, "follow the money."

Owning the Past

"I certainly did not know that you could actually buy museum-quality antiquities!" said Baron Lorne Thyssen, in an interview with *Apollo Magazine*, May 11, 2014. The wealthy donor to the new excavations near Ur is a notorious collector of ancient art and heir to one of the richest families in the world. The Thyssen family owns the world's largest and most valuable private collection of ancient relics, rivaled only by that of Queen Elizabeth.

As if it weren't enough for Baron Lorne Thyssen to amass a huge private collection, he is now in the business of selling these artifacts. He opened a retail front in London devoted to Greek antiquities. I'm sure you are wondering how this is even legal. When you are part of the 1 percent, it appears you are above the law. Perhaps it is his lineage that gives him this sense of entitlement. The Thyssens are one of the elite bloodlines who may actually believe they can trace their lineage to ancient Mesopotamia. Thyssen family members have made their home in various countries and spread in a corporate imperialist fashion, much like the Rothschild banking family. The Thyssen family has many notable members, all of whom descend from Friedrich Thyssen, who established steelworks, elevators, escalators, industrial conglomerates, banks, and massive art collections.

Fritz Thyssen was eventually arrested for refusing to accede to the demands of French authorities occupying the Ruhr. In 1921, the German government charged him with betraying the Ruhr district to the French during the war. It was Fritz who funded the newly formed Nazi Party with $25,000, which was a significant amount of money in the mid-1920s. In 1931, Fritz Thyssen joined the Nazi Party and soon became close friends with Adolf Hitler. He continued to use his offshore banks to pump money into the Nazi war machine. Over the years, Thyssen came to be known as "Hitler's most important and prominent financier" (Rogers, 2002). When asked about Hitler, Thyssen was actually quoted as saying, "I realized his orator gifts and his ability to lead the masses. What impressed me most, however, was the order that reigned over his meetings, the almost military discipline of his followers" (Neumann, 2013). Thyssen also persuaded the Association of German Industrialists to donate three million reichsmarks to the Nazi Party for the 1933 Reichstag election. As a payback, he was in turn elected a Nazi member of the Reichstag and appointed to the Prussian State Council, the largest German state.

After World War II, Thyssen was tried as a Nazi supporter, which he did not deny, admitting his support for the exclusion of Jews from German businesses and mistreatment of his own Jewish employees in the 1930s. As I detail in my 2013 report *The Sumerian Controversy*, Prescott Sheldon Bush (Member of "The Order" 1917), father of George Herbert Walker Bush, was a business partner of Fritz Thyssen (Lynn, 2013). Big oil, big banks, fraternal orders—they all have a place in this story. Yet, the question remains: why are they really funding archaeological excavations?

History belongs to 100 percent of us. It is not the domain of only the 1 percent. Archaeology can be a valuable tool of influence. If this were not the case, ISIS would not have destroyed or vandalized ancient World Heritage sites, nor would they have murdered scholars. Archaeological discoveries are sources of national pride and have the power to unify populations. As Orwell said, "He who controls the past controls the future. He who controls the present controls the past." If you systematically erase the past, you can control the future by filling in the blanks with whatever you want people to believe. This is the weaponization of history. Corporate elites are routinely purchasing and stealing the cultural heritage of vulnerable populations. Don't be fooled if some of these artifacts do end up in exhibits. The scholars who are permitted to examine them are a select few from an approved network. Remember, though, the researchers themselves are part of the problem, as they are cogs in the machine, but the real problem lies in the unseen hands that guide the machine. The best way uncover who these hidden hands belong to is to follow

Sumerian Tablets Stored in a Museum.

the money to find out who is funding exhibits. In some cases when history is under attack, it is a case not of who funded the museum but rather who defunded it.

Another filter, though likely unintentional, is that funding for jobs is limited for historical research. There are simply not enough historians and archaeologists with the necessary skills and qualifications to decipher tablets and other artifacts. As a result, there are countless Sumerian cuneiform tablets stashed in the basement archives of museums, like the ones shown here. These tablets are made from delicate clay that is in a constant state of disintegration. The time to decipher these is running out.

Destroying the Past

As discussed in chapter 3, Sumerian elites believed they were able to channel beings whom they called "antediluvian sages"

(Lenzi, 2013). Over many thousands of years, the *nişirtu*, the treasured secret of Enki, was kept and passed down through the mystery schools where elite scribal scholars recorded and translated the knowledge over and over. Eventually, these texts would be housed in great libraries, like the Royal Library of Ashurbanipal, where they would make their way to seekers and magicians throughout the ancient world and beyond.

Persian lore recounts that Alexander the Great had such a deep admiration for the Royal Library of Ashurbanipal at Nineveh that he made it his life's goal to build one just as grand, if not grander. This eventually led to the construction of the Library of Alexandria. So why was Ashurbanipal's library so awe-inspiring? The Royal Library of Ashurbanipal contained thousands of clay tablets (mostly fragments) with various texts dating as far back as the seventh century BCE, including the famous poem the Epic of Gilgamesh. The English traveler Sir Austen Henry Layard unearthed many tablet fragments that told variations of the Babylonian legends of the Deluge and of the Creation. The texts on fragments of the First and Fifth Tablets of Creation describe the fight between the "Gods and Chaos." The third tablet described the "Fall of Man."

Scholars are still trying to decipher all that was found at the site because those who handled the original artifacts left them a scattered mess. Fragments of tablets now sit in museum archives like puzzle pieces in an eight-year-old's bedroom. There is no telling what more we have to learn from these rare documents. Could some unexamined texts still hold the key to understanding human origins? Will we ever know, or is the quest for such answers still the domain of an elite group of academics fighting for what Indiana Jones, archaeologist in the classic Spielberg film franchise, called "fortune and glory"?

The Dirty Business of Archaeology

Amazing discoveries happen sometimes as if by accident. In 1846, Layard traveled to the East. He had always been attracted to countries with warm climates, and the opportunity to unearth an ancient city lured him to Mesopotamia. Although he was neither a historian nor an archaeologist, he found his way to the capital of the Assyrian kingdom: Nineveh. It had sat for nearly three thousand years, waiting to be opened. Layard is celebrated as an archaeological hero since his discovery. However, a lot of the credit should go to an Ottoman archaeologist, Hormuzd Rassam, who helped to uncover the site in 1854. Before looking at the content of the Library of Ashurbanipal, let's first look at a hidden truth about the discovery of this legendary site.

The life of Hormuzd Rassam (1826–1910) shows some dark sides of British imperialism in the nineteenth century and, indeed, archaeology, which were present even for those who warmly embraced Great Britain and her imperial mission. Rassam was born in 1826 in Mosul, part of the Mesopotamian province in the Ottoman Empire, which is now northern Iraq. He was the eighth and last child of Antun and Theresa Rassam, who originally worked as designers of a type of fabric that owes its name to the city of Mosul: mousseline, or muslin.

Rassam's parents were members of the Chaldean Catholic Church and the Assyrian Church of the East. The Chaldean Catholic Church split from the Assyrian Church of the East before 1800 and then became part of the Catholic Church, in contrast to its "mother church." Rassam's father was even archdeacon of the Assyrian church of the East in Mosul. Because of their faith and Assyrian ethnicity, the family was in the minority in Ottoman Mesopotamia. Thanks to increasing British intervention in this area during the beginning of the nineteenth century, this minority position could be exploited by the Rassams. The British saw the members of the many different Christian churches in Mesopotamia as religiously "purer" than the western Catholic Church and felt connected to them as a Protestant nation.

In these years, Hormuzd Rassam learned English from Maria Badger and also converted to the Church of England. His faith would later play an important role in his archaeology, as he saw it as a means to confirm the historical authenticity of the Bible. Connected to Rassam's conversion to Protestantism was the awakening of his fanatical love for Great Britain. Due to the strategic position of Mesopotamia as a route to the important colony of India, Great Britain was more and more interested in the area. To Rassam, the British were the protectors of the pure Christian faith in Mesopotamia and stood in stark contrast to what he viewed as the corrupt Muslim rulers of the Ottoman Empire. The British were also in a strong rivalry with the Catholic French, who also sought influence in the area.

In 1842 he met Sir Austen Henry Layard, who had become fascinated by the history of the area as a traveler in Mesopotamia. The two established a close relationship. Three years later, Layard returned to excavate hills that were relics of Babylonian and Assyrian cities like Nineveh and Nimrud, near Mosul. He had not forgotten Rassam and employed him as secretary, supervisor, and site manager. Rassam had a great insight into the relations between and use of the local tribes and could speak many languages. From October 1845 to June 1847 Rassam was employed by Layard, until he returned to

Great Britain. In September 1849 Layard went back to Mosul again, accompanied by Rassam. Here they would dig until the spring of 1851.

For various reasons Layard did not return to Mesopotamia after this second campaign, but he focused on a political and, later, diplomatic career. The British Museum, which wanted to continue the Mesopotamian excavations, put Rassam in charge of the dig in Layard's place. This was the opportunity for Rassam to develop as an independent archaeologist. During his time working independently, Rassam discovered many important sites and artifacts, including a temple in Nineveh dedicated to Ishtar (the goddess of love and war) and in Nimrud a temple dedicated to Nabu (the god of writing), in addition to a lot of other sculptures.

Perhaps his greatest discovery in these months took place on the hill of Kuyunjik, which had been shared by the British and French since the beginning of the excavations. Already during Layard's years at Kuyunjik, the French had apparently already given up "their" part of the hill. Rassam suspected that this part would still yield important finds. He later discovered a palace that had belonged to the last Assyrian kings. The most famous remnants of these are the reliefs with the lion hunt of King Ashurbanipal, partly still on display at the British Museum. Another section unfortunately ended up in the Tigris during transport.

In 1854, Rassam paused his archaeological quests and exchanged them for a number of posts in the colonial and diplomatic services. Initially he was employed as a translator by James Outram (1803–1863), a British political agent in Aden, in the current Yemen. There, he was quickly promoted to the first assistant of Outram and also appointed magistrate, as which he was responsible for the postal service, waterworks, and municipal buildings in the area. His talent for local diplomacy led him to be selected for the diplomatic mission that was to deliver a letter from Queen Victoria to the Ethiopian emperor Tewodros II (Theodore II, 1818–1868). The emperor held a number of leading Europeans imprisoned in Ethiopia, including the British consul, and the letter asked for their release.

After a considerable delay due to diplomatic jockeying, Rassam and his company were allowed to enter Ethiopia at the end of 1865. In January 1866 he delivered the letter to an at-first benevolent emperor. Unfortunately for Rassam the emperor changed his mind, and in April 1866 he had the whole company, including Rassam, picked up again. They were finally rescued in April 1868 by British troops out of India.

In the meantime, archaeology had not stood still. In particular, the deciphering of the cuneiform script had made a leap, and a discovery of a primitive version of the Bible story of the Flood had fueled European public interest in the Mesopotamian past. Rassam's second expedition had a false start due to difficulties in obtaining a permit from the Turkish government. This changed in 1877 when his old friend Layard, now an important diplomat, became the British ambassador in Constantinople (Istanbul). In the five years that followed, he set up a large number of excavations led by supervisors whom he trusted.

Rassam worked in the customary manner for the time: he had local workers dig and followed the walls he found. He judged valuable objects that he found on the spot: the pieces that were "scientifically interesting" were packed and sent to Great Britain, while the others were handed over to the local authorities. When he found some sixty to seventy thousand unbaked clay tablets with cuneiform, he baked them on the spot to preserve them.

This does not mean that he was not often mistrusted by local authorities. When he found a monumental bronze (door) threshold, rumors immediately broke out that it was solid gold. Under armed surveillance, a committee of local goldsmiths established that the metal was indeed bronze, but it was long rumored that Rassam had appropriated a golden threshold.

Among his most important finds in these years were a wide variety of cylinders with cuneiform inscriptions. The best known is the so-called Cyrus Cylinder, which records how the Persian king Cyrus the Great conquered the new Babylonian empire in 539 BCE and subsequently freed the Jews. In addition, Rassam discovered a large number of temples and believed he had found the location of the Hanging Gardens of Babylon. He is also credited with finding the famous Epic of Gilgamesh.

In 1882 Rassam would definitively settle in Great Britain—in the south English coastal town of Brighton, to be precise. He had seven children with his wife, one of whom would become a professional opera singer. Rassam died on September 8, 1910, and was buried at the cemetery of Hove, a small town next to Brighton. The manuscript for his autobiography has unfortunately been lost.

But even before he passed away, Rassam had already been discredited by several British colleagues and, as is clear from the incident with the bronze threshold, he was mistrusted by the inhabitants of Mesopotamia. A few years after Rassam's discovery of the palace of Ashurbanipal, George Rawlinson (1812–1902) attributed the discovery to his own brother Henry. Brother George would also wrongly attribute the deciphering of the cuneiform script to Henry. Instead of defending Rassam, Henry agreed that Rassam had been merely a simple worker at the dig. In addition, Rassam always had very limited financial resources for his excavations. While Layard was able to include another artist for archaeological drawings and reconstructions in his first, barely funded expedition, Rassam was on his own.

The worst blow to Rassam's image, however, would come in 1893. While he was already publicly associated with the fiasco of his Ethiopian mission despite the government praising his conduct in the matter, Wallis Budge (1857–1934), curator at the British Museum, began to spread rumors about Rassam. According to Budge, Rassam had deprived Great Britain during his excavations in Mesopotamia by settling the most important and best pieces with his relatives and sending only rubbish to the British Museum. Rassam sued him for libel and won, partly supported by prominent archaeologists such as Layard. However, the damage to his reputation had already been done. The discoverer of the Epic of Gilgamesh and countless temples and palace complexes fell into oblivion in an obscure end for an archaeologist who deserved better, in his own time and after.

One of Rassam and Layard's most important discoveries was the Royal Library of Ashurbanipal, located in Nineveh (modern-day Iraq). It was named after Ashurbanipal (668–627 BCE), the last great king of the Neo-Assyrian Empire. His name means "the god of Assyria is the creator of an heir" and he was the son of King Esarhaddon of the Neo-Assyrian Empire. In the Old Testament, he is called Asenappar (Ezra 4:10), while the Greeks knew him as Sardanapolos and the Romans as Sardanapulus. His reign saw the greatest territorial expansion of the Assyrian Empire, including Babylonia,

Persia, Syria, and Egypt—although Egypt was lost as a result of an uprising under the reign of Pharaoh Psammetichus I.

Ashurbanipal was a popular king who ruled over free citizens, but he was known for his cruelty to those whom he defeated in battle. The best known example is a relief depicting a defeated king wearing a dog chain and forced to live in a kennel after capture. Under the Ashurbanipal regime, the land of Elam, which had long been an invincible enemy of Assyria, was destroyed and Urartu, another experienced opponent, was dominated. However, toward the end, the Assyrian Empire had grown too large and was already crumbling.

What Was in the Library?

Among the ruins of the palace of Ashurbanipal, Layard and Rassam found several rooms with thousands of cuneiform tablets. (Scientists estimated that about thirty thousand clay tablets were kept in the library!) When the city later perished under the onslaught of Median and Babylonian warriors, the clay books in the ruinous Nineveh were burned, and so tempered and thus preserved. But many, unfortunately, broke into pieces. Carefully packed in boxes, these clay books were sent to London, where it took researchers thirty years to study and translate them into modern language.

The legendary library of King Ashurbanipal kept invaluable information about the culture of Sumer and Akkad. The tablets told the world that the wise mathematicians of Babylon knew not only four arithmetic operations—they could calculate percentages, measure geometric area, determine squaring and square root extraction, and perform sophisticated multiplication exercises with their own ancient table. In addition, our seven-day week was born in Mesopotamia. Babylonian scholars even laid the foundations of modern science based upon the structure and development of celestial bodies.

It was the Assyrians who could claim the title of the first printers. After all, for state and economic needs, it was necessary to write, rewrite, and send out a number of royal decrees to all the ends of the great Assyrian state! And to speed up the process, the Assyrians cut out the necessary inscriptions on a wooden board, and then made impressions on clay tablets. In this we have a prototype of a printing press.

It is interesting that in the Library of Ashurbanipal, books were kept in strict order. At the bottom of each table, the full title of the book was indicated, and next to it was the page number. In many tablets, each last line was repeated at the beginning of the next table. There was even a catalogue in which the title of the book was recorded, the number of lines, and the branch of knowledge to which the book belonged. Finding the necessary record was not difficult: each shelf had a clay tag with the name of the department, just like in a modern library.

The library kept historical texts, scrolls of laws, medical reference books, travel descriptions, dictionaries with lists of Sumerian syllabic signs and grammatical forms, and even dictionaries of foreign words. Assyria was associated with almost all the countries of the Near East. All the tablets of the Library of Ashurbanipal were made of the highest-quality clay. At first, the clay was kneaded for a long time, and then it was made into uniformly sized plates, measuring roughly thirty-two centimeters wide by twenty-two centimeters long by two and a half centimeters thick. When the workpiece was ready, the scribe wrote with a triangular stylus on the unbaked tablet.

Some of the books in the Library of Ashurbanipal came from countries defeated by Assyria and some from the temples of other cities or from private individuals. After all, once books appeared, book lovers did also. King Ashurbanipal, a truly rare case among the rulers of the ancient Near East, was considered the most educated person in his time. His father Asarhaddon wanted to see his son as high priest, and therefore young Ashurbanipal studied all the sciences of that time. As a result of this upbringing, he had a love of books, so he took several rooms on the second floor of his palace and transformed them into a library.

It is noteworthy that almost all the tablets of the Library of Ashurbanipal are either copies of the Sumerian-Babylonian texts or ancient tablets from the state and temple archives. By order of the king in all corners of his vast state, numerous scribes made copies of literary monuments. With great diligence, many of the tablets displayed an inscription confirming the identity of the copy and the original, since the ancient script was written down and then verified. Ashurbanipal tirelessly took care of replenishing his collection, ordering, "Any precious tablets that are not in Ashur, find and deliver to me."

The book depository of Ashurbanipal resembled huge wine cellars. On long benches there were rows of clay vessels, and in them book tablets. Many library shelves were also made of clay, since in Mesopotamia trees barely grew and wood was very expensive. On other benches there were smaller vessels, and in them autographed royal records of military campaigns, decrees and letters, and lists of the kings who had ruled in Mesopotamia. In the smallest vessels were songs of the ancient Sumerians, collections of proverbs, laments, and hymns to the gods.

In the last ten years of Ashurbanipal's reign, the scribes of Nineveh stopped writing the annals of the great king. To date, no king of Assyria and no known Mesopotamian sovereign has had so much inscribed about his military campaigns and his memorable actions and intellectual training. It was written that Ashurbanipal possessed the ability to decipher the hidden secret of all the art of the scribe, the celestial and terrestrial signs, and to read the writing of the stones of before the Flood, including the subtle tablets in Sumerian. This was key.

Ashurbanipal could not only read and write, he also knew Sumerian, a language dead for fifteen centuries, which remained liturgical and was used primarily for scientific descriptions throughout Mesopotamia, much the way Latin later functioned across Europe in medieval times as the language of the elites and intellectuals. All this was to disappear from all memory for thousands of years after the fall of the Assyrian Empire in 610 BCE. After years of speculating and searching, the library was finally found in 1847 on the eastern bank of the Tigris, facing the modern city of Mosul.

Iraqi Museum Looting

Founded in 1923, the Iraq National Museum had a challenging past. It was moved to its present location in 1966 and was enlarged in 1986. The museum had nearly 10,000 artifacts from prehistoric through Islamic periods on public display. This huge number accounted for less than 5 percent of the museum's total holdings. This was before the 1990–91 Gulf War. While the exterior structure of the museum was damaged in bombings during the war, its many thousands of cultural treasures survived unharmed, thanks to a devoted staff. In the years that followed the war, the museum acquired many new pieces leading up to the 2003 Iraq War, when many artifacts were moved from Iraq's regional museum for safekeeping.

In March 2003, the museum closed to the public. Most of the objects in the public galleries were moved to safe storage. The location of these important artifacts was known only to five staff members, all of whom swore on the Qur'an not to reveal it. However, not all of the objects could be moved, so larger artifacts were protected with foam rubber pads. In addition to securing the artifacts, staff members contemplated sealing the museum entrances with bricks, but they decided not to so that in case of a fire, emergency services could get in.

After the Gulf War, U.S. forces had been criticized for damaging archaeological sites in Iraq. As a result, McGuire Gibson of the Oriental Institute at the University of Chicago accompanied a delegation from the American Council for Cultural Policy to the Department of Defense to provide locations of four thousand—and later five thousand—archaeological sites that should be protected from military action in the event of war (Bogdanos, 2005). Gibson also warned that there would be looting. According to the DoD, U.S. troops were under orders not to damage archaeological and cultural sites. However, the DoD added that they would not intervene if Iraqi civilians started looting.

The account of what happened next is the official story. It seems that on March 19, 2003, coalition forces invaded Iraq and by April 5 they had reached the outskirts of Baghdad (Bogdanos, 2005). At the same time, the security guards evacuated the museum. Three days later, on April 8, Iraqi troops arrived at the museum grounds. Even in the official story, there is a disagreement over who these troops were. Some say they were irregular Fedayeen, while others say regular Republican Guard (Bogdanos, 2005). At any rate, the Iraqi forces around the museum were engaged in two days of heavy fighting with U.S. troops. Then, a few days later on Thursday, April 10, fighting continued outside while thieves had their run of the museum. They freely took what they wanted until chased off by the museum staff when they returned on April 12. At this time, the fighting had died down, so the museum staff put up a large sign that warned looters that the museum was under the protection of the U.S. military. This was not really the case until four days later on April 16, when four U.S. tanks arrived on the scene.

Rumors started circulating both at home and abroad. They suggested that the U.S. troops had purposely not secured the museum so that wealthy elite and politically influential antiquities collectors could "shop" for what they wanted. They also accused some of the U.S. troops of helping to collect these artifacts. Many artifacts were taken, as if by order. Some artifacts were left behind, even ones that could have been sold in lucrative deals. It was widely reported that the looters came in and knew the locations of very specific artifacts, many of which were not on public display but still targeted with precision. Additionally, offices and labs of the museums were thoroughly ransacked. Technical and computing equipment was also stolen, and safes were emptied.

Of the stolen artifacts were forty of the best quality pieces, "clearly by someone who recognised their significance" (Bogdanos, 2005, 213). Many of the most important artifacts had been gathered together in advance and put in the museum's restoration room, as if the entire thing had been planned (Bogdanos, 2005, 214–15). This would have made them much easier to remove from the premises. In addition, these artifacts were so important and immediately recognizable that they simply could not have been successfully sold on the open market. This made experts like Colonel Matthew Bogdanos take notice. Bogdanos is current assistant district attorney in Manhattan (since 1988) and a colonel in the U.S. Marine Corps Reserves. In 2003 he was on active duty and led an investigation into the looting of the museum. After looking at the evidence, Bogdanos believed that this premeditation and understanding of what artifacts to take implied that there were already buyers in place for the artifacts before the theft (Bogdanos, 2005, 215). At least 3,138 artifacts were stolen from restoration and above-ground storage rooms.

In addition to the main restoration room thefts, Bogdanos identified one other as most likely also preplanned. Out of four storerooms in the basement, looters went directly to the one containing the museum's collection of coins, jewelry, and cylinder seals. The thieves appeared to know in advance exactly what they were looking for and exactly where to find it. Further, the thieves were well equipped with the keys needed to open the storage lockers, allowing them to make off with 10,686 items, including 5,144 cylinder seals (Bogdanos, 2005). Imagine the information on over five thousand cylinder seals! This was a devastating loss to all of human history, not just Iraq's. What were the thieves looking for? I hesitate to call them looters because looting implies someone opportunistically stealing at random. This was not the case: this was an orchestrated attack on one of the most culturally rich historical locations in the entire world on behalf of wealthy elites.

It is easy for mainstream scholars and pundits to scoff at the idea of people stealing artifacts or that governments could be involved in doing so. No matter how hard the mainstream media or academic industrial complex tries to convince the public that there is really nothing interesting happening and that they should just take their word for it and move along, people are still beginning to see it for what it really was: identity theft. Through the theft, corruption, and distortion of artifacts and the historic narrative, the powers that be take with them our cultural identity, leaving us to wander deeper into the dark, wondering: Who are we? What are we? Where do we come from? And why are we here? Sadly, history is filled with destruction and lost wisdom: from the earliest library in ancient Mesopotamia to perhaps the greatest known library at Alexandria to the most recent as late as 2018, when in a single incident, the world lost more artifacts than those lost in Alexandria and Iraq combined!

A Modern Catastrophe

On September 2, 2018, at around 7:30 p.m., the world lost more history than in the Library of Alexandria and the Library of Ashurbanipal combined in the single greatest historical losses ever recorded. The 200-year-old National Museum of Brazil went up in flames and burned to the ground, and with it over twenty million artifacts spanning 11,000 years of not only Brazilian history, but also Egyptian, Greco-Roman, paleontological, geological, and biological. This tragedy is much more massive in terms of number of artifacts than even the burning of the Library of Alexandria, yet it has barely received any media attention, especially outside of Brazil.

I'm sure this sounds implausible because the burning of the Library of Alexandria has taken on legendary status. Yet primary accounts estimate the number of scrolls lost in Alexandria at around forty thousand. Modern scholars, such as Professor Luciano Canfora from the University of Bari in Italy, have also argued that the number may be much smaller than the ancient source accounts because the individual literary works or books were comprised of multiple scrolls. In our modern minds, we naturally imagine individual books being burned, when in fact each scroll could have represented a single chapter, further inflating the number. One of the highest estimates of the losses at Alexandria is from Aulus Gellius, in approximately 169 CE, who claimed that 700,000 scrolls were burned during the sack of Alexandria (Canfora, 1990). Regardless of which accounting you accept, the mountain of history and wisdom lost in the Library of Alexandria is still nowhere close to the twenty million recently lost in Brazil.

How could this happen? The details are so shocking, they leave one to wonder if this was a case of criminal negligence or criminal intent. The museum, located in Rio de Janeiro, was founded in 1818 by King Dom João VI. It was not a simple tourist attraction; it was also an important research center affiliated with the University of Brazil (now UFRJ). According to the National Museum of Brazil's website, the collection housed more than twenty million items covering many areas of science such as archaeology, ethnology, geology, paleontology, zoology, and biological anthropology (Localizacao, 2018).

Burning of the 200-year-old National Museum of Brazil. (Felipe Milanez [CC BY-SA 4.0 creativecommons.org, via Wikimedia Commons])

The fire burned out of control overnight until late the following morning, but small flares continued to burn parts of the institution's facilities, causing the ashes of documents to fall in several neighborhoods of the city. Researchers and officials from the museum met with fire officials to try to assist in saving the museum. The goal was to prevent the fire from reaching a part of the museum containing the combustible chemicals used in the preservation of rare animal specimens (Localizacao, 2018). As of the writing of this book, the cause of the fire is still a mystery. The Brazilian police have yet to determine if it was a criminal act or not.

Unfortunately, most of the historic building was made of wood and the collection itself contained flammable material. Thus, the fire spread quickly. However, there are disconcerting details about the event, as pointed out by *O Globo*, Rio de Janeiro's main newspaper. For example, only four guards were on-site. Also, the museum's smoke detectors were not working. Firefighters arrived soon after the fire started, but according to them, the two fire hydrants near the National Museum did not have enough pressure, even though according to the University of Rio de Janeiro (UFRJ) rector Roberto Lehrer, there was a reserve of water in the museum (*O Globo*, 2018). The fire commander-in-chief, Colonel Roberto Robadey Costa Jr., said that the lack of water delayed their ability to fight the fire by half an hour, leaving firefighters with little choice but to collect water from a nearby pond in a futile effort to extinguish the blaze (*O Globo*, 2018). The following day's dawn rainfall helped to extinguish further outbreaks.

In the days after the fire, hundreds of protesters took to the streets to voice their anger with the government and Brazilian president Michel Temer for not investing enough to help secure the museum in the years leading up to the fire.

Instead, the government chose to take millions of taxpayer dollars to pay for the 2014 World Cup and 2016 Rio Olympic Games (*O Globo*, 2018.).

Officials confirmed that 90 percent of the entire collection is gone. Treasures include the skull of Luzia, the oldest human fossil found in the Americas; the largest Egyptian collection in Latin America, containing mummies and rare Egyptian objects purchased by Dom Pedro I and Dom Pedro II; also, Incan artifacts and Andean mummies; a large collection of Greco-Roman art and artifacts of Empress Teresa Cristina; a paleontology collection that includes the eighty-million-year-old fossil of the dinosaur *Maxakalisaurus topai*. The five-ton meteorite Bendegó, the largest ever found in Brazil, was the only item left untouched after the fire (*O Globo*, 2018).

There are countless important artifacts and documents lost forever. While it may be difficult to imagine entire museum collections burning to the ground, it is perhaps even more difficult to imagine what other items could have been lost. What about the artifacts stored away from public viewing? The museum, as an independent part of the university, was a research institution. Countless artifacts that were not in the public view are also gone. Were they burned too? Or could this have been one of the most sophisticated art heists or cover-ups of all time?

What Is True?

We may never know the answers to these questions, but to question the prevailing narrative is important. We are living in an era where, increasingly, it seems facts do not matter.

Even in communities of alternative researchers there is a need for alternative research. Based on the evidence in the archaeological and historical records, I believe that the Anunnaki were clearly a group of advanced living beings who settled in a mountain valley in the Near East around 8200 BCE. These people brought and shared technologies never before seen by other more primitive bands of humans in the regions resettled after their homelands flooded. These amazing individuals had kept alive their sacred knowledge of the arts and sciences after being displaced from their northern homeland more than ten thousand years ago due to a near-extinction event, possibly triggered by a meteor.

Over time, these displaced scholars and scientists would shape the lives of the Mesopotamian people and assume leadership positions from whom subsequent leaders claimed lineage in order to maintain legitimacy. In addition to carrying with them the arts and sciences, these settlers brought the occult traditions of what would later become the mystery schools. Part of this mystery practice included the ability to contact off-world entities they believed to be nonhuman sages. These sages would guide the rulers, serving as a hidden hand in what would become a hierarchical bureaucratic government, which grew to be, in many ways, the model for all other administrative social systems.

The power these beings wielded inflated their egos, and the clash of culture combined with a new social stratification of lower, middle, and upper classes created stress. This led to the eventual dehumanization of the locals by the upper classes, who treated them as slaves and developed prejudices about whom they could and could not marry. This subjugation further instilled into the local "black-headed people" or Adamah that the elites themselves were gods, their having been mystified with magic and technologies. These enslaved people worked primarily in agriculture, or "The Garden," and would eventually find mercy in one of the elites named Enki.

Enki would break with his class and, understanding that knowledge is power, he rebelled against his own by teaching the Adamah the sacred arts. Meanwhile, the civilization was rapidly expanding, thanks to the "genius of a few" and the "labor of the many." After breaking with their own and giving the Adamah forbidden knowledge, the rebel "gods" around Enki would start to assimilate and be absorbed into the local culture through marriage, their offspring literally demonized. Over time, the story of how humanity was brought out of the wild and organized into civilizations would take on a legendary status. The gods would be celestialized, mythologized, and also demonized after centuries of rewriting and revising the tablets containing their stories.

Were they responsible for "creating" man? Not in a biological sense. However, as we have seen over and over in the scientific literature, the idea that life on Earth was "seeded" from outside our planet by an extraterrestrial intelligence cannot be ruled out. In fact, it seems that it is the most likely scenario, one that will need further research and serious consideration. Even so, that was the past, but the present is only a more complex derivative of this first world system. Today, there are still social stratification, prejudice, exploitation of the labor force, division, lies, manipulation of the masses, and even the mystery traditions. People still contact—or at least believe they are in contact with—these strange semi-biological entities from a different dimension. They may now be called the machine elves, but they are really all the same. They are the Seven Sages or Apkallu, the Archons of the Gnostics, the serpent gods of the Far East and Central America, the Titans of the Greeks, the Snake Brothers of the Hopi, the Jinn of Islam, the demons of Christianity, and the Elohim of the Old Testament.

They are the Watchers, and they are still here.

AFTERWORD:

Time for Connection

We are all connected: To each other, biologically. To the earth, chemically. To the rest of the universe, atomically.
—NEIL DEGRASSE TYSON, American astrophysicist

History is a dynamic and living field. It is a mistake to think that because it deals with dead people and dusty old relics that it is stagnant. Contrary to what most of us were taught as schoolchildren, history is not simply an exercise in the rote memorization of dates and facts. History is alive with discovery, debate, and discourse! As a historian, I can assure you that right now, scholars are actively debating and questioning almost every historical fact out there. Don't let anybody tell you it's all figured out, now go memorize and repeat it. That is control. We must continue to fight for free-thinking. We must read the authors and the theories that the mainstream shuns. Do not staunchly adhere to any one idea, whether alternative or mainstream, simply because it is fun or exciting. This close-minded divisiveness is fueling the "us versus them" mentality we are currently experiencing in all aspects of contemporary culture.

Now, more than ever, is the time for connection—between ideas and between people. Researchers must remain open-minded when entertaining theories and claims about the Anunnaki, but they must also approach the subject through a more critical lens. Many can point to the problems with mainstream research, but it is often more difficult to shine the light on ourselves. As a renegade, I do not put unthinking stock in the claims of traditional academia; however, I also do not blindly accept the word of any one alternative or independent researcher because the cult of personality threatens the validity of alternative research. "The problem lies in the poison that is ideologies. They have the same effect as dictatorial religions. . . . The 'dogmatists' reign supreme'" (von Däniken, 2018, 174).

Theorists of all backgrounds should not position themselves as gurus rather than scholars because gurus seek followers, while scholars seek challengers. It is through the respectful challenging of ideas that we can arrive at a more complete picture of the truth. A guru is threatened by someone challenging their ideas because they see it as hostile to their authority. A scholar, however, welcomes a challenge because they see it as an opportunity to grow closer to the truth.

Another important distinction between a guru and a scholar is that a guru wants to be the only source for truth, while a scholar knows that they are only one rung on the ladder humanity is building to climb over the giant wall of ignorance. Take, for example, Carl Sagan, often credited with saying that we stand the shoulders of giants, but ironically that comment was a secondary quote of Isaac Newton from a letter to his rival Robert Hooke in 1676:

> *What Descartes did was a good step. You have added much several ways, and especially in taking the colors of thin plates into*

*philosophical consideration. If I have seen a little further it is by
standing on the shoulders of Giants.*

Even so, Newton built his quote on the shoulders of a twelfth-century giant, theologian and author John of Salisbury, who wrote something similar in a Latin treatise on logic called *Metalogicon* in 1159:

*We are like dwarfs sitting on the shoulders of giants. We see more,
and things that are more distant, than they did, not because our
sight is superior or because we are taller than they, but because they
raise us up, and by their great stature add to ours.*

Even if alternative theories about history seem contrary to our belief systems, it is necessary to at least entertain them. Doing so not only challenges your thinking, it also spurs creativity. My suggestion to anyone interested in theories of the Anunnaki as our extraterrestrial creators is "do the research yourself" and consider many different viewpoints. Think creatively and critically. Resist the urge to simply focus on one or two dots that seem interesting to you. Instead, challenge yourself to zoom out to see the bigger picture. By focusing on what connects us and our ideas, we will find that we are all more linked than we realize and humanity's ultimate truth will finally reveal itself to those willing to conceive the inconceivable.

Let's create a strong public discourse about these and other issues about our past so that we are the history makers. Academics play an important role in this pursuit, but their role should be as a skilled and knowledgeable guide, a public servant and not an infallible dictator. The more we can teach others that history, as well as all academic pursuits, is something to *do* as opposed to something to *view*, the more we can elevate the overall intellect of humanity. When it comes to our history, we must stop being simply watchers and instead become participants.

BIBLIOGRAPHY

Actor, Jeffrey K. *Elseviers Integrated Review Immunology and Microbiology*. Philadelphia, PA: Elsevier/Mosby, 2012.

Allegro, J. M. *The Mushroom and the Bride.*" New York, The Citadel Press, 1970.

Allen, Richard Hinckley. *Star-names and Their Meanings*. New York: Stechert, 1899.

Annus, Amar. "On the Origin of Watchers: A Comparative Study of the Antediluvian Wisdom in Mesopotamian and Jewish Traditions." *Journal for the Study of the Pseudepigrapha* 19, no. 4 (2010): 277-320. doi:10.1177/0951820710373978.

Armstrong, Karen. *Fields of Blood: Religion and the History of Violence*. London: Vintage, 2015.

Arrhenius, Svante. *Worlds in the Making: The Evolution of the Universe*. New York: Harper, 1908.

Bahn, Paul G. *The Cambridge Illustrated History of Prehistoric Art*. S.l.: Cambridge, 1998.

Barton, George Aaron. *Miscellaneous Babylonian Inscriptions*. New Haven, CT: Yale Univ. Pr., 1918.

Basalla, George. *Civilized Life in the Universe: Scientists on Intelligent Extraterrestrials*. Oxford: Oxford University Press, 2006.

Bauval, Robert. "Investigation on the Origins of the Benben Stone: Was It an Iron Meteorite?" *Discussions in Egyptology*, 1989, 5–7. *gizamedia.rc.fas.harvard.edu/documents/legon_de_14_1989.pdf.*

Bauval, Robert, and Adrian Geoffrey. Gilbert. *The Orion Mystery: Unlocking the Secrets of the Pyramids*. London: Arrow books, 1994.

Beck, H. *Reallexikon der Germanischen Altertumskunde*. Berlin: W. De Gruyter, 2000.

Becker, Carl. "Everyman His Own Historian." *The American Historical Review* 37, no. 2 (1932): 221. doi.org.

Bocquentin, Fanny, and Andrew Garrard. "Natufian Collective Burial Practice and Cranial Pigmentation: A Reconstruction from Azraq 18 (Jordan)." *Journal of Archaeological Science: Reports* 10 (2016): 693–702. doi:10.1016/j.jasrep.2016.05.030.

Bogdanos, Matthew. "The Casualties of War: The Truth about the Iraq Museum." *American Journal of Archaeology* 109, no. 3 (2005): 477–526. doi:10.3764/aja.109.3.477.

Bogdanos, Matthew, and William Patrick. *Thieves of Baghdad: One Marine's Passion to Recover the World's Greatest Stolen Treasures*. New York: Bloomsbury Pub., 2006.

Brady, Bernadette. *Brady's Book of Fixed Stars*. York Beach, ME.: Samuel Weiser, 1998.

Braudel, Fernand. *The Structures of Everyday Life: Civilization and Capitalism, 15th–18th Century, Volume 1*. New York: Harper & Row, 1982.

Breisach, Ernst. *Historiography: Ancient, Medieval & Modern*. Chicago: University of Chicago Press, 1983.

Brumfiel, Geoff. "Russian Meteor Largest in a Century." *Nature*, 2013. doi:10.1038/nature.2013.12438.

Budge, E. A. Wallis. *The Book of the Dead: The Hieroglyphic Transcript of the Papyrus of Ani*. Whitefish, MT: Kessinger Pub., 2003.

Budge, Ernest Alfred Wallis. *An Egyptian Hieroglyphic Dictionary*. New York: Ungar, 1960.

Butler, Sally A. L. *Mesopotamian Conceptions of Dreams and Dream Rituals*. Münster, Germany: Ugarit-Verlag, 1998.

"Capricornus," Wikipedia. February 1, 2019. *wikipedia.org*.

Campbell, Joseph. *The Power of Myth*. Logan, IA: Turtleback Books, 2012.

Campbell, Stuart, Robert Killick, and Jane Moon. Manchester, n.d.

Canfora, Luciano. *The Vanished Library a Wonder of the Ancient World*. London: Vintage, 1990.

Capt, E. E. Raymond. *Glory of the Stars: A Study of the Zodiac*. Muskogee , OK: Artisan Publishers, n.d.

Cardwell, Donald S. L. *Wheels, Clocks, and Rockets: A History of Technology*. New York: Norton, 2001.

Carr, Edward Hallett. *What Is History Now?* Basingstoke, England: Palgrave, 2002.

Charles, R. H. *The Book of Enoch*. London: Society for Promoting Christian Knowledge, 1917.

Charlesworth, James H. *The Old Testament Pseudepigrapha*. Peabody, MA: Hendrickson Publishers, 2010.

Choudhuri, Supratim, and Michael Kotewicz. *Bioinformatics for Beginners: Genes, Genomes, Molecular Evolution, Databases, and Analytical Tools*. Elsevier, 2014.

Ćirković, Milan. "Cosmic Irony: SETI Optimism from Catastrophes?" *Contact in Context: A Journal of Research on Life in the Universe* 2, no. 1 (January 2004): 1–8. September 23, 2003. *arxiv.org.*

Clark, Andrew J. H., and David H. Clark. *Aliens: Can We Make Contact with Extraterrestrial Intelligence?* New York: Fromm International, 2000.

Clarke, Arthur C. *Profiles of the Future: An Inquiry into the Limits of the Possible.* London: Victor Gollancz, 1982.

Clay, A. T. "Ellil, the God of Nippur." *The American Journal of Semitic Languages and Literatures* 23, no. 4 (1907): 269–79. doi:10.1086/369595.

Clottes, Jean, and J. David. Lewis-Williams. *The Shamans of Prehistory: Trance and Magic in the Painted Caves.* New York: Harry N. Abrams, 1998.

Cornford , Francis, (trans.) "Tiamaeus." *Timaeus*, by Plato. Project Gutenberg. Accessed December 9, 2019. *www.gutenberg.org.*

Cory, Isaac P. *The Ancient Fragments: . . . Containing of Sanchoniatho, Berossus, Abydenus, Megasthenes, and Manetho. Also the Hermetic Creed, the Old (Egyptian) Chronicle, the Laterculus of Eratosthenes, the Tyrian Annals, the Oracles of Zoroaster, and the Periplus of Hanno.* 1828.

Cremo, Michael A., and Richard L. Thompson. *Forbidden Archeology: The Hidden History of the Human Race.* Los Angeles: Bhaktivedanta Institute, 1993.

Darlison, Bill. *The Gospel and the Zodiac: The Secret Truth about Jesus.* London: Duckworth Overlook, 2007.

David, Gary A. *Eye of the Phoenix: Mysterious Visions and Secrets in the American Southwest.* Kempton, IL: Adventures Unlimited Press, 2008.

Dick, Steven J. "Comment: Don't Expect ET to Look Like Us." *New Scientist* 198, no. 2658 (2008): 21. doi:10.1016/s0262-4079(08)61343-3.

Eiberg, Hans, Jesper Troelsen, Mette Nielsen, Annemette Mikkelsen, Jonas Mengel-From, Klaus W. Kjaer, and Lars Hansen. "Blue Eye Color in Humans May Be Caused by a Perfectly Associated Founder Mutation in a Regulatory Element Located within the HERC2 Gene Inhibiting OCA2 Expression." *Human Genetics* 123, no. 2 (2008): 177–87. doi:10.1007/s00439-007-0460-x.

"Eridanus (constellation)," Wikipedia. January 29, 2019. *wikipedia.org*.

Foster, Benjamin Read. *Before the Muses: An Anthology of Akkadian Literature*. Baltimore, MD: CDL Press, 2005.

Fritz, Kurt Von. "Herodotus and the Growth of Greek Historiography." *Transactions and Proceedings of the American Philological Association* 67 (1936): 315. *doi.org*.

Garrard, Andrew, Douglas Baird, Susan Colledge, Louise Martin, and Katherine Wright. "Prehistoric Environment and Settlement in the Azraq Basin: An Interim Report on the 1987 and 1988 Excavation Seasons." *Levant* 26, no. 1 (1991): 73–109. doi:10.1179/lev.1994.26.1.73.

Gesche, Petra D. *Schulunterricht in Babylonien Im Ersten Jahrtausend v. Chr.* Münster, Germany: Ugarit-Verl., 2000.

Griggs, Jessica. "Time for SETI to Start Listening for Alien Conversations." *New Scientist* 200, no. 2680 (2008): 14. doi:10.1016/s0262-4079(08)62737-2.

Hancock, Graham. *Fingerprints of the Gods*. Crown, 1996.

Hancock, Graham. *Fingerprints of the Gods: The Evidence of Earth's Lost Civilization*. New York: MJF Books, 2011.

Hancock, Graham, and Robert Bauval. *The Message of the Sphinx: A Quest for the Hidden Legacy of Mankind*. Toronto: Doubleday Canada, 1997.

Hecht, Jeff. "Modern Optics May Make Optical SETI Practical." *Laser Focus World* 32, no. 7 (July 1996).

Kaler, Jim. "Cursa." Enif. *stars.astro.illinois.edu*.

King, L. W. (trans). "The Code of Hammurabi." The Avalon Project—Laws of War: Laws and Customs of War on Land (Hague IV); October 18, 1907. Accessed May 12, 2018. *avalon.law.yale.edu*.

Kotze, Zacharias. "The Evil Eye of Sumerian Deities." *Asian and African Studies* 26, no. 1 (n.d.): 102–15. *doi.org*.

Kovacs, Maureen G. *The Epic of Gilgamesh*. Stanford, CA: Stanford Univ. Press, 2004.

Kramer, Samuel Noah. *History Begins at Sumer*. Philadelphia: University of Pennsylvania Press, 1988.

Kramer, Samuel Noah. *The Sumerians: Their History, Culture, and Character*. Chicago: University of Chicago Press, 1963.

Krasner, Barbara. *Ancient Mesopotamian Daily Life*. New York: Rosen Publishing, 2016.

Krueger, Derek. *Symeon the Holy Fool: Leontius's Life and the Late Antique City*. Berkeley: University of California Press, 1996.

Kulik, Alexander. *3 Baruch: Greek-Slavonic Apocalypse of Baruch*. Berlin: De Gruyter, 2009.

Kunitzsch, Paul, and Tim Smart. *A Dictionary of Modern Star Names: A Short Guide to 254 Star Names and Their Derivations*. Cambridge, MA: Sky Pub., 2006.

Leakey, R. E. F. "Early Homo Sapiens Remains from the Omo River Region of South-west Ethiopia: Faunal Remains from the Omo Valley." *Nature* 222, no. 5199 (1969): 1132–133. doi:10.1038/2221132a0.

Lenzi, Alan. "Advertising Secrecy, Creating Power in Ancient Mesopotamia: How Scholars Used Secrecy in Scribal Education to Bolster and Perpetuate Their Social Prestige and Power." *Antiguo Oriente* 11 (2013): 13–41.

Lenzi, Alan. "The Uruk List of Kings and Sages and Late Mesopotamian Scholarship." *Journal of Ancient Near Eastern Religions* 8, no. 2 (2008): 137–69. doi:10.1163/156921208786611764.

Lexham Press. Accessed December 19, 2018. *lexhampress.com.*

Lieder, Nancy. Pole Shift in 2003 Date. *www.zetatalk.com.*

Linenthal, Edward. "Committing History in Public." *The Journal of American History* 81, no. 3 (December 1994): 986. *doi.org.*

Livengood, Jonathan Mark. "On Causal Inferences in the Humanities and Social Sciences: Actual Causation." PhD diss., University of Pittsburgh, 2011. November 10, 2011. *d-scholarship.pitt.edu.*

"Localização," Museu Nacional–UFRJ. Accessed September 29, 2018. *www.museunacional.ufrj.br.*

Lynn, Heather. *The Sumerian Controversy.* Vol. 1. Cleveland, OH: Midnight Crescent Publishing, 2013.

Malina, Bruce J., and John J. Pilch. *Social-Science Commentary on the Book of Revelation.* Minneapolis: Fortress Press, 2000.

McDonough, Thomas R. *The Search for Extraterrestrial Intelligence: Listening for Life in the Cosmos.* New York: Wiley, 1987.

McKenna, Dennis. "Dr. Dennis J. McKenna—Is DMT a Chemical Messenger from an Extraterrestrial Civilization?" Address, Entheogenic Plant Sentience—Private Symposium, Tyringham Hall, Milton Keynes, 2017.

Melvin, David P. "Divine Mediation and the Rise of Civilization in Mesopotamian Literature and in Genesis 1–11."

Journal of Hebrew Scriptures 10 (2010). doi:10.5508/jhs.2010 .v10.a17.

Michalowski, P. "The Unbearable Lightness of Enlil." *Intellectual Life of the Ancient Near East: Papers Presented at the 43rd Rencontre Assyriologique Internationale, Prague*, July 1, 1996, 237–47.

Michalowski, Piotr. *The Lamentation over the Destruction of Sumer and Ur*. Winona Lake, IN: Eisenbrauns, 1989.

Moore, Susan. "Baron Lorne Thyssen-Bornemisza De Kászon: April Apollo." *Apollo Magazine*. May 11, 2014. Accessed May 27, 2014. *www.apollo-magazine.com*.

"Mul-Apin 1, " Ancient Mesopotamian Gods and Goddesses. *oracc.museum.upenn.edu*.

Neumann, Franz L., Herbert Marcuse, Otto Kirchheimer, and Raffaele Laudani. *Secret Reports on Nazi Germany: The Frankfurt School Contribution to the War Effort*. Princeton NJ: Princeton University Press, 2013.

"Ninurta's Return to Nibru," ETCSL Translation : T.1.6.1. Accessed August 7, 2018. *etcsl.orinst.ox.ac.uk*.

Nowicki, Stefan. "Menu of the Gods. Mesopotamian Super-natural Powers and Their Nourishment, with Reference to Selected Literary Sources." *Archiv Orientalni* 82, no. 2 (2014): 211-II-409. Accessed September 2, 2018.

O'Brien, C. A. E. *The Genius of the Few: The Story of Those Who Founded the Garden of Eden*. Edited by Barbara Joy O'Brien. San Bernardino, CA: Borgo Press, 1989.

Ossendrijver, M. "Ancient Babylonian Astronomers Calculated Jupiter's Position from the Area under a Time-velocity Graph." *Science* 351, no. 6272 (2016): 482–84. doi:10.1126 /science.aad8085.

Paulose, Anu. "Adam and Eve: An Adaptation." *Lehigh Preserve* 20, no. 2 (2012): 55–63.

Payne, Susan. *Viruses: From Understanding to Investigation*. Elsevier Science Publishing, 2017.

"The Pennsylvania Sumerian Dictionary," University of Pennsylvania Museum of Anthropology and Archaeology. *psd.museum.upenn.edu*.

Peters, Joris, Klaus Schmidt, Oliver Dietrich, and Nadja Pöllath. "Göbekli Tepe: Agriculture and Domestication." *Encyclopedia of Global Archaeology*, 2014, 3065–68. doi:10.1007 /978-1-4419-0465-2_2226.

Peters, Ted. *Science, Theology, and Ethics*. Milton Park, Abingdon, England: Taylor and Francis, 2017.

"Phoenix (constellation)," Wikipedia. February 19, 2019. *wikipedia.org*.

Pickover, Clifford A. *Sex, Drugs, Einstein, & Elves: Sushi, Psychedelics, Parallel Universes, and the Quest for Transcendence*. Petaluma, CA: Smart Publications, 2005.

Plato, and Oskar Piest. *Timaeus*. New York: Liberal Arts Press, 1959.

Popova, O. P., P. Jenniskens, V. Emelyanenko, A. Kartashova, E. Biryukov, S. Khaibrakhmanov, V. Shuvalov, Y. Rybnov, A. Dudorov, V. I. Grokhovsky, D. D. Badyukov, Q.-Z. Yin, P. S. Gural, J. Albers, M. Granvik, L. G. Evers, J. Kuiper, V. Kharlamov, A. Solovyov, Y. S. Rusakov, S. Korotkiy, I. Serdyuk, A. V. Korochantsev, M. Y. Larionov, D. Glazachev, A. E. Mayer, G. Gisler, S. V. Gladkovsky, J. Wimpenny, M. E. Sanborn, A. Yamakawa, K. L. Verosub, D. J. Rowland, S. Roeske, N. W. Botto, J. M. Friedrich, M. E. Zolensky, L. Le, D. Ross, K. Ziegler, T. Nakamura,

I. Ahn, J. I. Lee, Q. Zhou, X.-H. Li, Q.-L. Li, Y. Liu, G.-Q. Tang, T. Hiroi, D. Sears, I. A. Weinstein, A. S. Vokhmintsev, A. V. Ishchenko, P. Schmitt-Kopplin, N. Hertkorn, K. Nagao, M. K. Haba, M. Komatsu, and T. Mikouchi. "Chelyabinsk Airburst, Damage Assessment, Meteorite Recovery, and Characterization." *Science* 342, no. 6162 (2013): 1069–73. doi:10.1126/science.1242642.

Porada, Edith, and Anton Moortgat. "Vorderasiatische Rollsiegel. Ein Beitrag Zur Geschichte der Steinschnei-dekunst." *Journal of the American Oriental Society* 61, no. 2 (1941): 107. doi:10.2307/594256.

Praetorius, Dean. "Scientist: We May Have 2 Suns By 2012." The Huffington Post. May 25, 2011. *huffingtonpost.com*.

Reymond, Eve Anne Elisabeth. *The Mythical Origin of the Egyptian Temple*. Manchester, England: Manchester Univ. Press., 1969.

Rogers, Toby. "Heir to the Holocaust." *Clamor*, May/June 2002.

Salla, Michael. "An Exopolitical Perspective on the Preemptive War against Iraq." *www.exopolitics.org*, February 3, 2003.

Santillana, Giorgio De., Hertha Von. Dechend, and Damián Alou. *El Molino De Hamlet: Los Orígenes Del Conocimiento Humano Y Su Transmisión a Través Del Mito*. México D.F.: Sexto Piso, 2015.

Sapir, E. "The Status of Linguistics as a Science." *Language* 5, no. 4 (1929): 207. doi:10.2307/409588.

Schmidt, Gavin A., and Adam Frank. "The Silurian Hypothesis: Would It Be Possible to Detect an Industrial Civilization in the Geological Record?" *International Journal of Astrobiology*, 2018, 1–9. doi:10.1017/s1473550418000095.

SETI Institute. "Mission." Accessed December 19, 2018. *www.seti.org.*

Shepard, Leslie. *Encyclopedia of Occultism and Parapsychology: A Compendium of Information on the Occult Sciences, Magic, Demonology . . . with Biographical and Bibliographical Notes and Comprehensive Indexes.* Detroit, MI: Gale, 1982.

Sitchin, Zecharia. *The Cosmic Code: Book VI of the Earth Chronicles.* New York: Harper, 2007.

Sitchin, Zecharia. *The 12th Planet.* Bronx, NY: Ishi Press International, 2016.

Stanford, J. D., R. Hemingway, E. J. Rohling, P.g. Challenor, M. Medina-Elizalde, and A. J. Lester. "Sea-level Probability for the Last Deglaciation: A Statistical Analysis of Far-field Records." *Global and Planetary Change* 79, no. 3-4 (2011): 193-203. doi:10.1016/j.gloplacha.2010.11.002.

Steele, Edward J., Shirwan Al-Mufti, Kenneth A. Augustyn, Rohana Chandrajith, John P. Coghlan, S. G. Coulson, Sudipto Ghosh, Mark Gillman, Reginald M. Gorczynski, Brig Klyce, Godfrey Louis, Kithsiri Mahanama, Keith R. Oliver, Julio Padron, Jiangwen Qu, John A. Schuster, W. E. Smith, Duane P. Snyder, Julian A. Steele, Brent J. Stewart, Robert Temple, Gensuke Tokoro, Christopher A. Tout, Alexander Unzicker, Milton Wainwright, Jamie Wallis, Daryl H. Wallis, Max K. Wallis, John Wetherall, D. T. Wickramasinghe, J. T. Wickramasinghe, N. Chandra Wickramasinghe, and Yongsheng Liu. "Cause of Cambrian Explosion—Terrestrial or Cosmic?" *Progress in Biophysics and Molecular Biology* 136 (2018): 3–23. doi:10.1016/j.pbiomolbio.2018.03.004.

"Story (n.1)," Etymonline. Accessed September 26, 2018. *www.etymonline.com.*

Strassman, Rick. *DMT: The Spirit Molecule*. Rochester, VT: Park Street Press, 2001.

Teal, Emily. "Medicine and Doctoring in Ancient Mesopotamia." *Grand Valley Journal of History* 3, no. 1 (October 2014). *scholarworks.gvsu.edu*.

Tinney, Steve. *The Nippur Lament: Royal Rhetoric and Divine Legitimation in the Reign of Isme-Dagan of Isin (1953–1935 B.C.)*. Philadelphia: Samuel Noah Kramer Fund, 1996.

Trigger, Bruce G. *Understanding Early Civilizations: A Comparative Study*. Cambridge: Cambridge, England University Press, 2010.

"Ubaid Period," Wikipedia. January 14, 2019. *wikipedia.org*.

"URAP 2013 Report Ur Region Archaeology Project." *URAP 2013 Report Ur Region Archaeology Project*. Manchester, England, 2013.

U.S. Department of Commerce, and National Oceanic and Atmospheric Administration. "How Much of the Ocean Have We Explored?" NOAA's National Ocean Service. January 1, 2009. Accessed January 5, 2019. *oceanservice.noaa.gov*.

von Däniken, Erich. *The Gods Never Left Us: The Long Awaited Sequel to the Worldwide Best-Seller Chariots of the Gods*. Wayne, NJ: New Page Books, a division of the Career Press, Inc., 2018.

Wazana, Nili. "Anzu and Ziz: Great Mythical Birds in Ancient Near Eastern, Biblical, and Rabbinic Traditions." *Journal of the Ancient Near Eastern Society* 31 (2009): 111–35.

Weinstein-Evron, Mina, and Shimon Ilani. "Provenance of Ochre in the Natufian Layers of El-Wad Cave, Mount Carmel, Israel." *Journal of Archaeological Science* 21, no. 4 (1994): 461–67. doi:10.1006/jasc.1994.1045.

Willgress, Lydia. "Prince Charles and Camilla Avoid Eating Garlic to Stop Them 'Stinking' during Engagements." *The Telegraph*. September 27, 2016. Accessed August 12, 2018. *www.telegraph.co.uk*.

Wrangham, Richard. *Catching Fire: How Cooking Made Us Human*. New York: Basic Books, 2010.

Zaitsev, Alexander L. "Sending and Searching for Interstellar Messages." *Acta Astronautica* 63, no. 5–6 (2008): 614–17. doi:10.1016/j.actaastro.2008.05.014.

Ziskind, Jonathan R. "The Sumerian Problem." *The History Teacher* 5, no. 2 (1972): 34. doi:10.2307/491500.

ABOUT THE AUTHOR

 **DR. HEATHER LYNN** is an author, historian, and renegade archaeologist, on a quest to uncover the truth behind ancient mysteries. After earning her associate degree in archaeology, she continued to study anthropology and history, earning her Master of Arts in history. Her thesis examined the intersection of class inequality, consumer culture, propaganda, and public education in early modern Europe. She went on to pursue her doctorate in education at the University of New England. She is a lifelong learner and holds certificates in human osteoarchaeology from Leiden University and archeoastronomy from Politecnico di Milano.

Lynn is a member of professional organizations including the American Historical Association, the Society for Historical Archaeology (SHA), Association of Ancient Historians, and the World Archaeological Congress. Her research includes hidden history, ancient mysteries, mythology, folklore, the occult, symbolism, paleocontact, and consciousness. In addition to regular appearances on radio programs like *Coast to Coast AM*, Lynn has been a historical consultant for television programs, including History Channel's *Ancient Aliens*. She also speaks at various conferences and events. Her own show, *Digging Deeper*, is now available on YouTube, iTunes, TuneIn, Stitcher, and Spotify.

Website: *www.drheatherlynn.com*